Andrei Tarkovsky's Sounding Cinema

Andrei Tarkovsky's Sounding Cinema adds a new dimension to our understanding and appreciation of the work of Russian director Andrei Tarkovsky (1932–1986) through an exploration of the presence of music and sound in his films.

The first comprehensive study in English concentrating on the soundtrack in Tarkovsky's cinema, this book reveals how Tarkovsky's use of electronic music, electronically manipulated sound, traditional folk songs and fragments of canonized works of Western art music plays into the philosophical, existential and ethical themes recurring throughout his work. Exploring the multilayered relationship between music, sound, film image and narrative space, Pontara provides penetrating and innovative close readings of *Solaris* (1972), *Mirror* (1975), *Stalker* (1979), *Nostalghia* (1983) and *The Sacrifice* (1986) and in turn deeply enriches critical understanding of Tarkovsky's films and their relation to the broader traditions of European art cinema.

An excellent resource for scholars, researchers and students interested in European art cinema and the role of music in film, as well as for film aficionados interested in Tarkovsky's work.

Tobias Pontara is Professor in Musicology at the University of Gothenburg, Sweden.

Music and Sound on the International Screen
Series Editors: Michael Baumgartner
Cleveland State University
Ewelina Boczkowska
Youngstown State University

Around the world, music and sound play an essential role in the experience of cinema and other screen media, yet research on music in screen media has been largely centered on the United States. *Music and Sound on the International Screen* expands the horizons of film music scholarship by publishing cutting-edge monographs and edited collections on topics in music, sound, and screen media beyond Hollywood. Written by established and emerging international scholars, the books in this series encourage vigorous and sustained discourse around the historical, social, cultural, and aesthetic aspects of music in the context of the moving image.

**Music, Collective Memory, Trauma and Nostalgia
in European Cinema after the Second World War**
Edited by Michael Baumgartner and Ewelina Boczkowska

Andrei Tarkovsky's Sounding Cinema
Music and Meaning from *Solaris* to *The Sacrifice*
Tobias Pontara

For more information about this series, please visit: www.routledge.com/music/series/MSIS

Andrei Tarkovsky's Sounding Cinema
Music and Meaning from *Solaris* to *The Sacrifice*

Tobias Pontara

NEW YORK AND LONDON

First published 2020
by Routledge
52 Vanderbilt Avenue, New York, NY 10017

and by Routledge
2 Park Square, Milton Park, Abingdon, Oxon, OX14 4RN

Routledge is an imprint of the Taylor & Francis Group, an informa business

First issued in paperback 2021

© 2020 Taylor & Francis

The right of Tobias Pontara to be identified as author of this work
has been asserted by him in accordance with sections 77 and 78 of
the Copyright, Designs and Patents Act 1988.

All rights reserved. No part of this book may be reprinted or
reproduced or utilized in any form or by any electronic, mechanical,
or other means, now known or hereafter invented, including
photocopying and recording, or in any information storage or
retrieval system, without permission in writing from the publishers.

Trademark notice: Product or corporate names may be trademarks
or registered trademarks, and are used only for identification and
explanation without intent to infringe.

Library of Congress Cataloging-in-Publication Data
Names: Pontara, Tobias, author.
Title: Andrei Tarkovsky's sounding cinema : music and meaning
   from *Solaris* to *The Sacrifice*/Tobias Pontara.
Description: New York : Routledge, 2020. | Series: Music and sound
   on the international screen | Includes bibliographical references
   and index.
Identifiers: LCCN 2019040645 (print) | LCCN 2019040646 (ebook) |
   ISBN 9780367277291 (hardback) | ISBN 9780429297618 (ebook)
Subjects: LCSH: Tarkovskiĭ, Andreiĭ Arsen'evich, 1932–1986—
   Criticism and interpretation. | Motion picture music—History
   and criticism.
Classification: LCC ML2075 .P6 2020 (print) | LCC ML2075 (ebook) |
   DDC 791.4302/4—dc23
LC record available at https://lccn.loc.gov/2019040645
LC ebook record available at https://lccn.loc.gov/2019040646

ISBN: 978-0-367-27729-1 (hbk)
ISBN: 978-1-03-208377-3 (pbk)
ISBN: 978-0-429-29761-8 (ebk)

Typeset in Baskerville
by Apex CoVantage, LLC

To my parents, Aslög and Giuliano

Contents

List of Figures	viii
List of Music Examples	ix
Acknowledgments	x

1 Interpreting Tarkovsky's Cinema Through Its Music   1

2 Bach at the Space Station: Diegetic Ambiguities and Multiplying Gaps in *Solaris*   20

3 Memories, Dreams and Mysteries: Music and Dimensions of Human Experience in *Mirror*   46

4 Beethoven Overcome: Transcendence and Utopia in *Stalker*   75

5 Musical Offerings, Soothing Sounds and Sacrificial Acts: Managing the Nostalgia of *Nostalghia*   96

6 The Voice of Truth: Liminal Music, Spiritual Authenticity and Gradual Awakening in *The Sacrifice*   118

7 Music, Meaning and Troubled Utopias in Tarkovsky's Cinema   141

Appendix: The Structure of Mirror	174
References	180
Index	188

Figures

2.1	Kris Kelvin and Hari levitating in the space station's library in *Solaris*	21
2.2	Kelvin and Hari after having watched Kelvin's homemade film in *Solaris*	25
2.3	The surface of the planet Solaris	31
3.1	Maria's vision of herself as levitating over the marital bed in *Mirror*	50
3.2	Alexei's dream-vision of the mother in *Mirror*	60
3.3	Evaporating heat mark on the table left behind by the inexplicably disappearing woman in *Mirror*	64
3.4	The orphaned boy Asafiev climbing a hill against a distinctly Bruegelesque background landscape in *Mirror*	67
4.1	Monkey resting her head against the tabletop after having telekinetically moved the glasses in the last scene of *Stalker*	78
4.2	Black-and-white shot of the family's bedroom at the beginning of *Stalker*	89
5.1	Domenico in flames calling out for his dog Zoe toward the end of *Nostalghia*	103
5.2	Andrei's family, a dog and a horse at the beginning of *Nostalghia*	105
5.3	Andrei in front of the family dacha inside San Galgano Abbey in the end scene of *Nostalghia*	107
6.1	A delirious anticipation of nuclear disaster in *The Sacrifice*	126
6.2	Alexander and Maria levitating over Maria's bed in *The Sacrifice*	131
6.3	Near the end of *The Sacrifice* Alexander turns the shakuhachi flute music on after having set fire to his house	133

Music Examples

3.1 Johann Sebastian Bach, *St. John Passion*: opening
    chorus mm. 37–39   57
3.2 Eduard Artemiev: music for *Mirror*   61
4.1 "Stalker's theme." Adapted from *Stalker* (1979).
    Composer: Eduard Artemiev   87

Acknowledgments

During the process of writing this book, I have benefited enormously from the feedback of numerous colleagues and friends. Giorgio Biancorosso and Berthold Hoeckner read earlier versions of the chapters on *Solaris* and *Stalker* (Chapters 2 and 4). These chapters would not be what they are now without the provocatively astute comments of Giorgio and Berthold. Joakim Tillman's perceptive comments on the *Stalker* chapter impelled me to make some substantial and much-needed last-minute revisions to the text. Erik Wallrup gave essential feedback on the chapter on *The Sacrifice* (Chapter 6) and directed my attention to several details in the film that I had managed to overlook. Ewelina Boczkowska and Michael Baumgartner did the same with earlier versions of the chapter on *Nostalghia* (Chapter 5). That chapter could certainly not have been completed in its present form without the meticulous scrutinization of Ewelina and Michael. I am deeply grateful to Everett Thiele, who read the whole manuscript and whose professional advice on matters of style has been invaluable. Thanks also to Genevieve Aoki, my editor at Routledge, and to Peter Sheehy, senior editorial assistant at Routledge. I am further grateful to Steven Reale, Susan McClary, Alf Björnberg, Andreas Nordin, Mia Liinason, Lars Lilliestam, Mats Björkin, Karin Wagner, Jan Eriksson, Åsa Bergman, Ola Stockfelt, Per-Henning Olsson, Mattias Lundberg, Ulrik Volgsten, Olga Sasunkevich and two anonymous reviewers.

My colleague and dear friend Erkki Huovinen has, beyond any doubt, been my most important inspiration and resource as I have struggled to write and finalize this book. I count myself lucky to have such a brilliant scholar and truly generous person among my friends. Finally, I am deeply grateful to Boel Melin, my wife and partner of 20 years, who has endured more conversations on Tarkovsky at the dinner table than she would probably care to remember.

I have received invaluable critical feedback on several of the chapters in connection with presentations at international conferences, most notably Music and the Moving Image in New York and the annual Film-Philosophy Conference, which in 2018 was held at "my" department – the

Department of Cultural Sciences – at the University of Gothenburg and was organized by film scholar and departmental colleague Anna Bachman Rogers.

This book was able to be completed in part due to a sabbatical leave funded by the Swedish Foundation for Humanities and Social Sciences (Riksbankens Jubileumsfond), which gave me the opportunity to focus full time on my research on Tarkovsky during the whole of 2018.

An earlier version of Chapter 2 was published as "Bach at the Space Station: Hermeneutic Pliability and Multiplying Gaps in Andrei Tarkovsky's Solaris" in *Music, Sound and the Moving Image* (Liverpool University Press, 2014), 1–23.

An earlier version of Chapter 4 was published as "Beethoven Overcome: Romantic and Existentialist Utopia in Andrei Tarkovsky's Stalker" in *19th-Century Music* (University of California Press, 2011), 302–315.

A shorter version of Chapter 5 will be published as "The Music of Sacrificial Acts: Displacement, Redemption, Beethoven and Verdi in Andrei Tarkovsky's Nostalghia" in Michael Baumgartner and Ewelina Boczkowska (eds.), *Music, Memory, Nostalgia and Trauma in European Cinema after the Second World War* (New York: Routledge, 2019).

1 Interpreting Tarkovsky's Cinema Through Its Music

A book might begin in any number of ways. Academic books on films by prominent directors, for example, sometimes begin with a more personal account of how the author first encountered and came to appreciate the films in question. This is one of those books. My first meeting with Andrei Tarkovsky's work occurred when I was around 16. At that age, I was mostly interested in ice hockey and in making grandiose plans about my imagined future career as an international star flutist, so it still sometimes puzzles me that I so clearly remember the long evening I spent at the cinema watching *Nostalghia* with my parents and older brother. As I recall, I actually sat through the whole film without falling asleep. But I was not overly enthusiastic. In fact, I thought it was the most boring film I had ever seen, and it would probably be something of an understatement to say I was not exactly eager to make closer acquaintance with Tarkovsky's cinema.

Many years would pass before I came across a Tarkovsky film again. But eventually I did, and this time I was alone. Housesitting for my parents (and taking care of the cat) for some weeks in July while they were away on vacation, my plan was to work around the clock to finalize the PhD I had been struggling with for several years. This particular day, however, exhausted after too many hours of intense reading and writing, I decided to skip my evening work period. Instead, I looked through my parents' rather limited DVD collection, consisting mostly of Italian neorealist films, a few films by Hitchcock and three or four Swedish pictures. And then there was Tarkovsky's *Stalker*. Why not give Tarkovsky another chance, I thought to myself. It turned out to be the right choice. I was not really aware of it at the time, but in retrospect that evening stands out as imbued by a state of intensified presence. It was as if those hours spent watching Tarkovsky's film were carved out from my usual everyday life in a particularly distinct way, perhaps as an exemplary instance of what John Dewey once famously called "an experience." *Stalker* had taken me over completely, and it was immediately clear to me that I had never seen anything remotely like this before. And the film continued to hold an almost magical sway over me. For weeks I kept thinking about it. But

2 *Tarkovsky's Cinema Through Its Music*

most of all, I thought about the final scene, where the Stalker's daughter moves drinking glasses across a table by what seems to be pure telekinesis while a mixture of Beethoven's "Ode to Joy" and the sound of a passing train is heard on the soundtrack. Indeed, I thought about it so much that three years later I had written an essay focusing specifically on that scene. And as with so many other people captured by Tarkovsky's cinema, one film led to another. Since first seeing *Stalker*, I have watched and re-watched Tarkovsky's films so many times that it is probably accurate to describe the last ten years of my life as my personal Tarkovsky decade.

During this decade, my research on Tarkovsky has slowly transformed from something of a side project, carried out on evenings and weekends, into a full-time occupation. Since I am a film musicologist, it is perhaps natural that I became interested in the place and function of music in Tarkovsky's films, and this interest grew as I gradually came to realize that this is an understudied area within the continuously growing scholarship on Tarkovsky. The overall aim of the present book is, accordingly, to contribute to Tarkovsky studies by filling this gap. For reasons that will become apparent later, I focus on the director's last five films, which will be discussed in chronological order, from *Solaris* to *The Sacrifice*. But as I will also go on to elaborate, as much as I am concerned with how music works in Tarkovsky's cinema, my primary interest lies in exploring how paying specific attention to music can enable new critical understandings of his films. Thus, this is at one and the same time a book about music's place and function, its role and significance, in Tarkovsky's cinema and a book that via a specific focus on music seeks to unlock fresh critical perspectives on his films. It is, in other words, a book that aims to interpret Tarkovsky's cinema through the lens of its music.

In a sense, acquainting oneself with Tarkovsky's work is a fairly manageable enterprise. After all, compared to most other directors, Tarkovsky's cinematic oeuvre is quite modest. Between 1962 and 1986 he completed only seven full-length feature films. Despite this limited output, Tarkovsky has every so often been described as one of the greatest filmmakers of the twentieth century. While the critical reception of Tarkovsky's cinema has by no means been unanimously enthusiastic, and while the broader audience has been continuously divided in its responses, his films are now widely regarded as important landmarks in the history of cinema and have long held the status of "film classics." Firmly grounded in a Russian tradition, but also in the broader institution of European art cinema, they are often described as being essentially different in kind from the narratively oriented and action-based motion pictures of classical Hollywood as well as the commercially driven mainstream cinema of the contemporary global entertainment industry.[1] This is a view that Tarkovsky himself endorsed, tirelessly repeating as he did that the making of a film is, or at any rate should be, an uncompromisingly artistic endeavor and that cinema should consequently be regarded as an art form in its own right. Most of the writing on Tarkovsky's films proceeds from this assumption, and during the last three decades a growing body of literature has appeared in which his films are treated with the same reverence and attention to detail as any symphony by Beethoven, novel by Joyce or painting by Picasso.

In this growing scholarly interest for the Russian director – an interest that has been particularly intense during the last decade, so much so that Terence McSweeney (2015, 18) can speak of "a renaissance of Tarkovsky studies" – the ways that music functions in his films have received less attention. Thus, even though Tarkovsky's inventive use of sound has been rather extensively discussed (Truppin 1992; Chion 1994; Synessios 2001; Beer 2006; Robinson 2006; Smith 2007; Quandt 2008; Sarkar 2008; Fairweather 2012; Çolak 2013; Stadler 2018), to date there exists no more than a handful of articles and book chapters that focus specifically on the topic of music in Tarkovsky's cinema (Egorova 1997; Shpinitskaya 2006; Noeske 2008; Pontara 2011; Shpinitskaya 2014; Pontara 2014, 2019). And the single book-length study published, though often impressive in the depth of its analyses, is characterized by a rather selective approach in which several films receive very close attention while others are discussed more in passing, if at all (see Calabretto 2010a).[2] Maybe there is good reason for this scholarly neglect. As Tarkovsky himself once said: "In my heart of hearts I don't believe films need music at all" (Tarkovsky 1986, 159). This statement could be taken to imply that music does not deserve any particular attention in the study of his films. Moreover, while his belief in music's insignificance for cinema was evidently difficult to live up to fully in practice, Tarkovsky does seem to have worked toward a gradual realization of it. As with so many other works of the European art cinema tradition, music is used with the utmost carefulness in Tarkovsky's films, and from his third feature, *Solaris*, onward this caution becomes increasingly evident with every new film. So why should we devote our precious scholarly time to studying something that takes up a comparatively small proportion of his films, and that the director himself obviously regarded as of negligible importance?

The simple answer to this question is: because it is there. Even if Tarkovsky believed, in principle, that film can and perhaps even should do without music, this does not mean that he regarded the music he actually did put into his films as a redundant extra layer that could ultimately be dispensed with. In fact, he held quite the opposite view. Immediately after the passage quoted earlier, he made the following statement: "Music has always had a rightful place in my films, and has been important and precious" (Tarkovsky 1986, 159). From the fact that, quantitatively speaking, music plays a fairly modest role in Tarkovsky's cinematic output, it does not follow that it is an insignificant or unimportant phenomenon in his films. Rather, just as in certain films by Ingmar Bergman or Pier Paolo Pasolini, and no doubt in European art cinema more generally,

4 *Tarkovsky's Cinema Through Its Music*

the scarcity with which music occurs often creates a heightened sense of its importance for the scenes it underscores or accompanies. And, just as in Bergman and Pasolini, the appearance of music in Tarkovsky's films (whether classical, electronic or some kind of traditional music) always leaves the strong impression that it was very carefully chosen for the purpose of the shot or scene at hand; this impression does not go away just because the director himself declared that film as an art form should ideally be realized without the aid of music. It is precisely because of the scarcity with which it occurs that music often takes on an intriguing presence in these films. That said, the function and meaning of the musical passages and fragments scattered throughout Tarkovsky's cinema are never a matter of straightforward description. Instead, these musical excerpts are in every instance open to a multiplicity of interpretations or, alternatively, and as Tarkovsky himself would have it, can be experienced for the sheer aesthetic and emotional impact they bring to his films.

That Tarkovsky the filmmaker had an ambivalent attitude toward music does not mean that music was unimportant for Tarkovsky the person. On the contrary, he was a great lover of classical music and, as Vida T. Johnson and Graham Petrie point out in their now classic book *The Films of Andrei Tarkovsky: A Visual Fugue,* Tarkovsky early on developed a strong affection for Tchaikovsky and other Russian composers, after which he moved on "to Beethoven, Mozart, and, most important, Bach" (Johnson and Petrie 1994, 18). While Bach would remain the unchallenged hero of Tarkovsky's musical pantheon, later in his life he developed a growing impatience with much of Western art music, and Romantic music in particular, associating it with an unhealthy individualistic aesthetic characterized above all by a neurotic obsession with one's own raptures and agonies. The uneasiness Tarkovsky felt with the music of Beethoven and later composers is evident from several statements he made in different interviews as well as in his book on cinema, *Sculpting in Time.* Thus, in the latter we find passages like the following: "Compare Eastern and Western music. The West is forever shouting: 'This is me! Look at me! Listen to me suffering, loving! How unhappy I am! How happy! I! Mine! Me!'" (Tarkovsky 1986, 240). Similarly, in an interview in Stockholm in 1985, he described the music of Wagner and Beethoven as

> an unending monologue about oneself: look how poor I am, all in rags, how miserable, what a Job I am, how unhappy, how I suffer – like nobody else – I suffer like the ancient Prometheus . . . and here is how I love, and here is how I. . . . You understand? I, I, I, I, I.[3]

Bach's music, on the other hand, is free from such hysterical self-absorption, because Bach, like Leonardo da Vinci, is "an ideal representative of art" who has nothing to do with the "human vanity which is so typical of the west."[4] As I will argue in the chapters that follow, these views on classical music are reflected in the different ways brief fragments from canonized musical works are incorporated into Tarkovsky's films.

In his first two feature films, Tarkovsky fundamentally adhered to the standard conventions of musical underscoring in film. In *Ivan's Childhood* (1962) and, to a somewhat lesser extent, in *Andrei Rublev* (1966), music is used in the rather traditional sense of conveying a mood and underscoring dramatic events, as well as expressing the emotional state of the characters. The music for both *Ivan* and *Rublev* was composed specifically for the films by Vyacheslav Ovchinnikov, who also produced music for such basically mainstream films as Sergei Bondarchuk's epic filmization of Tolstoy's *War and Peace* (1966). With *Solaris* (1972), a major change in Tarkovsky's handling of music occurs. From this film on, conventional musical underscoring virtually disappears from his films, and it is also with *Solaris* that Tarkovsky's practice of inserting fragments from the classical musical canon begins, a practice he would employ to a greater or lesser degree throughout the remainder of his artistic career.

For Tarkovsky, music functions most effectively in film when it is used as a refrain; that is to say, when the same musical material is allowed to reappear during the course of the film.[5] Used in this way,

> music does more than intensify the impression of the visual image by providing a parallel illustration of the same idea; it opens up the possibility of a *new*, transfigured impression of the same material: something different in kind. Plunging into the musical element which the refrain brings into being, we return again and again to the emotions the film has given us, with our experience deepened each time by new impressions. With the introduction of the musical progression, the life recorded in the frame can change its colour and sometimes even its essence.
>
> (Tarkovsky 1986, 158)

This way of treating music is evident in all of Tarkovsky's last five features. In *Solaris*, *Mirror* (1975) and *Stalker* (1979), recurring snippets of classical music are mixed in complex ways with other kinds of music and with more or less musicalized sound effects. Most notable in this regard are the electronic scores composed for the three films by Eduard Artemiev, and a substantial part of the chapters on these films will focus on the relationship between classical and electronic music, as well as on the connections between these musics and other sonic phenomena that occur regularly in Tarkovsky's cinema, such as the rhythmic clanking of passing trains and the sounds of wind, rain, fire and dripping water. Central to my argument will be the claim that in *Solaris*, *Mirror* and *Stalker*, Tarkovsky works with a more or less clearly expressed dichotomy between "classical" and "electronic" musical worlds. But, as I will argue in the final chapter of this book, these dichotomies are very differently treated and expressed

6   *Tarkovsky's Cinema Through Its Music*

in the films, and they also play into the wider themes and concerns of the films in rather disparate, even contradictory, ways.

In his last two films, *Nostalghia* (1983) and *The Sacrifice* (1986), Tarkovsky comes closer to actualizing his conviction that cinema does not really need music. The presence of music in these two films is pared down to a minimum, comprising only a few passages of Western classical music alongside Russian and Chinese folk music in *Nostalghia* and a mixture of Japanese flute music, Swedish herding calls and Bach in *The Sacrifice*. Nevertheless, even in these films the music can be said to play an extremely important role, both in how classical music helps to frame the films by occurring at the very beginning and end of them (which also happens in *Solaris* and *Mirror*) and in how different types of music are linked with hallucinatory, dream-like or even other-worldly experiences undergone by the characters.

The stylistic changes that occur in the treatment of music from *Solaris* onward justify the selection of films singled out for analysis in this book. Thus, while *Solaris*, *Mirror*, *Stalker*, *Nostalghia* and *The Sacrifice* will all receive their own chapters, *Ivan's Childhood* and *Andrei Rublev* are largely passed by in silence.[6] What interests me is the at once ascetic and strongly (though never unequivocal) symbolic use of music in Tarkovsky's last five features and how an examination of the music's representational significance can function as a point of departure for exploring questions of meaning and representation in the films more broadly. In pursuing such a line of inquiry, however, the following chapters will also address more specific questions that concern the connection between the music and other parts of the soundtrack, as well as how the music relates to the film image, the stylistic designs and the formal and narrative structures of the films.

A central question in this context, one that to a greater or lesser extent will be taken up in all the chapters, is the question of music's diegetic status in the films, i.e. how the various occurrences of classical, electronic and traditional music relate to the complex and at times indeterminate nature of the films' fictional realities or story worlds. Or, to give the stricter definition of diegesis that I will assume throughout this book: "the *narratively implied spatiotemporal world of the actions and characters*" (Gorbman 1987, 21; emphasis in original). Contemporary film music studies, and audiovisual studies more broadly, has been much occupied with questions about music's diegetic status, and, beyond the basic conceptual distinction between diegetic and nondiegetic music introduced by Claudia Gorbman in her 1987 book *Unheard Melodies: Narrative Film Music*, a diversity of additional concepts have been suggested, either to capture more precisely those instances of music in film that do not fit easily into the distinction (e.g. Biancorosso 2001; Holbrook 2004; Taylor 2007; Stilwell 2007; Smith 2009; Heldt 2013; Buhler 2018) or else to recontextualize, redefine or even reject the distinction

Tarkovsky's Cinema Through Its Music   7

altogether (e.g. Chion 1994; Rosar 2009; Winters 2010; Kassabian 2001, 2013; Cecchi 2010; Sbravatti 2016; Penner 2017). As will become clear in the coming chapters, in this book my approach to this conceptual panoply is pragmatic in character, meaning that the concepts applied in each chapter are above all chosen for their critical usefulness; i.e. for their fruitfulness in developing the specific interpretation in question. Far from being irrelevant to the understanding of Tarkovsky's films, a probing into music's diegetic status can function as an important means to work out new and rewarding critical perspectives on the films. At the same time, and as I argue more extensively in Chapter 7, a pragmatic selection of concepts based on their critical efficacy still needs to heed the requirement that such concepts are diegetically plausible, which in the context of Tarkovsky's films means that they must convincingly position the music in relation to a diegesis (cf. Pontara 2016). Again, however, as I argue in Chapter 2 (and again in Chapter 7), precisely because of the indeterminate nature of the films' fictional realities, what constitutes the diegesis in a Tarkovsky film is often itself to a high degree dependent on the interpretive framework from which the film is assessed, and thus the diegesis is not simply "narratively implied" in the way it is in most mainstream films. Consequently, in several of the chapters the interpretive process is characterized by a complex balancing act, one in which the critical relevance of the concepts applied, their diegetic plausibility and the interpretatively constructed diegesis constitute interrelated and mutually reinforcing elements.

In weaving music into a broader interpretive argument, each chapter takes a pronouncedly hermeneutical approach toward the film studied. Accordingly, Chapters 2 to 6 provide in-depth close readings of each of Tarkovsky's last five films, focusing on how the philosophical, existential and ethical themes recurring throughout the films are reinforced, deepened and sometimes problematized by the way music is introduced and treated in them. A basic premise underlying this hermeneutical approach is that the multifarious instances of music in Tarkovsky's cinema can productively be theorized as what musicologist Lawrence Kramer, in a now classic phrase, has termed "hermeneutic windows" (Kramer 1990, 6). As such, they constitute a kind of interpretive keys or entry points from which more elaborate readings of the films can be developed. As I hope to show, the readings thus established are not only plausible, but also comprise new and intriguing ways of comprehending and experiencing the films (though the extent to which they rest on analyses of music's diegetic status varies between the chapters). In other words, by accessing each of Tarkovsky's films from *Solaris* to *The Sacrifice* through the lens of the soundtrack, and the music in particular, the book aims at a significant reinterpretation of Tarkovsky's cinematic output as a whole. Thus, rather than being simply a study about music in Tarkovsky's cinema, the present

8   *Tarkovsky's Cinema Through Its Music*

book is concerned with how our understanding and appreciation of Tarkovsky's work can be reinvigorated by looking more closely at the place, role and function of music in his films.

However, speaking about "readings" and "interpretations" immediately raises a contested issue with regard to Tarkovsky's cinema, one that I need to consider at some length here. It appears that the kind of hermeneutical approach advocated in this study is inconsistent with Tarkovsky's own views on how his films should be approached, views that are inextricably tied to his philosophy of art and cinema, and at the center of which stands a strong skepticism, dislike even, of critical interpretations (cf. Miall 2008, 321). This anti-interpretive stance has, sometimes rather uncritically, been adopted as a basic premise in much research on Tarkovsky, as is evident not least in "the frequently repeated aphorism that the films need to be felt rather than 'read'" (McSweeney 2015, 17). Consequently, the approach developed in this book would seem to put me in the position of writing against the grain of contemporary academic discourse.

In Tarkovsky's view, cinema should be regarded as an art form in its own right, one that above all is distinguished by its ability to capture time "in its factual forms and manifestations" (Tarkovsky 1986, 63). The true filmmaker is an artist who works with time in much the same way a sculptor works with a piece of clay or marble. Consequently, the essence of the filmmaker's work can be defined as a "sculpting in time" (Tarkovsky 1986, 63). This centrality of time to Tarkovsky's cinematic aesthetic is perhaps most evident when we consider one of Tarkovsky's most characteristic hallmarks, the so-called long take. In film after film, Tarkovsky creates lengthy sequences marked by such protraction and density that time itself becomes almost tangible, generating in the spectator an impression that each shot is saturated by a unique temporal rhythm or "time pressure" (Tarkovsky 1986, 117). In the words of Tarkovsky himself: "The distinctive time running through the shots makes the rhythm of the picture; and rhythm is determined . . . by the pressure of the time that runs through them" (Tarkovsky 1986, 117).[7] From such a perspective, any film worth the name shapes time in its own characteristic way and thereby develops its temporal, rhythmic and aesthetic distinctiveness. Moreover, unlike literature, film "does not have to use words" but instead "manifests itself to us directly" (Tarkovsky 1986, 60). Cinema has its own "poetic meaning" (Tarkovsky 1986, 82) and "like music, allows for an utterly direct, emotional, sensuous perception of the work" (Tarkovsky 1986, 176), a view echoed by Robert Bird when he writes that "Tarkovsky's films are accessible only through their *direct apprehension* as art works" (Bird 2008, 21; emphasis added). In short, given that the true cinematic artwork is a unique temporal and "emotional reality" (Tarkovsky 1986, 176), such a work must be felt rather than explicated.

Tarkovsky's Cinema Through Its Music   9

Not surprisingly, then, the search for explanations of what various things in his films might mean clearly was something that outraged Tarkovsky:

> Everybody asks me what things mean in my films. This is terrible! An artist doesn't have to answer for his meanings. I don't think so deeply about my work – I don't *know* what my symbols may represent. What matters to me is that they arouse feelings, any feelings you like, based on whatever your inner response might be. If you *look* for a meaning, you'll miss everything that happens. Thinking during a film interferes with your experience of it. Take a watch to pieces, it doesn't work. Similarly with a work of art, there's no way it can be analysed without destroying it.
>
> (Gianvito 2006, 71)

Reducing Tarkovsky's films to a question of simple symbolism or allegory – to representational meaning – is thus to engage in insensitive and unproductive over-intellectualization that fails to acknowledge the emotional impact of his cinematic language and the intriguing complexity of the rich, multilayered sonic and visual images that lie at the heart of his films. Echoing Susan Sontag's famous rejection of interpretation, Tarkovsky describes the critic's search for meaning and content as a violation of the cinematic work and of the spectator's experience, a corrupting activity that, in Sontag's words, "amounts to the philistine refusal to leave the work of art alone" (Sontag 2001, 5). Interpretation and analysis are futile endeavors, for "the moment a viewer understands, deciphers, all is over, finished: the illusion of the infinite becomes banality, a commonplace, a truism. The mystery disappears" (Tarkovsky, quoted in Johnson and Petrie 1994, 38).

Tarkovsky is not, however, entirely consistent in his rejection of critical and symbolic interpretation. Most conspicuously, he occasionally provided such interpretations himself. Thus, Sean Martin notices that for Tarkovsky "the Zone . . . while being just 'a zone', also symbolised the trials and tribulations of life, while the watering of the tree in *The Sacrifice* 'for me is a symbol of faith'" (Martin 2011, 33). Furthermore, in *Sculpting in Time* Tarkovsky sometimes seems to *welcome* critical interpretations of his films, as for example when he claims that "in the multiplicity of judgements passed upon it, the work of art in its turn takes on a kind of inconstant and many-faceted life of its own, its existence enhanced and widened" (Tarkovsky 1986, 46). And, later in the book, he asserts that it gladdens him if his films are able to stimulate "various interpretations" (Tarkovsky 1986, 168). Rather than referring to the readings of academics and critics, however, Tarkovsky is here talking about the personal responses and reactions of the individual cinema-goer. In fact, the affirmation of interpretive multiplicity found in *Sculpting in Time* may be

10 *Tarkovsky's Cinema Through Its Music*

one of the reasons why he tends to reject critical interpretations of a more scholarly kind. For Tarkovsky, such interpretations are by and large characterized by a pretentious style of writing that pretends to tell the reader how things actually are, and claims to occupy a privileged position with regard to what the films mean and how they should be understood. In other words, while Tarkovsky celebrates the indefinite array of imaginative and emotional responses people might have when watching his films, he has no patience with the knowledge production of professional critics and scholars, which is perhaps too often cast in terms of what music sociologist Tia DeNora has described as an "'I'm telling you, it's there' form of analysis" (DeNora 2000, 29).[8] In a book like the present one, which performs exactly the kind of "scholarly" readings of which Tarkovsky is so suspicious, it is thus particularly important to clarify one's interpretive position. Accordingly, I will here briefly outline the methodological and epistemological framework underlying my interpretive arguments in the chapters to come.

This book does not have the ambition to say how things "really" are or what they "essentially" mean in Tarkovsky's films. On the contrary, the readings I develop in the coming chapters are all initiated by and grounded in a highly personal and emotional experience of each film. This experience has been of tremendous importance throughout the interpretive process in that it has functioned as the basic precondition for genuine critical dialogue with the films. Such an admission is tantamount to acknowledging that, on a very fundamental level, my interpretations are not qualitatively different from the "non-scholarly" responses of countless Tarkovsky aficionados. There is thus an inescapable subjective dimension to what is offered in the pages to come. I believe, however, that this is both necessary and desirable, because the moment the critic loses contact with her personal responses, she inevitably starts to disentangle herself from the aesthetic and emotional reality of the film, a reality that can only exist as a lived experience within herself. In this spirit, the readings in Chapters 2 to 6 all result from a critical engagement with each particular film that rests on a decidedly subjective basis. Thus understood, my approach is basically a form of reader-response criticism, something that also explains the structure of the book, which, rather than being arranged in accordance with a set of overarching thematic issues, consists of a collection of relatively free-standing case studies (as will be further discussed at the end of this chapter).

However, to claim that there is always a subjective dimension to critical enquiry is not the same as claiming that interpretations never can be justified, or that no epistemic values can be assigned to them. The readings in this book are developed within a theoretical framework inspired by American philosopher Joseph Margolis's philosophy of interpretation. According to Margolis, "the goal of interpretation" should be "the imputation of a coherent design under conditions descriptively insufficient for

Tarkovsky's Cinema Through Its Music 11

that purpose" (Margolis 1992, 41). Interpretation should thus be understood as a constitutive activity; it constructs, or in David Bordwell's (1989) words "makes," meaning rather than uncovers it. Implicit in the concept of imputation also lies an endorsement of a specific kind of interpretive relativism; in Margolis's words, a "tolerance of alternative and seemingly contrary |interpretive| hypotheses" (Margolis 1992, 41). This brand of interpretive relativism rejects the idea that interpretations "take truth-values" (Margolis 1992, 44), or, amounting to much the same thing, that there are pre-existing properties of artworks to which the conclusions of our interpretive efforts should ideally correspond. But even if truth should not be invoked as the ultimate goal of interpretation, it is still the case that "epistemic values of some sort can be assigned interpretations" (Margolis 1992, 48), and this claim is what distinguishes Margolis's "robust relativism" (as he labels it) from the more easy-going variants of relativism advocated by many postmodern thinkers. Thus, although interpretive arguments cannot or should not be evaluated in terms of truth and falsity, they can be rationally justified by being judged in accordance with criteria of *critical plausibility*. In short, while interpretation is essentially a constructivist activity, in that it attributes rather than detects meaning, specific interpretations are plausible only to the extent that they fulfill certain justificatory requirements.

According to Margolis, a plausible interpretation must fulfill the following two requirements: (1) it must be consistent or compatible with "the describable features" of a given artwork; and (2) it must conform with "relativized canons of interpretation that themselves fall within the tolerance of a historically continuous tradition of interpretation" (Margolis 1992, 48). Regarding the first requirement, interpretations, even if not strictly true or false in themselves, may nevertheless exhibit epistemic integrity as long as they can be shown to be "compatible with what is (minimally) descriptively true of a given work" (Margolis 1992, 43). This requirement may appear rather uncontroversial, but as I will show later, descriptive misrepresentations of music in Tarkovsky's cinema occur with some frequency in the scholarly literature. Such misrepresentations affect the credibility of the interpretations they underpin, since plausible interpretations must be compatible with descriptive accuracy not only of the music itself but also with regard to how music relates to other parts of the soundtrack, as well as to narrative and film image. The tenor of Margolis's second requirement is perhaps less clear. As I have discussed elsewhere, it involves a complex theory of how the conceptual schemes, perceptual abilities and general epistemic outlook of a society at any given historical juncture are conditioned and "fore-structured" (Margolis 2009) by deeply entrenched cultural myths, myths that can subsequently become "'objective' for criticism" (Margolis 1980, 152).[9] But, minimally, it could be understood as saying that any interpretation aspiring to plausibility must be developed in accordance with, or with explicit reference to, a

12　*Tarkovsky's Cinema Through Its Music*

specific body of previous interpretations that are internally related in some relevant way. (I take it that this is at least partly what is meant by the expression "relativized canons of interpretation.") In other words, a plausible interpretation must be critically relevant; it must adjoin with appropriate scholarly contexts and contribute to ongoing intellectual traditions. The latter statement also implies that a plausible interpretation must have critical force, which means that beyond interacting and measuring up with an emerging or established canon of scholarly works – and, more broadly, proceeding within a theoretically and intellectually "continuous tradition of interpretation" – it must advance a substantially novel understanding of the film under consideration. Engaging throughout with a now well-established "canon of interpretation" in Tarkovsky studies – i.e. with major scholarly works like Le Fanu (1987), Söderbergh Widding (1992), Green (1993), Johnson and Petrie (1994), Synessios (2001), Jónsson and Óttarsson (2006), Bird (2008), Dunne (2008), Redwood (2010), Skakov (2012), Mroz (2013), Bould (2014), Sitney (2014a) and McSweeney (2015) – the present book distinguishes itself from its predecessors by its consistent exploration of themes, dimensions and patterns of signification that arguably first become fully apparent when Tarkovsky's films are systematically approached from the perspective of the music (and sound) they contain.

To sum up, the model of interpretation underpinning the readings in this book is one that, while acknowledging and embracing the ineradicable subjective element of all interpretation, stipulates some basic criteria that the readings are required to meet. The advantage of this model is that it sets up clear methodological guidelines for justifying the interpretive arguments advanced, while also leaving ample room for the creativity and imagination of the interpreter.

* * *

As I mentioned earlier, in the course of developing my interpretations, the place and function of the music in each film will be examined in detail. The present book is in fact the first comprehensive study that systematically discusses music in Tarkovsky's cinema, and thus addresses an overlooked area in the steadily growing scholarly literature on Tarkovsky. This in itself should be sufficient reason for its existence. Add to this the often sweeping, and at times downright inaccurate, statements and analyses that with some regularity occur in even the best texts on Tarkovsky, and the rationale behind a book like the present one should be obvious. In order to draw attention to the somewhat unsatisfactory situation within Tarkovsky studies when it comes to the soundtracks, and especially the music, I will briefly discuss a few examples from the scholarly literature that demonstrate how easy it is to misconstrue even the apparently most descriptive levels of Tarkovsky's films (thus violating Margolis's first requirement).

Tarkovsky's Cinema Through Its Music   13

One film of Tarkovsky that has suffered especially with regard to misrepresentations of its soundtrack is *Stalker*. This might not be entirely surprising given the 2001 DVD re-release of the film by the Russian Cinema Council (RusCiCo). In connection with this re-release, and to the chagrin of many Tarkovsky aficionados, parts of the original mono soundtrack were altered in the new 5.1 standard surround-sound format that accompanied the updated version of the film. One major, and apparently completely unauthorized, alteration concerned the celebrated scene where the film's three main characters – Stalker, Writer and Professor – travel into the mysterious Zone on a motorized railway trolley. In Tarkovsky and Artemiev's original version of this scene, the sound of the trolley's rhythmic clacking against the rails is increasingly superimposed by electronically manipulated sounds, signaling a gradual transition from the world of the everyday into the magical realm of the Zone. However, in the new surround-sound version of this scene, a passage of electronically composed music has been added to the soundtrack. While some viewers may consider this an improvement over the original version (the persons responsible for the change obviously did), it is ultimately inconsistent with the director's original intentions.[10]

The new 5.1 version has apparently caused some confusion among film and film music scholars as well, with some writers commenting, knowingly or not, on the "wrong" version without any clarification that it is a distortion of the film as originally conceived by Tarkovsky. Thus, in an otherwise brilliant essay on the musicalization of the soundtrack in contemporary cinema, Kevin Donnelly provides the following description of the railway trolley scene:

> Some art films followed a long-standing tradition of imbuing sound effects with weighty emotional and symbolic significance, endowing sound with a primarily aesthetic role. Tarkovsky's *Stalker* is a case in point, during the sequence of the lengthy train journey to "the zone" where the soundtrack is dominated by the non-quite-regular diegetic clacking of the train on the track. The metallic sounds remain in the foreground, undergirded by some subtle chords, mixed from a small orchestra and synthesized nondiegetic music by Eduard Artemiev.
>
> (Donnelly 2013, 359)

Donnelly here refers to what is sometimes called the "Stalker theme," a slowly unfolding and electronically manipulated melody that is heard at the very beginning of the film and then again during the three men's sojourn in the Zone. In the 5.1 version, this theme does appear in the railway trolley scene, but Tarkovsky and Artemiev had obviously conceived the scene differently, since in the original version the "Stalker theme" is not heard on the soundtrack. There is no evidence that Artemiev would have approved such retroactive alterations, either. (Tarkovsky himself had

14   *Tarkovsky's Cinema Through Its Music*

been dead for 15 years at the time of the re-release.) However, without an explicit qualification that the version commented upon is an alteration of the original soundtrack, such misrepresentations may easily create an impression that they are concerned with *Tarkovsky*'s film when in fact they are describing a distorted version of it. And to the extent that they function as the basis or starting point for more elaborate interpretations of the film, such interpretations themselves risk being compromised, especially if they make reference to the intentions of Tarkovsky and his collaborators.

Also writing about the music in *Stalker*, Thomas Redwood comments on the twice-recurring combination of train sound and classical music in the film's post-credits scene. He states that the second shot of this scene "introduces the rumbling of train wheels accompanied by a fragment of Ravel's *Bolero*," while "at the end of shot VIII we hear the train wheels in motion again, this time accompanied by Wagner's *Meistersinger*" (Redwood 2010, 120). These descriptions are repeated in one of the book's appendices (Appendix D), where the post-credits scene is laid out in detail (Redwood 2010, 247–248). Now, it is true that Ravel's *Bolero* occurs in connection with the sound of moving trains in *Stalker*. But this happens much later in the film, in the extended scene where the purportedly magical Room at the heart of the Zone is gradually revealed to us. In the second shot of the opening scene, it is not Ravel's *Bolero* that we hear, but instead a brief and almost imperceptible passage from *The Marseillaise*. And while the eighth shot does contain music by Wagner, the snippet we hear at this moment is from *Tannhäuser*, not from *Meistersinger*. In what otherwise is a very perceptive and meticulous formal analysis of the "narrational importance of stylistic devices" in *Stalker* (Redwood 2010, 53), such misrepresentations stand out as perplexing and unfortunate anomalies.

Other films by Tarkovsky have suffered from inaccurate descriptions of the music they contain. In what is probably the most extensive and detailed analysis to date of the music in *Solaris*, Tatiana Egorova states that Bach's choral prelude "Ich ruf zu dir, Herr Jesu Christ" (BWV 639) appears three times in the film:

> The choral prelude in F minor appears in the film three times: firstly, with the captions (in its original form), secondly at the golden section point – the scene in the library (combined with Artemiev's music) and lastly in the finale (dissolved in Artemiev's music).
>
> (Egorova 1997, 234)

The chorale actually appears four times. Its second appearance is not in connection with the "scene of weightlessness" (Egorova 1997, 234) in the library, but in an earlier scene where the film's protagonist, Kris Kelvin, and the Solaris-generated version of his deceased wife, Hari, watch

Tarkovsky's Cinema Through Its Music   15

the homemade film that Kelvin has brought with him to the desolate space station. By omitting this scene, Egorova fails to provide a proper grounding for her subsequent analysis of the library scene, in which she states that "listening to the music and looking closely at Brueghel's picture, Hari suddenly begins to 'recollect' her human past" (Egorova 1997, 235). In fact, Bach's music is not actually heard on the soundtrack during Hari's contemplation of the painting; it does not appear until the following sequence, when Hari and Kelvin are seen levitating in the library. But more importantly, the statement that Hari "listens to" or "hears" Bach's music in the library scene is only convincing, to the extent that it can be at all, if we understand this hearing as being of a metadiegetic kind; that is, as something imagined or recollected from Hari's subjective point of view. But this way of construing Bach's music appears rather ad hoc unless the earlier "home movie" scene is taken into account. As I argue in Chapter 2, this is the only scene in the film where we can plausibly claim that Bach's music is manifestly diegetic (i.e. is actually heard by both Hari and Kris), and it is thus crucial for the claim that Hari imagines or recollects this music in the later scene. In itself, it might not be enough to plausibly justify this claim. Without reference to the "home movie" scene, however, the claim comes across as at best an inspired whim, and at worst a seriously mistaken and completely unfounded account.[11]

Egorova and Donnelly are not specialists on Tarkovsky's films. However, even such authorities on Tarkovsky and otherwise perceptive writers as Vida T. Johnson and Graham Petrie are occasionally guilty of misrepresentations. For instance, when discussing the use of Beethoven's "Ode to Joy" in *Nostalghia*, they rightly observe that it appears twice in close connection with the moving and disconcerting character Domenico (although the first time what we actually hear is an instrumental passage from the finale of the Ninth Symphony rather than the "Ode to Joy" itself). A few sentences later, however, they state that "another gravely beautiful extract from the *same music* [is heard] as Andrei succeeds in placing the candle on the far ledge of the pool" (Johnson and Petrie 1994, 200; emphasis added). In fact, what we hear at this point in the film is not Beethoven's music at all but a brief passage from the beginning of Giuseppe Verdi's *Requiem*. Thus, when Johnson and Petrie go on to claim that the subsequent appearance of this "same music" is what "completes Domenico's action and compensates for his failure" (Johnson and Petrie 1994, 200), this claim is critically undermined by the erroneous observation they use to back it up.

A host of other examples could be provided of inaccurate "observations" regarding the music in Tarkovsky's films (and I will note some further instances in the chapters to come). The purpose of this brief survey is not to single out any particular scholar for castigation, but rather to indicate the extent to which the presence of music in Tarkovsky's cinema

16   *Tarkovsky's Cinema Through Its Music*

has been inaccurately handled and analyzed by scholars, which demonstrates the need for a comprehensive study focusing specifically on this dimension of Tarkovsky's films. Moreover, in a book like this one, which takes a decidedly interpretive and hermeneutical approach to Tarkovsky's films, it is clear that misrepresentations like those noted must be rigorously avoided.

* * *

This book is organized as a series of separate case studies. Chapters 2 to 6 survey Tarkovsky's last five feature films in chronological order, while Chapter 7 sums up and further discusses the most significant results that have emerged in the preceding chapters. Chapter 2, on *Solaris*, stands out from the others in that it simultaneously functions as a practical illustration of the interpretive approach described earlier and as a hermeneutical examination of the film from the perspective of its music. The chapter centers on the fourfold appearance of Johann Sebastian Bach's choral prelude "Ich ruf zu dir, Herr Jesu Christ" (BWV 639) and asks how this music relates to the fictional world, or diegesis, of the film. I answer this question by developing two radically different accounts of the chorale's diegetic status, demonstrating how these accounts effectively rely on the interpretive perspective or context through which the music is assessed and, consequently, how they imply very different ways of experiencing the film. In the chapter's penultimate section, this hermeneutic pliability, as I will call it, of the chorale's diegetic status is discussed in relation to Robynn Stilwell's concept of the "fantastical gap," a concept reserved for film music that is felt to be inherently ambiguous with regard to its diegetic status, as opposed to more plainly identifiable diegetic and nondiegetic music (Stilwell 2007). However, not everything about this music is a question of hermeneutic pliability. In the final section of the chapter, I return to what I claim is a basic dichotomy in the film between the "tonal and imaginative spheres" (Egorova 1997) of classical and electronic music, a dichotomy that will surface several times during the chapter in connection with the different interpretive constructions of the chorale's diegetic status. Since I regard this dichotomy as a central element in the film, I contend that any interpretative construal of Bach's music (and by extension, any interpretation of the film that makes reference to Bach's music) that involves a denial of it is destined to be implausible, which in effect means that our interpretive freedom, even if considerable, is not unlimited.

In Chapters 3 to 6, the theoretical discussion running alongside my analysis of *Solaris* is largely set aside in favor of more straightforward case studies, each of which advances a specific interpretive perspective on the film under consideration. Surveying all instances of classical and electronic music in *Mirror*, Chapter 3 aims to foreground the very different roles played by the two types of music in the film and, by implication, how they are involved in the construction of different thematic threads throughout the film. I argue that classical music is connected with life experiences that, because they are familiar and *nameable* human emotions and mental states, are recognizable in such a way that the character can "inhabit" them and "feel at home." In contrast, as the film unfolds, Eduard Artemiev's electronic score becomes increasingly associated with a strong sense of incomprehensibility and alterity, in that it accompanies encounters with things – dreams, supernatural presences, the impenetrable forces of human destruction – that transgress the limits of human understanding and comprehension. By tying both types of music closely to the interiority of the film's main character (even though I identify a few instances that seem to fit less well into this perspective), the chapter works toward the conclusion that *Mirror* explores two radically different, and ultimately irreconcilable, dimensions of human experience.

Chapter 4 takes as its point of departure the very last scene of *Stalker*, which portrays a young girl mysteriously moving glasses across a table just by fixing her eyes on them; the soundtrack simultaneously features the sound of a passing train and a fragment of the "Ode to Joy" from Beethoven's Ninth Symphony. This combination of classical music and train noise forms what I call a sonic figure, a kind of unified sound gestalt that in fact has already appeared several times in the film, and can plausibly be understood as a symbol of the technological, political and ideological developments of post-Enlightenment society. However, when accompanying the magical actions and the ineffable silence of the young girl, these signifiers of triumph and progress appear strangely illusory, creating the impression that the grand projects they denote were never more than a mistaken substitute for a truer, more lasting reality. The chapter then widens its focus and demonstrates how during the course of the narrative a musical dichotomy is gradually established between the recurring sonic figure and the film's electronic score. I argue that this dichotomy effects a division between an authentic subjectivity (electronic music) and the alienating forces (the sonic figure) that threaten to destroy it. In a further step, these complexities of the soundtrack are discussed in relation to the broader ethical and ideological concerns of the film. This discussion eventually brings me back to the film's final scene, which, viewed in relation to the film as a whole, leads me to conclude that *Stalker* can indeed be understood as expressing a central tenet of the utopian aesthetics of early Romanticism: the idea of transcendence.

As I conjecture in the final chapter of this book, of all of Tarkovsky's films *Stalker* is possibly the one in which a utopian impulse is most explicitly at work. *Nostalghia*, on the other hand, can arguably be described as his most despairing picture. Chapter 5 examines how excerpts from canonized works by Beethoven and Verdi are merged with snippets of Russian folk song and how the juxtaposition of these two musical realms

18   *Tarkovsky's Cinema Through Its Music*

serves to emphasize and underscore the film's central existential and ethical themes. The chapter focuses in particular on how music and sound are involved in the film's representation of the condition of nostalgia, which in Tarkovsky's hands becomes an extraordinarily complex and multifaceted phenomenon. The film's two protagonists both die at the end, but the final scene seems to suggest that the main character, the Russian poet-musicologist Andrei, has achieved some kind of reconciliation between his intense yearning for a more authentic life (expressed through his longing for his homeland and his family) and the alienated state of his present exiled condition.

Tarkovsky's final film also has a tormented character at its center, but one who gradually comes to realize the presence of a higher spiritual truth. Chapter 6 focuses on the multiple occurrences of Swedish herding calls in *The Sacrifice*. I argue that these calls can plausibly be described as what I term transcendental diegetic music, and that, while essentially belonging to the film's diegesis, they nevertheless enter the empirical reality of the characters from a position outside of this reality. Thus understood, the herding calls represent the kind of authentic spirituality that Tarkovsky, in *Sculpting in Time*, interchangeably describes as "the infinite," "the limitless" and "absolute spiritual truth" (Tarkovsky 1986, 37). From these considerations, I build a narrative interpretation, the aim of which is to show how the herding calls – understood as the voice of absolute spiritual truth – are increasingly acknowledged by the film's main character, and in this way come to play a crucial role as they guide him toward the radical sacrificial acts in which he eventually engages.

As pointed out earlier, the results and conclusions of this book are not prefigured by a thematically structured approach, but instead emerge out of a free-standing, focused and critical dialogue with each particular film. In the seventh and final chapter, however, the analyses undertaken in Chapters 2 to 6 form the basis of a more extended discussion of questions of music, meaning and interpretation in Tarkovsky's cinema. In summarizing the results of these preceding chapters, three broad themes are identified and elaborated upon. First, picking up the thread from Chapter 2, I discuss the concept of hermeneutic pliability in relation to Tarkovsky's cinema as a whole, examining to what extent the malleable diegetic status of the Bach chorale prelude in *Solaris* also characterizes the music in the other films. Secondly, I develop a more overarching account of how patterns of meaning and representation cluster around different types of music in Tarkovsky's cinema, and identify and discuss the presence of two recurring representational devices related to music in his films: musical dichotomies and musical syntheses. Finally, I conclude the chapter, and the book, with an argument that purports to show how music is centrally involved in what I describe as a "troubled utopianism" present to greater or lesser extent in all of Tarkovsky's last five films.

Notes

1. It is interesting to note, however, that references and tributes to Tarkovsky's films appear with some regularity in contemporary mainstream cinema. One of the more striking examples is Alejandro González Iñárritu's 2015 film *The Revenant*. Another even more recent film that in a humorous manner pays tribute to Tarkovsky is David Leitch's *Atomic Blonde* (2017). Working perhaps more self-consciously within a European art cinema tradition, Lars von Trier in his later films has been strongly influenced by Tarkovsky, an influence that is explicitly acknowledged in films like *Antichrist* (2009) and *Melancholia* (2011), both of which are dedicated to the Russian director. In *Nymphomaniac* (2013), von Trier develops an intricate play with references to Tarkovsky's use of Johann Sebastian Bach's chorale prelude "Ich ruf zu dir, Herr Jesu Christ" in *Solaris*. For further examples of directors who have been inspired by Tarkovsky's cinematic aesthetic, see Nick James's excellent 2015 essay "The Tarkovsky Legacy": www.bfi.org.uk/news-opinion/sight-sound-magazine/features/deep-focus/tarkovsky-legacy (accessed 2019-04-08).
2. An additional "problem" with this book concerns its accessibility, since all the contributions are in Italian.
3. Andrei Tarkovsky, "I'm Interested in the Problem of Inner Freedom." Interview with Jerzy Illg and Leonard Neuger in Stockholm 1985. *Nostalghia.com*: http://nostalghia.com/TheTopics/interview.html (accessed 2018-12-12).
4. "Andrei Tarkovsky on *The Sacrifice*." (Tarkovsky in interview with Annie Epelboin in Paris 1986). *Nostalghia.com*: http://nostalghia.com/TheTopics/On_Sacrifice.html (accessed 2018-12-12).
5. On this topic, see also Fairweather (2012, 32–44).
6. If not otherwise specified, all references to Tarkovsky's films in this book (including specific time specifications) are based on the DVDs in the *Andrei Tarkovsky Collection* issued by Artificial Eye in 2011.
7. For an elucidating discussion of Tarkovsky's concept of time pressure, see McSweeney (2015, 25–42).
8. DeNora's criticism is specifically directed at the branch of musicology that is sometimes called "musical hermeneutics" and that "approach[es] music as if it were a text and ascribe[s] to it clearly delineated narrational, representational, or figurative meanings" (Pontara 2015, 4).
9. See Pontara (2015). See also Casey (1997), Carroll (1999) and Krausz (1999, 109). Although Margolis seems to prefer the term "myth," he concedes that his understanding of cultural myths is partly covered by terms like "archetype" and "ideology" (Margolis 1980, 151–152). Furthermore, one can note that Margolis's theory of cultural myths has much in common with Michel Foucault's ideas about epistemes, discursive formations and the historical a priori.
10. Another peculiar alteration of the soundtrack was the removal of Beethoven's music from the last scene. For more information on this strange handling of the original soundtrack, see *Nostalghia.com*: www.nostalghia.com/TheNews2002.html (accessed 2018-12-13). See also Chapter 4, footnote 17.
11. Egorova's discussion (1997, 237) of *Mirror* provides what could perhaps be called a paradigmatic example of how a lack of descriptive adequacy can undermine an interpretive argument. Here she develops an elaborate reading around the music in the film's pre-credits scene, which shows an adolescent boy being cured of his stuttering. The reading is sophisticated enough, the only problem being that the scene does not contain any music.

2 Bach at the Space Station
Diegetic Ambiguities and Multiplying Gaps in *Solaris*

One of the most memorable scenes from Andrei Tarkovsky's *Solaris* (1972) pictures a man and a woman levitating in a beautifully furnished room (Figure 2.1). The room in question is a library on an almost-deserted space station, the engines of which have been temporarily shut down, resulting in a brief moment of zero gravity. Behind the levitating couple we see miniature reproductions of a series of paintings by Pieter Bruegel the Elder, and during the scene two brief shots are inserted, providing us with close-ups of specific details from one of the paintings, the famous *Hunters in the Snow* (1565). A fully lit candelabrum comes drifting through the air, followed by a copy of Cervantes's novel *Don Quixote*. Before long, the engines restart, and the couple are now seen seated peacefully on a sofa, the man's head resting on the woman's knees. Next to them on the floor is the candelabrum, some of its candles still burning.

This whole sequence proceeds without any dialogue, and other sounds are also reduced to a minimum. Instead, the soundtrack is dominated by the chorale prelude "Ich ruf zu dir, Herr Jesu Christ" (BWV 639) from Johann Sebastian Bach's *Orgelbüchlein*. This piece of music has been heard twice before, and it will be heard again at the very end of the film. In this scene, and in the other scenes where it occurs, it plays a vital role in the construction of an emotional atmosphere marked by tenderness and intimacy, while also betraying the male protagonist's strong yearning to escape the desolated space station and return to the tranquility and fertile soil of his earthly familial home.

When the Bach chorale is mentioned in the literature, it is almost always to point out its role as a representative of Earth and the authentic human values associated with Earth, such as love, spirituality and art. Tatiana Egorova, for example, describes the chorale as "a symbol which has absorbed the greatest timeless values of human culture" (Egorova 1997, 234), and she also emphasizes its close connection to the protagonist's "memory of the Earth, Home [and] Father" (Egorova 1997, 235). Similarly, Metin Çolak stresses how "Bach's prelude reminds us of regaining the essence of life" (Çolak 2013, 16), while Peter Green describes Bach's music as providing "a counterpart to the visual iconography used

Figure 2.1 Kris Kelvin and Hari levitating in the space station's library in *Solaris*
Source: Films Sans Frontières

to evoke memories of Earth" (Green 1993, 76). This understanding of Bach's music in *Solaris* seems to me to be essentially correct, and it also corresponds closely to Tarkovsky's own view of the chorale's role and function in the film (Gianvito 2006, 136). There is, however, another issue connected with the chorale that is seldom raised in the literature, one that is primarily concerned not with the representational function or symbolic value of the music but rather with its *placement* within the cinematic totality of the film. In this chapter, I will focus on this issue by asking how the chorale relates to the narrative of *Solaris*. More specifically, my question is this: should the chorale prelude be understood as part of the narrated world of the film, or is it more plausible to describe it as some kind of extra- or nondiegetic music, that is, as something to which the spectators of the film, but not the characters inhabiting the narrated world, have access? Or to put it another way, how should we locate this music in relation to the film's diegesis, understanding the diegesis as the "narratively implied spatiotemporal world of the actions and the characters" (Gorbman 1987, 21)? As will become clear, the answer to this question will fundamentally depend on the interpretive framework we bring to the film.

But let us return to the space station's library for some initial reflections about the music accompanying the levitating couple. Sonically, the Bach chorale is placed very much in the spectator's perceptual foreground, but in a way that seems to disfavor rather than support an understanding of it as belonging to the diegesis. And where would the music come from, anyway? There is no organ in the library or anywhere else on this

22 *Bach at the Space Station*

sinister station, and even though the station does seem to be equipped with a film projector (see later in this chapter), it is unclear if this is one of those devices that emit sound. If the choice is between diegetic and nondiegetic music, it appears more sensible to ascribe the chorale a nondiegetic status. Thus understood, it is, in Robynn Stilwell's words, not "part of the film's story world" but rather an "element of the cinematic apparatus that represents that world" (Stilwell 2007, 184). Conceived of as occupying a position external to the world of the station, it may be taken as commenting on, framing or narrating something about that world and the people inhabiting it.[1] Perhaps, however, the Bach chorale actually is diegetic music of a more subtle kind. It might be an instance of what film music scholars call *metadiegetic* music: music heard, remembered or otherwise imagined by a character within the diegesis. As such, the music would most obviously be understood as an integral part of the male protagonist's experience, something that he feels, undergoes, perceives and engages with. In the levitation scene, at least, this may be an entirely plausible way of making sense of this music.

In what follows, my objective is to show how situating Bach's music within different interpretive frameworks may shape the way we understand its diegetic status in the film. I begin with a brief overview of the narrative of *Solaris* and the occurrences of Bach's music in the film. The main part of the chapter then develops two radically different interpretive perspectives on the film and its music, each of which implies a different construal of the music's diegetic status. According to the first perspective, the chorale is best understood as a nondiegetic representation, while in the second perspective, it gradually emerges as metadiegetic music. My claim is that these perspectives are both acceptable, and that nondiegetic and metadiegetic accounts are equally plausible. Moreover, there are almost certainly other accounts of Bach's music, and its diegetic status, that merit consideration. In the chapter's penultimate section, this *hermeneutic pliability* of the Bach chorale is discussed in relation to film musicologist Robynn Stilwell's concept of the "fantastical gap," a concept reserved for music in film that is experienced as genuinely indeterminable or ambiguous with regard to the more stable states of plainly identifiable diegetic and nondiegetic music. I argue that it is precisely the open and indeterminate nature of Tarkovsky's film, and more specifically the difficulty of determining what its narrative is about and hence what constitutes its diegesis, that enables a plurality of widely divergent but nevertheless equally plausible interpretive constructions of the Bach chorale, a plurality that in turn gives rise to a multiplicity of ambiguities or "fantastical gaps" with regard to its diegetic status. However, not everything about this music is a question of hermeneutic pliability. In the final section of the chapter, I return to what I claim is a basic dichotomy in the film between the "tonal and imaginative spheres" (Egorova 1997, 230) of classical and electronic music, a dichotomy that will surface several times during the chapter in

Bach at the Space Station 23

connection with the different interpretive constructions of the chorale's diegetic status. Since I regard this dichotomy as a central element in the film, I contend that any interpretative construal of the Bach chorale that involves a denial of it is destined to be implausible, which in effect means that our interpretive freedom, even if considerable, is not unlimited.

Bach in *Solaris*: A Brief Overview

In *Solaris*, astronaut and psychologist Kris Kelvin is sent to an almost-deserted space station located just above the surface of the mysterious planet Solaris, his specific mission being to investigate the "solaristic" science carried out there and decide whether the research program should continue or be shut down. Once at the station, however, Kelvin soon loses control of the situation. Like the three remaining crew members (one of whom has actually died by the time of Kelvin's arrival), his mind is almost immediately affected by the strange powers of Solaris: when the space station's personnel are asleep, the planet mysteriously starts to interact with their psyches by transforming figures from their dreams into material beings. Kelvin soon encounters a rematerialization of his long-lost love Hari, who committed suicide a decade before Kelvin's departure to Solaris. Kelvin's initial reaction betrays an almost panicked denial of what is going on, in that he immediately tries to get rid of the resurrected Hari by ejecting her from the station in a small space capsule. But when Hari continues to rematerialize (back on Earth, Kelvin's abandonment of Hari seems to have been at least a contributing cause of her suicide), the guilt-ridden Kelvin starts to develop an ever-increasing attachment to her and, as a result, gradually grows more and more indifferent to his initial mission assignment. The power the planet holds over Kelvin, represented mainly through his growing affection for Hari, eventually escalates to the point where it is revealed that his apparent return to Earth is actually an illusion. The zooming out of the end scene takes the spectator by surprise, revealing that what at first appears to be Kelvin's beloved family house is actually a replica located on a tiny island on Solaris's vast oceanic surface.

By Tarkovskian standards, *Solaris* contains a fairly large amount of music, especially if compared to his final two works, *Nostalghia* and *The Sacrifice*. If for the moment, however, we disregard the electronic score (consisting of both music and non-musical sounds) saturating portions of the film, what remains amounts to four appearances of Bach's chorale prelude. The first of these occurs in connection with the opening credits, in a sense setting the tone for what is to come. The significance of this opening sequence is vividly described by Mark Bould:

> Houselights go down, credits roll. White Cyrillic text seems to glow against the pitch-black backdrop. For three whole minutes. Thirty

24 *Bach at the Space Station*

seconds of actors' names scrolling up the screen, and then the film's title and crew credits fade in and out, one after another, in the centre of the screen. There is something very deliberate about this darkness. It takes us deeper than the mere dimming of an auditorium. Accompanied by Bach's Chorale Prelude in F Minor, a plea for a divine infusion of faith in a time of despair, it quietens us. The sacramental organ music ministers. It slows our pace, prepares us. Sound and vision transport us into another world.

(Bould 2014, 28)

After this first playing of Bach's music, we have to wait a long time before we encounter it again. When it next occurs, we are already an hour and a half into the film. Here it accompanies a short home movie that Kelvin has brought with him to the station and that he and Hari are now watching. Approximately half an hour later, the chorale makes its third appearance in connection with the spectacular scene where Kelvin and Hari drift weightlessly through the station's library. Finally, the chorale appears as a bridge into the film's final scene (briefly described earlier), where it accompanies and underscores what may be understood as Kelvin's ultimate submission to the attracting forces of Solaris.

The Implied Filmmaker – Nondiegetic Bach

When we first hear Bach's music in *Solaris*, we have not yet entered into the story world where a discussion of its location along the diegetic/nondiegetic axis would become directly relevant.[2] It is with the chorale's second appearance that the intricacies begin. Constituted as a film within a film, the scene presents us with the short home movie from Kelvin's childhood, and we see Kelvin together with his parents in autumn and winter landscapes of a distinctly Bruegelesque kind. The film includes a short concluding sequence presumably shot by the adult Kelvin himself, since what we now see is Hari in front of his parents' house. Actually, Bach's music has already begun to assert itself in the preceding scene, where it emerges from an electronic soundscape accompanying a panoramic view of Solaris's surface. While the electronic sounds quickly fade away, the chorale continues to play in the short intervening episode where we see Kelvin and Hari preparing to watch the home movie. We then hear it during the whole sequence featuring the film, after which it continues for a few seconds in connection with a medium-close-up shot of Kelvin and Hari as they watch the monitor (Figure 2.2).

Interestingly, the end of the Bach chorale is synchronized with subtle changes in lighting as the home movie stops. Thus, at least one element of the *mise-en-scène* might actually prompt us to think of the music as constituting a soundtrack to the homemade film and, consequently, as being diegetic in a more straightforward sense.[3] (Regarding the beginning

Figure 2.2 Kelvin and Hari after having watched Kelvin's homemade film in *Solaris*
Source: Films Sans Frontières

of the chorale, we could perhaps envisage it as a sound advance to the diegetic screening of the film.) On the other hand, the timbral qualities of this music mark it as nondiegetic rather than diegetic; sonically, the music simply does not appear to be issuing from any loudspeakers in the room where Kelvin and Hari are watching the film. So already on this level an uncertainty arises as to the music's relation to the diegesis, since it seems to be cued in different ways by the image and soundtrack. The cues that would favor a plainly diegetic understanding of Bach's music might nevertheless be too subtle to be convincing. Moreover, in the third and fourth playings of the chorale, such cues are nonexistent. In light of this, it seems reasonable to explore the prospects for a nondiegetic construal of this music, even though it seems unlikely that we could give a convincing description of it as performing the functions traditionally associated with nondiegetic music in classical narrative cinema. The Bach of *Solaris* does not have much in common with how such music typically behaves in a classical narrative film. Here I will focus instead on a somewhat different strategy, namely to construe it as a statement about or an attitude toward the film, with its themes issuing from what has been termed an "implied filmmaker."

According to Jerrold Levinson, we need to make a distinction between the "cinematic narrator" and the "implied filmmaker" and between the types of film music – narrative and non-narrative – that can be ascribed to each. The basic criterion for distinguishing between the two is whether or not the music makes something fictional, or fictionally true, in the

26   *Bach at the Space Station*

world of a film. Levinson suggests that music ascribable to the implied filmmaker is typically non-narrative, and can instead be understood "as a direct reflection of authorial stance or personality" (Levinson 2004, 510). Thus, whereas the implied filmmaker is equivalent to the director *as hypothesized* by a properly informed viewer or audience,[4] the cinematic narrator is to be thought of as responsible for the film's narration while at the same time existing on "the fictional plane of the characters" (Levinson 2004, 487). Nicholas Reyland argues that this division may be too crude, quoting Edward Branigan, who states that "between the 'extra-fictional' narrator (the implied filmmaker) and the narrative presenter . . . 'many fine gradations' exist" (Reyland 2012a, 61). For our present purposes, we will accept the distinction, since it entails that, in contrast to the cinematic narrator, the implied filmmaker should be understood as an agency that "presents the world of the film, at one doxastic remove, from a position external to it" (Levinson 2004, 488). Thus, to the extent that we can convincingly construe Bach's music as reflecting a standpoint or an attitude issuing from Tarkovsky himself (or a hypothesized Tarkovsky), we will conceive of it as coming from outside of the film's story world.

But can we plausibly interpret it in this way? As a musical style topic in cinema, Bach's music (and classical music more generally) has been associated with everything from aristocratic and upper-class locations to cultivated but dangerous psychopaths.[5] Two films that immediately spring to mind here are Stanley Kubrick's *Barry Lyndon* (1975) and Jonathan Demme's *Silence of the Lambs* (1991). This use of the music to establish setting or delineate character should be ascribed to Levinson's cinematic narrator, since it clearly takes part in constituting the fictional world of the film. There are, however, other uses of Bach's music that may better be understood as an expression of an implied filmmaker. For example, in the European art cinema of the 1960s and 1970s, Bach was sometimes used to signify moments of revelation and intense emotionality, often in a way that was closely tied to the personal convictions, experiences and worldviews of the filmmaker. Perhaps the best example of this is Swedish director Ingmar Bergman. In films such as *Through a Glass Darkly* (1961), *Hour of the Wolf* (1968), *Cries and Whispers* (1972), *Autumn Sonata* (1978) and later *Saraband* (2003), Bach's music at times takes on the character of a lamentation, revealing and highlighting the "spiritual condition of individuals and circumstances" (Bird 1996) in a way that can be experienced as a direct communication from the director to his audience.[6]

Tarkovsky may in fact have been influenced by Bergman's use of Bach in *Through a Glass Darkly* (where the only music heard is the Saraband from the second Cello Suite in D minor) in his own treatment of it in *Solaris*.[7] In both films, Bach's music accompanies the opening credits and then reappears three times at important nodes in the narrative, including at the very end. Moreover, in Tarkovsky, as in Bergman, the association of Bach with emotional sincerity and intensified inwardness marks not only

Bach at the Space Station   27

several of his films, but to a certain extent his whole vision of art and life. For Tarkovsky, the two were inextricably linked. Thus, with a pathos that placed him very far from the prevailing aesthetic currents of the twentieth century, he could claim that "the aim of art is to prepare a person for death, to plough and harrow his soul, rendering it capable of turning to good" (Tarkovsky 1986, 43; see also Johnson and Petrie 1994, 32). In another formulation, art "is an instrument for knowing |the world| in the course of man's journey towards what is called 'absolute truth'" (Tarkovsky 1986, 37). In Tarkovsky's artistic testament, *Sculpting in Time*, claims like these are legion, suggesting that his aesthetic outlook is a kind of *Kunstreligion* that connects art and the experience of art to deep existential, spiritual and "eternal" truths (I will return to this topic in the last chapter of this book). Bach stands very much at the center of this conception. Even though Tarkovsky strenuously rejects much of the art and (especially) music of the Western world as being shamelessly self-centered and emotionally insincere,[8] he does make an important exception for the music of Bach, the truth and sincerity of which results from it enabling a "relationship with God |that| is absolutely outside of civilization" (Gianvito 2006, 141). For Tarkovsky, Bach's music discloses the truth within us.

If we return now to *Solaris*, we can note that the appearance of the Bach chorale prelude is confined to exactly those scenes where the space station and its spectral atmosphere are temporarily set aside and Kelvin is instead involved with the people and places of his earlier life on Earth. Musically and emotionally, there is also a clear contrast between, on the one hand, the poignancy, firmly grounded F-minor tonality and slowly unfolding melody in the chorale's upper part and, on the other hand, the monotonous electronic rumbling, buzzing and humming surrounding and permeating the station. Understood as a style topic that conveys a "chorale-like religiosity" (Reyland 2012a, 59), this organ piece may on a broader cultural or "mythic" level (cf. Barthes 1972) be taken to signify the eternal values and absolute spiritual truth that have been ascribed to Bach's music – and, *pace* Tarkovsky, classical music more generally – since the dawn of Romanticism. Thus, within the Earth-Space dichotomy of *Solaris*, the continuous reappearance of Bach's chorale may be understood as a leitmotif representing the earthly, but timeless, values of love, intimacy, authenticity and subjective truth, providing, in Robert Hatten's words, "a vision of grace in the midst of tragic grief" (quoted in Reyland 2012a, 65).[9] Or perhaps, considering the title of the work, it can more accurately be conceived of as a *plea* for such grace, as a call for salvation in times of deep despair and alienation. In any case, Tarkovsky himself seems to have had a similar reading in mind. Thus, in complete accordance with his belief that Bach's music was the absolute expression of an inner or subjective truth, he claimed that

> unlike the main idea of |Stanislaw| Lem's novel, the idea in our film
> was the following: human beings have to remain human beings, even

28   *Bach at the Space Station*

if they find themselves in inhumane conditions. . . . What could be more natural than to express this idea of humanity with the help of Bach's music?

(Gianvito 2006, 136)[10]

According to Levinson, when pre-existing music is encountered in a film it often conveys a much stronger "impression . . . of chosenness, on the part of the implied filmmaker" than music specifically composed and adapted for film (Levinson 2004, 483). To perceive Bach's music as being chosen in this sense seems a perfectly sensible option, an option that should be even stronger in an "art film" like *Solaris*, where the author can be understood as a "textual force 'who' communicates . . . and expresses" her or his intentions and visions through her or his handling of the filmic apparatus (Bordwell 2007, 154). Juxtaposing Tarkovsky's near-religious reverence for Bach's music with an account of how this music functions in the film, we may read the chorale as a musically expressed ethical statement issuing directly from the (implied) director: namely, that a person's most important obligation, always and under any circumstances, is to preserve the truth within him or herself, to hold on to that which makes him or her a human being. The music is heard as an important message of an implied (or actual) filmmaker, who, by using it, intends to tell us that this is what the scenes are all about, indeed what the whole film is about.

On this view, the music is strongly nondiegetic: we have constructed it as a statement of what is of importance in human life, a statement made by a persona that is actually "standing outside both the story and its narration" (Levinson 2004, 485).[11] Constructed as a statement issuing from an implied filmmaker, the music is *about* the *type* of circumstances in which Kelvin is caught up. As an "external meditation on the film's happenings" (Levinson 2004, 508), it shows us Tarkovsky's attitude toward the circumstances depicted and how one should behave under such circumstances.

Kelvin and the "ID-Machine" – Metadiegetic Bach

A construal of Bach's chorale prelude as nondiegetic in the sense previously mentioned is not easily reconcilable with a conception of it as metadiegetic, for it is hard to simultaneously perceive it as an utterance of an implied filmmaker *and* as something heard or otherwise experienced by a character in the diegesis. This is not to say that there is only one correct interpretation of the chorale, only that it may be very difficult to imagine it as being both of these things at the same time. To the extent that there exists an irreconcilability between the two perspectives, it is of a psychological rather than a logical kind. In philosopher Robert Stecker's words, it is a "seeing-as incompatibility," which is something very different from logical incompatibility (Stecker 1997, 129–132). Thus, far from claiming

Bach at the Space Station 29

that there is no viable way to interpret the chorale as metadiegetic, my aim in this section is precisely to develop such an interpretation.

With reference to French literary theorist Gérard Genette, Claudia Gorbman describes metadiegetic music as "[music] pertaining to narration by a secondary narrator," and she particularly associates such music with the "musical thoughts" of a character in the diegesis, suggesting by implication that metadiegetic music is music that is heard or imagined from the on-screen character's point of view (Gorbman 1987, 22–23). Robynn Stilwell, elaborating on Gorbman's definition, distinguishes between two types of metadiegetic music: (1) a "literal form," such as when, in *Amadeus* (1984), the audience hears the same music that Mozart hears in the act of composition; and (2) the more common situation, where an on-screen character associates music with something else, like, for example, a past event or the memory of another person. Stilwell then goes on to discuss a musical cue from the film *The Insider* (1999), which she considers to be "an even more abstracted form of metadiegetic sound," since here the music can be understood as expressing or underscoring *unarticulated* emotions (Stilwell 2007, 195–196). Ultimately, however, she remains skeptical of strategies leading to "ever finer gradations and attendant terminologies" within the category of the metadiegetic, preferring instead a modified version of Gorbman's conception:

> we might refine the concept of the metadiegetic as a kind of represented subjectivity, music clearly (through framing, dialogue, acting, lighting, sound design, or other cinematic process) situated in a character who forms a particularly strong point of identification/location for the audience. The character becomes the bridging mechanism between the audience and the diegesis as we enter into his or her subjectivity.
>
> (Stilwell 2007, 196)

Can Bach's chorale be "situated" in Kelvin in the way Stilwell describes here? On the one hand, the scenes featuring the chorale display no obvious features of dialogue, sound design or cinematography that would warrant describing the music as residing in Kelvin. On the other hand, by experiencing the film from within a certain interpretive framework, we may actually begin to see aspects of the film image as supporting a conception of the music as metadiegetic. For Tarkovsky, the narrative of *Solaris* was to be understood as an "inner journey" (see Gianvito 2006, 33, 167), and he probably would have approved of Steven Dillon's description of the film as "one of the most profound cinematic dreams ever conceived" (Dillon 2006, 2). It would be hard indeed to imagine a credible reading of *Solaris* that did not at some level involve a conception of the film as being about the inner world of Kelvin. Peter Green goes so far as to say that "the possibility that . . . all Kelvin's . . . seemingly real

30   Bach at the Space Station

experiences in the space station might be materializations of mental or subconscious states cannot be excluded" (Green 1993, 74). Along these lines, I suggest that a particularly plausible way of making sense of this film is to view it from a psychoanalytical perspective. Such a perspective is championed by Slavoj Žižek in an inventive Lacanian reading of *Solaris*.

According to Žižek, the planet Solaris can be regarded as "an exemplary case of the Lacanian Thing," since in it (or nearby) the distinction between a realistic conception of our life situation and the magical realm of floating phantasmagorias of the Lacanian Real collapses. Solaris, for Žižek, is an "Other-Thing . . . directly materializing our innermost fantasies which support our desire"; it is what he calls an "Id-machine," that is to say "a machine that generates and materializes in reality itself my ultimate phantasmatic objectal supplement or partner, which I would never be ready to accept in reality, although my entire psychic life turns around it" (Žižek 1999, 223). But even though this "Other-Thing" (Žižek also refers to it as the "Solaris-Thing") must be understood as being part of ourselves, and thus not something materially external to us, Žižek argues that it should not be directly equated with the Freudian unconscious. For, he says, "the Solaris-Thing is even more 'ourselves' than the Unconscious, since it is an otherness which directly 'is' ourselves, staging the 'objectively subjective' phantasmatic core of our being" (Žižek 1999, 226). In fact, Žižek comprehends the Solaris-Thing as something akin to the Kantian transcendental subject, in that it shares with this subject both its constituting powers and the impossibility of coming to know or grasp it. Like the noumenal subject of Kant, the Solaris-Thing is a "Thing which thinks" and, moreover, a thing which, while thinking, makes things happen (Žižek 1999, 225). It is at the same time our innermost core and a radical otherness, and, being such an "inner-alien" force, it "must remain at a distance if we are to sustain the consistency of our symbolic universe" (Žižek 1999, 226). From a Žižekian perspective, then, Solaris should be conceived of as a largely inaccessible dimension of Kelvin himself, a seething vessel for his most repressed desires, feelings and fears. When the forces of this giant Id-machine begin to spin out of control, they threaten to erode the fragile self-identity of Kelvin and his fellow crew members (one of whom, the doctor Gibarian, is actually driven to suicide).

In his essay, Žižek has next to nothing to say about the music in *Solaris*. This is unfortunate, for the threatening radical otherness of Solaris is effectively intensified by the electronic sounds that are so inextricably linked to the planet and its powers. Far more than just a symbol of the alien and unfathomable nature of Solaris (which is, of course, the standard way electronic music was put to use in a great many Hollywood films of the 1950s and 1960s), Eduard Artemiev's ANS-generated electronic sounds must be regarded as one of the main resources by which the film constructs the planet's otherness.[12] Indeed, some of these sounds can plausibly be understood as radiating directly from the planet itself, turning them into the metadiegetic "music" of the more unknown and anonymous regions of our protagonist's interior.

There are numerous instances in the film where electronic music appears to be a direct articulation of Solaris's enigmatic activities, something that is perhaps most evident in the recurring shots (nine in total, if the final scene is counted) of the planet's oceanic surface (Figure 2.3). These shots are almost invariably accompanied by a distinctive electronic rumble, aptly described by Egorova as "a compressed clot of sound energy" (Egorova 1997, 233). It is the consistent matching of this clearly demarcated and identifiable sound unit with the simmering and ever-changing surface of Solaris that creates the impression of a sound being produced by the planet itself. Moreover, there are several sequences in the film where characters seem to take notice of this reverberating sound "clot." For example, when Kelvin, after having watched the first part of Gibarian's taped message, takes the video cassette out of the recorder, the rumbling sound is briefly heard. Kelvin, who is about to leave Gibarian's disorganized living quarters, turns around with an expression of wariness on his face, scanning the room with his eyes as if to locate the source of the sound.

Other parts of Artemiev's score are more indirectly connected to Solaris's activities by being associated with the neutrino-constituted "guests"[13] rather than appearing in connection with images of the planet. An example of this is the octave interval heard when Kelvin, just after his arrival on the station, briefly spots a human ear belonging to one of the guests, who has taken up residence in cyberneticist Dr. Snaut's room;[14] another

Figure 2.3 The surface of the planet Solaris
Source: Films Sans Frontières

32 *Bach at the Space Station*

is the recurring "melodious chimes of little bells, crystal rods and goblets" (Egorova 1997, 234) associated with the young girl wandering around the station (and whose presence is due to the now deceased Gibarian). The most striking example, however, occurs just before the third playing of the Bach chorale when Hari, temporarily left alone in the library, is contemplating the reproduction of Bruegel's *Hunters in the Snow*. Here, the planet's inscrutable nature is sonically expressed through Hari's metadiegetic imaginations as she meticulously examines the painting. Saturated by a combination of electronically amplified natural sounds and more unequivocal electronic music, this scene can be understood "as an act of the ocean's 'surrogate creature', one which allows Solaris to begin 'to grasp the alien nature of human aesthetics'" (Thomson 2007, 13).[15]

Returning now to our Žižekian perspective, the narrative of *Solaris* can be construed as an inner drama in which Kelvin struggles to maintain what he perceives to be his authentic or real identity; an identity, moreover, formed by and grounded in, to use Žižek's words, his "concrete social or cultural background" (Žižek 2000, 251; see also Tarkovsky 1986, 193). For Kelvin, the core of this "background" is constituted by his intimate relationships with and commitments to a few people (Hari, his mother and perhaps most of all his father) and to his parents' dacha and the fertile nature surrounding it. And in almost direct opposition to the impersonal quality of the electronic sounds radiating from Solaris, Kelvin's recurring attempts to reconnect with the "authentic objects" of his earlier life are unvaryingly accompanied by the music of Bach. In this way, the two kinds of music come to represent two different levels of, or forces in, Kelvin's psyche: the one threatening to undermine his identity by its instant, but ultimately illusory, gratification of his innermost longings and desires (thus corresponding to Freud's concept of the primary process); the other striving to maintain the bonds to his earlier life on Earth in order to prevent that final psychic breakdown in which reality – and, hence, a sense of stable identity – no longer can be kept separate from pure fantasy and illusion.

Now the claim that Bach's music can be understood as metadiegetic connects with the observation that it is locatable to just those scenes in the film where Kelvin engages with different kinds of substitutes for the highly emotionally invested objects of his pre-Solaris life. It is through his deep and longstanding attachment to Hari, his parents, the family dacha and the countryside surrounding it that he has formed his identity – his conception of who he truly and essentially is. Bach's music is closely connected to this "Kelvian" life-world, and may even be regarded as an integral part of it.

To see how this can be so, let us return to the scene featuring the home movie. As a film-within-a-film, this scene juxtaposes the point-of-view perspective of Kelvin and Hari with that of the spectator. Accordingly, even if we may not actually feel that our viewing perspective is identical to that

Bach at the Space Station 33

of the characters, we must acknowledge the fact that, just like us, Kelvin and Hari are watching the film. In showing the film, Kelvin obviously hopes to help the replica-Hari of the space station to reclaim some of her identity as the real-person Hari of his earlier life, even if this means providing replica-Hari with images and memories that, strictly speaking, do not belong to her (though it seems as if she actually does start to internalize some of them). But it could be argued that this is not necessarily the basic motive for Kelvin's undertaking. As so often with Tarkovsky, the scene can be read in several ways. Thus, we may take it to be less about Hari's predicament than Kelvin's own salvation. Hari herself entertains this possibility during the gloomy celebration of Snaut's birthday in the library when she defends Kelvin against the accusations of the astrobiologist Sartorius. Saying that Kelvin is better than both Snaut and Sartorius because his love for her makes him more human than the two of them, she immediately qualifies this statement: "Or maybe it's not me he loves, but he's simply protecting himself." From this perspective, the screening of the home movie is motivated primarily by emancipatory needs; Kelvin strives to break free from the alienated atmosphere of the station and the phantasmagoric forces of Solaris – of which replica-Hari's appearance is but another manifestation – by constructing a relationship of authentic intimacy with the persons figuring in the film and, even more importantly, with the replica-Hari who is watching the film with him. On this reading, Bach's music acts as the subjective core of this staged intimacy; it is, so to speak, the musically articulated emotional interior that fuels Kelvin's struggles to protect his sense of self from the alienating forces of Solaris. Hence, Bach's chorale prelude should be regarded as an integral part of Kelvin's state of mind; it constitutes the emotional ambiance needed in order to endow his space station alliances with the reality and (imagined) authenticity of his pre-Solaris relationships on Earth.

The two additional scenes in which the music is heard may be read in much the same way. In the levitation scene, where Kelvin and Hari are seen floating weightlessly in the station's library, the music begins when the couple are already in the air, just after the camera's (and Hari's) close examination of Bruegel's painting. Again, we can understand this scene as Kelvin's attempt to resurrect the emotional reality or "feel" of his earlier life. And just like the first attempt, this second staging of intimacy and reconciliation will fail because however much Kelvin wants her to be real, the Solaris-derived Hari is precisely not that: she is and remains a phantom of the protagonist's guilt-ridden past. The important point, however, is that just as with the earlier scene, we may construct the present scene as one in which Kelvin is hearing – in the sense of in some way experiencing the import of – Bach's music. Thus, we may sensibly claim that at this moment Kelvin "wordlessly . . . 'takes over' part of the film's narration," putting us, the spectators, in the privileged position of being able "to read his musical thoughts" (Gorbman quoted in Stilwell 2007, 194). Or maybe

34   *Bach at the Space Station*

it is more accurate to say that it is his musically *rendered* thoughts we are presented to and that the music *focalizes* these thoughts, i.e. functions as a "representation or intimation of [Kelvin's] mental states and processes" (Heldt 2013, 127). Thus understood, Kelvin does not *literally* hear Bach's music; rather, the music is taken as "indicating something non-musical in the character's mind" (Heldt 2013, 128).[16] This, however, could still be described as a form of metadiegetic music, though one of a more subtle and "abstracted" kind (Stilwell 2007, 195–196). A similar metadiegetic account is valid also for the film's concluding scene, in which we first are made to believe that Kelvin has finally returned to Earth, only to soon find out that he is encircled by the Id-forces of Solaris more than ever before, in that he is now literally *on* the planet's surface. As if to signal Kelvin's immense relief and emotional excitement upon his imagined homecoming, the music swells in volume until it completely dominates the soundtrack.

In all three scenes, then, Kelvin's interaction with the phantasms produced by the Solaris-Thing awakens in him a very specific mental state, and this mental state is what is defined by Bach's music. Tarkovsky himself expressed something similar with regard to how music could function in his films when, in a discussion of *Mirror*, he wrote that he and Artemiev wanted the music to "accurately produce precise states of mind, the sounds of a person's interior world" (Tarkovsky 1986, 162).

This metadiegetic reading of Bach's music can be further substantiated if it is placed more explicitly within the context of our Žižekian perspective. For, whether or not we want to emphasize Kelvin as an agent who actively performs an act of intimacy, Bach's chorale can be construed as a product of the Solaris-Thing, as something emanating from the depths of Kelvin's unconscious. It may initially look as if Bach's music is set up in direct opposition to Artemiev's electronic sounds. The electronic sound world belongs to the impersonal Id-forces of the Solaris-Thing. Bach's music, on the other hand, is connected to Earth and the personal relationships left behind there, and by extension to Kelvin's repeated attempts to access what Nariman Skakov (2012, 86) describes as a "realm of true existence." But this radical opposition between the two kinds of music is more apparent than real, since what actually happens during the course of the film is that they increasingly come to merge with one another. More precisely, as the film proceeds Bach's music is "gradually deformed by Eduard Artemiev's electronic elaborations" (Bird 2008, 152). This process is rather subtle, and the first and second playings of the chorale do not display any obvious electronic distortions.[17] In its third occurrence, however, the chorale becomes increasingly infused with the electronic sounds of the ANS synthesizer, and toward the end of this sequence the chorale – here played while "the ocean of metamorphic plasma that covers [Solaris's] surface" (Bould 2014, 20) is shown – is bit by bit drowned out by the ominous rumbling sound emanating from the planet. With

Bach at the Space Station 35

the fourth and final occurrence of the chorale, its absorption into the alien electronic sound world of Solaris is completed. Here it has become inextricably merged with the "vibraphone-like countermelody" added by Artemiev and with the ANS-generated "vocal, string, and bell-like textures" (Barham 2009, 266).[18] Accordingly, just as it visually becomes clear that Kelvin is now on Solaris's surface, it aurally becomes clear that he is completely and irreversibly encircled by the Planet's powers.

This electronic take-over of Bach's music makes the chorale prelude and the state of mind it represents increasingly a part of the Solaris-Thing.[19] It is as if the core of Kelvin's interiority has transformed into an echo of itself, an echo returned in transmuted form by the enigmatic planet. Just as replica-Hari and the illusion of the family home on Solaris's surface are produced by the impersonal forces of the Solaris-Thing, so too is the "Bachian interior" of Kelvin. Bach's music and the state of mind it represents belong to an Id-constituted world of simulacra into which Kelvin inevitably and increasingly is drawn. Thus, "Tarkovsky's Kelvin gives himself over to the will of Solaris, in a sense becoming the planet's puppet" (Jordan and Haladyn 2010, 271).

Being produced by the planet itself, Bach's music belongs to the same category as the illusory replicas of Kelvin's lost "good objects" (the characters in the home movie, the Hari of the space station, the father and the house in the final scene). It is just as much a part of his experienced world as these objects are. Indeed, in the concluding scene everything we see and hear can be understood as the metadiegetic fantasies of the "Kelvian" Solaris-Thing. According to Sean Martin, "as *Solaris* progresses, it is less and less concerned with 'corresponding to reality', and more and more engaged in depicting Kelvin's inner world" (Martin 2011, 103). The final scene can be viewed as the culmination of this journey into interiority.[20]

Hermeneutic Pliability and Multiplying Gaps

In most classical and contemporary Hollywood cinema, it is a relatively straightforward matter to decide whether a piece of music is diegetic or nondiegetic, thoroughly acquainted as we all are with the conventions that signal the presence of each (Bordwell and Thompson 2010, 285; Dyer 2010, 99–100).[21] Within film musicology, however, there has been quite a lot of discussion regarding those instances where the distinction between the two is blurred, situations for which Robynn Stilwell has coined the term "the fantastical gap." As Stilwell (2007, 184) points out, such situations seem to presuppose the existence of more unambiguous forms of diegetic and nondiegetic music. In a similar fashion, and with direct reference to Stilwell, Daniel Yacavone claims that the "ambiguity and 'border crossing' not only confirms the diegetic/nondiegetic distinction, and the existence of a border area between the two, but also 'calls attention' to both" (Yacavone 2012, 33; see also Pontara 2016, 52).[22]

36   *Bach at the Space Station*

In a film like *Solaris* the required conventions are either lacking or play a subordinate role. Thus, the question of whether Bach's music is diegetic or nondiegetic may not catch on to our intuitions and so might be felt as having no obvious answer. One might even respond to it by saying that such attempts to place the music fundamentally miss the point; what is important are the aesthetic, emotional, poetic and, perhaps, symbolic aspects of this music. Another way to answer the question, however, is to do what I have been trying to do in the preceding pages, namely to show how the music's diegetic status changes in proportion to the varying interpretive accounts that justify it. In this line of reasoning, Bach's music *becomes* diegetic, nondiegetic or metadiegetic only within the scope or context of a specific reading, and this is what I refer to as the music's hermeneutic pliability.

One way to account for such hermeneutic pliability is to understand the appearances of Bach's chorale prelude in *Solaris* as "unique moments" in Nicholas Reyland's sense. These are "moments in films . . . where a striking shift in discourse occurs," and it is precisely by virtue of this discursive shift that they demand interpretation (Reyland 2012a, 61). Such moments, moreover, have an "in-built indeterminacy" that magnifies "the hermeneutics of multiple choice inherent in any act of criticism" (Reyland 2012a, 60). Reyland himself finds such a unique moment in a pivotal scene from Clint Eastwood's *Mystic River* (2003), where the discursive shift is brought about by the way the "music and camera work disrupt the stylistic conventions of this aesthetically conservative film," a disruption that "can be audio-viewed as implying some form of narratorial agency breaking the narrative flow" (Reyland 2012a, 59). As Reyland demonstrates, this disruption leads to a multiplicity of interpretive options. In particular, the "agency behind such musical interruptions may be read as an authorial intervention by a composer or filmmaker, implied or otherwise" *or* "one's sense of such an agent may alternatively be of a narrator that the music makes fictional" (Reyland 2012a, 60–62). In *Solaris*, the recurring intrusion of Bach's music into an otherwise very bleak audiovisual setting constitutes such a clear break within the film's discourse that it cannot fail to set our interpretive inclinations adrift. Our options here are hardly restricted to the two readings I developed earlier. The home movie scene alone may, as we have seen, afford at least three different constructions of the music: as diegetic, metadiegetic and nondiegetic. More unexpectedly, perhaps, it is possible to refashion a non- or metadiegetic construction of the chorale into one that functions as intra-diegetic in Ben Winters's sense. Bach's music would then play "an active role in the diegesis," shaping the narrative space and entering into causal relations with its characters, while "still appearing," in the manner of nondiegetic music, "to remain 'unheard' by [these] characters" (Winters 2010, 243). In short, multiple interpretive possibilities lead to a multiplicity of options regarding the

Bach at the Space Station 37

music's diegetic, nondiegetic, metadiegetic and perhaps intra-diegetic status.

What is and is not included in a film's diegesis, then, is not unaffected by the interpretations we make.[23] In the case of *Solaris*, such hermeneutic pliability renders the location of Bach's music within the cinematic totality increasingly ambiguous. It is therefore interesting to discuss this pliability in relation to Stilwell's concept of the fantastical gap for, as David Neumeyer says, "the fantastical gap is all about . . . ambiguities" (Neumeyer 2009, 31). Though Stilwell discusses numerous instances of diegetic/ nondiegetic ambiguity, most of her examples can be viewed as falling into one of two broad categories. In the first we find those very common situations where a musical cue starts out as diegetic or nondiegetic and then transforms into its opposite. Here the gap is essentially constituted as a movement, as a path from state A to state B; it is, in Stilwell's words, a "trajectory" or "transition between stable states" (Stilwell 2007, 200).[24] A paradigmatic example of this kind of gap is found in a scene from Woody Allen's *Bananas* (1971) in which what appears to be a bit of nondiegetic music is subsequently revealed to be the sound of a harpist practicing in the protagonist's wardrobe.[25] In the second category, however, there are instances where the gap is not so much a trajectory as a constant *vacillation* or indecisiveness vis-à-vis some stable states. In discussing *The Insider*, Stilwell provides an example of this second kind of gap, claiming that although the music in the pertinent scene "is *always* nondiegetic . . . it has clearly also traversed a gap into interiority with the suppression of the diegetic and the foregrounding of an instrument as soft as a mandolin" (Stilwell 2007, 195). In short, both poles (in this case, nondiegetic and metadiegetic music) are *continuously* present. What *all* instances of the fantastical gap have in common, however, is the obfuscation of the borders between music's different cine-ontological locations. Such blurring of boundaries "does always *mean*," and it becomes "fantastical" precisely because it "changes the state, not only of the filmic moment, but also of the observer's relationship to it" (Stilwell 2007, 186). Like Reyland's unique moments, fantastical gaps are "important moments of revelation, of symbolism, and of emotional engagement within the film and without" (Stilwell 2007, 200).

The complex cluster of ambiguities that accrue around Bach's music in *Solaris* changes "the filmic moment" again and again as well as "the observer's relationship to it" (Stilwell 2007, 200). As an illustration of this, we can look once more at the home movie scene. On a basic level, the gap may here be construed as a fairly standard one, in that the music can be seen as moving from a nondiegetic to a diegetic state. (It is nondiegetic when it emerges out of the electronic sound picture during the shot of Solaris's surface; it is diegetic when conceived of as part of the homemade film.) Already at this point, however, there is an element of complexity present, since the diegetic music simultaneously functions

38   *Bach at the Space Station*

nondiegetically to underscore the film Kelvin and Hari are watching. This complexity is further deepened when we realize that *throughout the entire scene* Bach's music may also plausibly be understood (from our perspective) as either diegetic, nondiegetic or metadiegetic. Thus, superimposed upon the more conventional movement from nondiegetic to diegetic music is the possibility of (1) the music being diegetic from the spectator's perspective and nondiegetic from the perspective of the characters; and (2) a spectatorial construction of the music as being either diegetic, nondiegetic or metadiegetic all along. And when we then add the possibility that the music may even be experienced as intra-diegetic, the ambiguities quickly start to multiply. Even though it is hardly possible to experience all these gaps simultaneously, the ensuing plurality of ambiguities must be seen as both constituted *by* and constitutive *of* the interpretive pliability of the scene. We should expect to find a similar diversity of gaps in the other scenes involving Bach's chorale (though, of course, without the added complexity that results from a sequence that depicts a film within a film).

A somewhat different kind of gap appears if we proceed from Tarkovsky's description of the narrative as an "inner journey" and then consider the Bach chorale as it materializes over the course of the film. Here we may recall Sean Martin's contention that "as *Solaris* progresses, it is less and less concerned with 'corresponding to reality', and more and more engaged in depicting Kelvin's inner world" (Martin 2011, 103). Similarly, Nariman Skakov describes a narrative path in which "the film's plot gradually disintegrates and the viewer is no longer able to distinguish reality from mere hallucinations or a real entity from its 'reflection'" (Skakov 2012, 74). Under such descriptions, *Solaris* can be seen to exhibit a characteristic feature of what Martin Fitzpatrick has called "subjunctive narration." Fitzpatrick defines a subjunctive narrative as an "uncertain narrative, marked by an inherent unknowability . . . in which significant information is not epistemologically secure," and in which perceivers "cannot precisely determine the facts of the case" (Fitzpatrick 2002, 244–245). Viewed from a perspective like that of Martin or Skakov, the narrative of *Solaris* presents a steadily escalating tour de force of "epistemic lacunae" (Fitzpatrick 2002, 245). For example, we may increasingly come to feel that Hari's presence on the station was really only a figment of Kelvin's imagination, without ever being able to conclusively settle such doubts. Perhaps, like Peter Green, one might even be inclined to contemplate "the possibility that . . . *all* Kelvin's . . . seemingly real experiences in the space station might be materializations of mental or subconscious states" (Green 1993, 74; emphasis added). But again, that is precisely the point: it *is* no more than a possibility. Such narrative "destabilizations" or "denarrations" (Reyland 2013, 39) undermine the spectator's ability to construct a stable and clearly bifurcated story world in which objective reality can be distinguished "from

Bach at the Space Station   39

mere hallucinations" (Skakov 2012, 74). This breakdown of the borders between the objective and the subjective creates a large-scale ambiguity within the film that gradually draws Bach's music into its orbit. Thus, being recognizably "extra-fictional" (Winters 2010, 237) when appearing in connection with the opening credits,[26] and at least potentially perceivable as firmly anchored in the diegesis during the home movie scene, the music eventually ends up in a maelstrom of epistemological uncertainties. To the extent that the film is constructed as a subjunctive narrative, it becomes increasingly problematic to decide whether the music is part of the film's story world, exists only in Kelvin's imagination, functions as intra-diegetic "musical wallpaper" (Winters 2012) or constitutes a message articulated by an implied filmmaker. In other words, what we have here is a gap that gradually develops over the course of the whole film: an ambiguity that we may never be able to resolve and that may eventually lead us away from considerations of the music's diegetic status and back to questions about why it is there in the first place – questions, that is, about the significance, the symbolism, the value, in short, the "point" (Fitzpatrick 2002, 247) of Bach's music in the film.

Finally, there is yet another, more speculative, way in which we may speak of a fantastical gap in *Solaris*, one that I would briefly like to explore here, since I think it provides an important corollary to Tarkovsky's own ideas about the nature of his films and the implications of these ideas for interpretation. As my two earlier readings have hopefully demonstrated, the film affords both a metadiegetic and a more purely nondiegetic conception of Bach's music. Like the ambiguities discussed until now, the gap that I will now explore is conditioned by such polarizations, but here it may be seen to arise only *after* we have substituted one interpretive framework for another. Now, if a prerequisite for speaking about the fantastical gap is that "there is no completely rational way to understand the placement of the music" (Stilwell 2007, 194), specific readings may very well be experienced as interpreting any would-be ambiguity out of existence. This is because once an interpretive framework has been provided, the music's relation to the story world will become largely fixed, and its placement will thus be "rationalized." Hence, if we find the previously mentioned Žižekian reading convincing, we will also be inclined to let it mold and determine our understanding and experience of the film and its details; and staying within the orbit of this particular reading, we may start to experience the music as metadiegetic to such a degree that a conception of it as nondiegetic seems quite unfitting. Conversely, being influenced by a reading that urges us to view the music as unambiguously non- or extradiegetic (for example, the "implied-filmmaker" reading), a claim to the effect that the music is or can be regarded as metadiegetic might begin to appear very far-fetched. However, having managed to entertain *both* these perspectives, we may eventually come to acknowledge the inherent disposition of the music to function in either of these ways.

40   *Bach at the Space Station*

In this scenario, the gap will reappear at a more abstract level, coming into existence only very gradually as an a posteriori shift in perception (or at least in conception) that juxtaposes ex post facto the two construals of the film and its music. Such an ambiguity of the music is, to borrow Giorgio Biancorosso's words, an ambiguity that can be "entertain[ed . . .] only in retrospect" (Biancorosso 2009, 24).

This kind of cross-version gap is essentially unlike all other variants of the fantastical gap discussed so far in that it is not experienced as a direct, in-the-moment ambiguity. To better grasp what is at issue, we may compare it to a parallel case in the realm of so-called absolute music (i.e. instrumental classical music). Here, we can imagine a person who after intensive study of, say, musicologist Susan McClary's reading of Johannes Brahms's Third Symphony, begins to hear the different musical themes as gendered, where before she perceived them as purely musical entities in accordance with a formalist aesthetic (see McClary 1993). For this person, as long as she stays within the perspective of McClary's reading, a "purely musical" way of hearing the themes is hardly available. Nor can she perceive the music as simultaneously gendered and purely musical, since the two alternatives are clearly irreconcilable. Whether this shift to a gendered way of listening is irreversible or not is of less significance here. The important thing to note is that in one interpretive context, the music is perceived as gendered, while in another it is not. And having experienced both these possibilities in turn, we may in retrospect acknowledge the process tracked by this experience as one of traversing the border between a non-gendered and a gendered perception of the music. The music clearly has the disposition to experientially sustain both these perceptions – and this is so even if, in the end, we come to reject one of them as untenable.

Insofar as this analogy is productive, it suggests that the experience of ambiguity in film need not be confined to single viewing or listening occasions, but can also emerge over a range of viewings. For such a cross-version ambiguity to be successfully explored, however, the film as a whole must be sufficiently indeterminate to allow for radical hermeneutic pliability. It must in a sense be music, or poetry. Tarkovsky himself repeatedly emphasized the poetic and indeterminate dimension of his films, as, for example, when he claimed they "are ambivalent and allow for widely different interpretations" (Tarkovsky 1986, 109). For Tarkovsky, "a film based on poetic principles would involve the spectator in an active role: 'He becomes a participant in the process of discovering life, unsupported by ready-made deductions from the plot or ineluctable pointers by the author'" (quoted in Martin 2011, 45–46). While in much mainstream cinema the fantastical gap must be seen as a function of how deep-rooted viewing conventions and standard cinematic cues are manipulated, in *Solaris* – and in Tarkovsky's cinema more generally – it is the very *absence* of such conventions that opens up the music to ambiguity.[27] When such hermeneutically grounded ambiguities start to develop across a range of viewings, they become the enabling conditions for an increasingly complex and dynamic dialogue, not only with the specific film in question, but also with other people – scholars, critics, aficionados – who return again and again to the films of this remarkable Russian director. Perhaps even more importantly, the multiplying gaps in *Solaris* offer a multitude of potential spaces for further engagement with all types of questions about film, music and meaning.

The Basic Musical Dichotomy of *Solaris* and the Limits of Hermeneutic Pliability

Having investigated the different ways in which the diegetic status of Bach's music can be constructed in *Solaris*, and the manifold cine-ontological ambiguities or gaps that ensue from these interpretive constructions, I will in this concluding section return to what I view as the common ground of all these constructions. Despite the differences between these perspectives, they all seem to rest on a basic dichotomy between classical and electronic music. Accordingly, in both my nondiegetic and metadiegetic constructions of the Bach chorale prelude, the music preserves its connection with Earth and the intrinsically human values related to Earth. In other words, even when changing its diegetic status, the music preserves its *meaning* as an expression of an allegedly authentic and inherently human pre-Solaris earthly existence. The dichotomy between the chorale prelude and the electronic music is established both by the radically different musical and expressive properties of the two types of music, and by the way electronic music is closely connected to the planet Solaris.[28] Although the gradual sonic take-over of Bach's music by Artemiev's electronic score would seem to mitigate, or even abolish, this dichotomy, what makes the take-over significant is precisely the feeling that the two types of music articulate radically different expressive and experiential dimensions. This difference, I would argue, is as much a reality in *Solaris* as it is a reality that Bach's music becomes increasingly saturated by electronic music as the film proceeds. In essence, what this means is that the hermeneutic pliability explored in relation to the diegetic status of Bach's music cannot be extended to all aspects of this music. It might not be a hard-core *descriptive* fact that Bach's music articulates Kelvin's longing for a more authentic pre-Solaris earthly life in the sense that it is a descriptive fact that the chorale appears four times during the course of the film, but to deny that this music is closely connected to imagery of Earth (whether Kelvin's or the implied filmmaker's) seems implausible. Similarly, with the electronic music a claim to the effect that it does not bear any special relation to the impenetrable planet Solaris appears fundamentally indefensible. It appears that any plausible interpretation of the film that, to a lesser or greater extent, relies on an account of its music must proceed

42   *Bach at the Space Station*

within the limits of this basic understanding of the two types of music. The openness of *Solaris* and the "uncertainty" of its narrative warrant an interpretive approach that stresses the constructivist and, in philosopher Joseph Margolis's words, imputational nature of interpretation, as well as the possibility of a multiplicity of equally plausible, though not necessarily congruent, interpretations (cf. Margolis 1992). It does not, however, follow from this that we are free to construct the film in whatever way we want. Championing hermeneutic pliability is not equivalent to claiming that anything goes.

The chapters that follow are all premised on the interpretive approach described and illustrated in this chapter (and laid out in more theoretical detail in Chapter 1). However, the present chapter's focus on conceptual issues and distinctions, and its somewhat taxonomic investigation of the possible cine-ontological states ascribable to Bach's music, will largely be put aside in favor of more straightforward case studies. Thus, in the next chapter on *Mirror*, even though I will discuss questions about the music's diegetic status, I will be less concerned with exploring alternative interpretive constructions. Instead, my aim will be to develop a specific reading of the film and its music. As we shall see, in *Mirror* as well a basic musical dichotomy can be found between classical and electronic music, a dichotomy that, moreover, exhibits important similarities to the one we have detected in *Solaris*. But there are also significant differences between *Mirror* and *Solaris* in this regard, differences that include both the relationship between the two types of music and the ways they are associated with central themes running through the films.

Notes

1. The emphasis on music's narrating role is central to most accounts of nondiegetic music. Such an emphasis can be seen as implied in the earlier quote from Stilwell. David Neumeyer is more explicit, defining nondiegetic music as music belonging to "the register of the narration or the narrator" (Neumeyer 2015, 38). As will become clear, however, certain types of nondiegetic music are better described as performing a non-narrative function. For a thorough discussion of the diegetic/nondiegetic distinction in relation to film music, see Heldt (2013, 48–118).
2. Unlike "Das alte Jahr vergangen ist" in *Mirror*, the chorale prelude does not here continue into the film's opening scene. *Solaris* also differs from *Mirror* in that the music and the opening credits are not preceded by a pre-credit sequence. For further discussion of Bach's music in *Mirror*, see Chapter 3.
3. This seems to be the position of Robert Bird, who speaks of Hari "seeing her prototype on [the homemade] film and hearing its soundtrack" (Bird 2008, 161).
4. In keeping with his theory of "hypothetical intentionalism" (see Levinson 1992), Jerrold Levinson says that "the implied filmmaker . . . is the image we construct of the film's maker – beliefs, aims, attitudes, values, and personality – on the basis of the film viewed in its full context of creation" (Levinson 2004, 488).

Bach at the Space Station   43

5. Following Ronald Rodman, we may think of a musical style topic as "the point where the non-referential structure of the music engages a referential component in the listener." Thus understood, musical style topics "have two important aspects: (1) they link music to non-musical concepts/ideas/objects and (2) this link must be recognized by the culture in which it is produced" (Rodman 2010, 117–118).

6. It should be emphasized, though, that in Bergman's films classical music very often appears in the form of diegetic performances (cf. Barham 2009, 261–262).

7. In fact, as Robinson (2006, 187) points out, Tarkovsky was well aware of Bergman's use of music and sound in *Through a Glass Darkly*.

8. On this point, see *Nostalghia.com* and the interview that Jerzy Illg and Leonard Neuger made with Tarkovsky in Stockholm in 1985. URL: www.nostalghia.com/TheTopics/interview.html (accessed 2019-04-08). I will return to Tarkovsky's criticisms of Post-Baroque Western art music in Chapter 4 and again in Chapter 7.

9. The quoted remark concerns a passage from the slow movement of Beethoven's "Hammerklavier" sonata. Regarding the leitmotivic function of the chorale and its connection with Earth, Roberto Calabretto has argued that such claims tend to misconstrue the import of Bach's music in the film. As Calabretto sees it, the music "non è . . . semplicemente un *Leitmotiv*, ancor più non è la colonna sonora arricchita da sentimenti umani della Terra da contrapporre alla musica elettronica che invece identifica Solaris, come molta critica ha incautamente dichiarato: Bach, al contrario, è l'essenza dell'universo, metafora dell'ordine natural e cosmico" (Calabretto 2010b, 14). ("[Bach's music] is . . . not simply a *leitmotif*; furthermore, it is not the sounding pillar enriched by the human feelings of Earth in contrast to the electronic music that characterizes Solaris, as many critics has incautiously declared: Bach, contrariwise, is the essence of the universe, a metaphor for the natural and cosmic order.") My translation.

10. Tarkovsky's words are in fact echoed by Hari when she and the three crew members meet in the library to celebrate Snaut's birthday. She tells Snaut and Sartorius that "Kris Kelvin is more consistent than both of you. In inhuman conditions, he has behaved humanly." For the differences between Tarkovsky's film and Lem's novel, see Johnson and Petrie (1994, 101–108), Bould (2014, 20–27, 77) and McSweeney (2015, 97–98). For a comparison between Tarkovsky's film and Steven Soderbergh's 2002 remake of it, see Dillon (2006, 1–44).

11. Ben Winters (2012, 44) considers the possibility that the non-narrative music of Levinson's implied filmmaker is the *only* kind of music that "we may legitimately talk about" as "operating at a level beyond or outside of the diegesis."

12. Egorova (1997, 232) goes so far as to say that Solaris's "formidable force . . . is *mainly* conveyed through the music" (emphasis added). Regarding the ANS synthesizer, it got its name after the initials of the famous Russian composer and pianist Alexander Nikolayevich Scriabin (see also Beer 2006).

13. Upon Snaut and Sartorius's first meeting with the Solaris-derived Hari at Sartorius's lab, Snaut reacts to Sartorius's depersonalizing expression "them" for the apparitions, suggesting that they use the word "guests" instead. Later in the same scene, Sartorius explains that "while our structure is made of atoms, theirs consists of neutrinos."

14. The interval first occurs a few minutes earlier when Kelvin enters the station through a pair of sliding doors.

15. The references in the quote are to Fredric Jameson's *Archaeologies of the Future: The Desire Called Utopia and Other Science Fictions* (London: Verso, 2005, 112, note 8).

44 Bach at the Space Station

16. I will return to Heldt's concept of internal focalization, derived from Edward Branigan, in the next chapter on *Mirror*. I should also note that Heldt is not discussing *Solaris*.

17. According to David Beer, however, Artemiev himself has claimed "that the entire soundtrack was electronic," which would suggest that all four occurrences of the Bach chorale were "played on the ANS" (Beer 2006, 115, note 257). Even so, the first two occurrences of the chorale appear, aurally, to be uncontaminated by electronic sound, especially if compared to the last two occurrences.

18. Egorova (1997, 235) provides an alternative and strangely inaccurate description, writing that "Bach's music has the function in this finale of a clear-cut *cantus firmus*, which is superimposed on a freely improvised, limited aleatoric texture from the chorus, synthesizers ANS and SINTI-100, and instrumental groups from a reduced symphony orchestra." To describe the texture as "aleatoric" is clearly a misrepresentation. Furthermore, Egorova's mention of the SINTI-100 (SYNTHI 100) is curious since there is no evidence that Artemiev used this type of synthesizer in constructing the score for *Solaris*. The SYNTHI 100 was, however, used in *Stalker* to process the sounds of the Tar and the traverse flute that form the basis of what is sometimes called the Stalker theme (see Chapter 4).

19. This, of course, is not the only way to view the relation between the two types of music in the film. As Barham points out, "the problem of interpreting this ending [of *Solaris*] is embodied in its sound: has the humanist Bach been appropriated by Artemiev's technological score, or vice versa? Or has rapprochement been reached between the two poles? Does the final gesture suggest merely the pessimism of Tarkovsky's outlook, or the redemption of technology in some transcendent metaphysical realm?" (Barham 2009, 267–268).

20. The sequence from this scene where Kelvin, now on his knees, embraces his father is usually taken to allude to Rembrandt's *The Return of the Prodigal Son* (1666–1669), and the most common interpretation is that Kelvin comes to some kind of reconciliation with himself at the end of the film (see, for example, Johnson and Petrie 1994, 110; Miall 2008, 327; Slevin 2010, 61; Skakov 2012, 98). The reading I have provided would go somewhat against the grain with its emphasis on the illusory character of this reconciliation (cf. Chion 2001, 158).

21. I will not go deeper into the issue here, but the statement just made may not be entirely convincing when it comes to recent digital cinema, where the separation of diegetic and nondiegetic sound effects and music has become increasingly relaxed (cf. Buhler 2018, 269ff.).

22. For Yacavone, the diegetic/nondiegetic distinction should be subsumed under the broader concept of a "film world," by which he means the experienced and uniquely presented totality of a given film. A film world is an "*irreducible* symbolic, aesthetic, and phenomenological whole" (Yacavone 2012, 36; see also Yacavone 2008, 86).

23. There is a difference here, of course, between classical narrative cinema and many films in the European art cinema tradition. As I will come back to in Chapter 7, in the former case the spectator's construction of the diegesis is to a much higher degree determined by the cues given in the film's narration. In other words, it is less a question of interpretive construction than of guided reconstruction.

24. Jeff Smith denies that such examples are (typically) instances of the fantastical gap, arguing instead that they should be viewed as a kind of spatially displaced diegetic music/sound (see Smith 2009, 14–19). See also Chapter 5, note 7.

Bach at the Space Station   45

25. See Biancorosso (2009) for a thorough examination of this scene.
26. But even here it can perhaps be imagined as a kind of metadiegetic music in the sense that it can be understood as a pre-narrative representation or intimation of the protagonist's state of mind (cf. the discussion of *Das alte Jahr vergangen ist* in Chapter 3).
27. For David Bordwell, interpretive ambiguity can in fact be viewed as one of the defining characteristics of art cinema (Bordwell 1985, 212–213).
28. The one scene in the film where electronic music and sound do not appear in connection with Solaris and/or the space station is the extended sequence at the film's beginning where pilot and astronaut Burton is driving though an endless cityscape. For Beer (2006, 111), this "suggests that the music is perhaps linked to broader understandings of the term *alien*." Thus, in contrast to Johnson and Petrie, who propose "that the earth and the alien are separate, I am suggesting that the earth also contains alien spaces. . . . The significance of the location of the first appearance of the dissonant electronic music then becomes apparent. Alien here then becomes synonymous with spaces that are uncomfortable, unusual, or in which the character is in constant motion and therefore cannot become familiar with their surroundings." For another extensive discussion of the scene and its soundscape, see Bould (2014, 46–50).

3 Memories, Dreams and Mysteries

Music and Dimensions of Human Experience in *Mirror*

One of the most commonly observed features of *Mirror* (completed in 1974 and released in 1975) is its strongly autobiographical nature, something that was emphasized not least by Tarkovsky himself (Tarkovsky 1986, 158). The film grew in part out of Tarkovsky's memories and dreams of his childhood, but it also deals with topics closely connected to the director's adult life, such as his complicated and guilt-ridden relationships with his aging mother, his ex-wife and his first-born son. Another characteristic of *Mirror* frequently remarked upon is the bewildering complexity of the film's design. As Terence McSweeney points out, "the film has no formal narrative in the traditional sense" (McSweeney 2015, 28). Instead, revolving around the recollections and reminiscences of the 40-year-old Alexei – often described in the literature as the film's "narrator"[1] – *Mirror* moves in a seemingly random way between three different time periods, and the result is less a clear and linear narrative than a complex assortment of memories, dreams and scenes from the narrator's present-day life interspersed with lengthy sequences of archival footage. This convoluted structure makes the film an extraordinary challenge for the first-time viewer, even though on closer scrutiny it turns out to be "surprisingly coherent" (Johnson and Petrie 1994, 116). The nature of this coherence is aptly described by Matilda Mroz when she writes that *Mirror* "proceeds through a series of episodes or moments that . . . relate to one another through rhythm, pattern, and theme, rather than linear chronology or narrative structure" (Mroz 2013, 91). By focusing specifically on the music in the film, my aim in this chapter is to draw attention to themes and patterns of signification in *Mirror* that have so far received little or no attention in the literature. However, in contrast to Mroz's more formal account of music's role and function in *Mirror*, according to which the music "is associated primarily with the aesthetic aspects of the film" (Mroz 2013, 123), I claim that the themes and patterns that emerge when the music is our primary focus are importantly related to the characters' interior lives and, consequently, should be understood as essentially narrative in character.

Musically, *Mirror* stands out among Tarkovsky's works; of the five films examined in this book, it is the one that contains the most music. As in *Solaris*, both classical and electronic music are heard on the soundtrack.[2]

Memories, Dreams and Mysteries 47

But whereas in *Solaris*, the classical music is limited to four occurrences of Johann Sebastian Bach's chorale prelude "Ich ruf zu dir, Herr Jesu Christ," in *Mirror* we find a variety of pieces by different composers. Again, whereas in *Solaris* electronic music is consistently associated with the planet Solaris and the desolated space station, in *Mirror* it occurs in connection with seemingly unrelated scenes and representations, such as dream-memories of early childhood, the inexplicable appearance and disappearance of mysterious characters and newsreel sequences depicting agitated mobs, exploding bombs and the tribulations of war.

The diversity of musical appearances in *Mirror*, in combination with the complexity of the film's organization, requires a somewhat more schematic approach than the one employed in the previous chapter as well as in the coming chapters on *Stalker*, *Nostalghia* and *The Sacrifice*. The main part of this chapter is accordingly divided into two sections focusing on classical and electronic music respectively. By covering almost all occurrences of music in the film, my aim is to foreground the very different roles played by classical and electronic music and, by implication, how they are involved in the construction of different thematic threads. Proceeding from a claim made by Tarkovsky in *Sculpting in Time*, I understand these thematic threads as being essentially involved in the film's multifaceted probing into the phenomenology of human experience:

> In *Mirror* I wanted to make people feel that Bach and Pergolesi and Pushkin's letter and the soldiers forcing the Sivash crossing, and also the intimate, domestic events – that all these things are in a sense equally important as human experience.
>
> (Tarkovsky 1986, 193)

In contrast to *Solaris*, however, classical and electronic music are (with one exception) kept distinctly apart in *Mirror*. There is no overlapping or blurring between the two musical realms in the film, and the classical music is not electronically elaborated upon as it is in *Solaris*. Being clearly separated from each other, I argue that the two types of music are tied to radically different kinds or dimensions of human experience. Thus, classical music is connected with experiences of belonging, loss and intimacy. Whether it be the music of Pergolesi, Purcell or Bach, the music underscores moments of deep attachment and intensified presence, simultaneously expressing and denoting a recognizable emotional life-world that the characters can inhabit and in which they feel at home (which does not mean that all instances of classical music are connected with states of satisfaction and joy). In contrast, electronic music is consistently, if never overtly, associated with moments of unease and tension, and in particular with experiences and phenomena that for various reasons seem to challenge the limits of human understanding and comprehension: dream-memories of early childhood, inexplicable appearances of unidentified characters and the senseless irrationality besetting the modern world

48   *Memories, Dreams and Mysteries*

(exemplified with shots of raging masses, exploding atomic bombs and bedraggled soldiers preparing for and marching to battle).[3]

Moments of Affection and Belonging: Classical Music

There are in total seven occurrences of classical music in *Mirror*. Music by Bach occurs four times in the film: two appearances of the chorale prelude "Das alte Jahr vergangen ist" (BWV 614), the opening chorus of *St. John Passion* and the recitative "Und siehe da, der Vorhang im Tempel zerriß" from *St. Matthew Passion*. Music from Henry Purcell's *The Indian Queen* appears on two occasions, while the final movement of Giovanni Battista Pergolesi's *Stabat Mater* occurs only once in the film. In this section, I will argue that, in *Mirror*, classical music is consistently associated with memories and visions of deep affection and belonging. It underscores scenes where the characters, though not necessarily happy or joyful, nevertheless seem to be in close connection with their innermost feelings. Accordingly, I divide the scenes in which classical music occurs into five different themes representing five different emotional and/or mental states: "loss and longing," "love and intimacy," "tranquility and belonging," "despair" and "reconciliation." In contrast to the electronic score, which I will interpret as articulating a sense of incomprehensibility and alterity attached to situations and experiences that lie beyond human comprehension, the classical music underscores moments of intensified presence and of strong emotional affinity with the persons who are the objects of the protagonist's affections. Unlike much of the electronic score, the classical music is closely tied to Alexei and his interior meditations, possible exceptions being the initial 60 seconds of Pergolesi's *Stabat Mater* and the two occurrences of Bach's chorale prelude.

Loss and Longing: "Das alte Jahr vergangen ist"

As in *Solaris*, the opening credits in *Mirror* appear on the screen to the accompaniment of music from Johann Sebastian Bach's *Orgelbüchlein*. And just as the chorale prelude "Ich ruf zu dir, Herr Jesu Christ" in *Solaris* can be understood as an apt reflection of the protagonist's situation, "Das alte Jahr vergangen ist" in *Mirror* also provides a key to the fundamental emotional disposition of the film's narrator. Though the prelude was originally intended as a New Year's hymn, the minor tonalities and the slowly evolving cantus firmus melody in its upper voice together express what can perhaps be described as a grief-stricken reflection.[4] The piece may accordingly be interpreted more as a mournful meditation over the year that has passed than as a joyful celebration of the year that is about to come. Thus understood, it is more backward-looking than forward-looking, and as such it reflects the emotional disposition of *Mirror*'s narrator exceedingly well. *Mirror* is a film built around Alexei's thoughts about

Memories, Dreams and Mysteries 49

an irretrievable past: a past that can never be fully recovered or revisited as it was, but exists only through distorted dreams and memories in the narrator's troubled mind (cf. Mroz 2013, 91–92).[5] As Tarkovsky himself wrote: "The episodes the narrator remembers at an extreme moment of crisis cause him pain up to the last minute, fill him with sorrow and anxiety" (Tarkovsky 1986, 134).

Unlike the other occurrences of classical music in *Mirror*, however, "Das alte Jahr vergangen ist" is just as much connected with Alexei's mother Maria as with Alexei himself. It is significant that its first appearance is not restricted to the opening credits, but continues into the post-credit scene where it accompanies the camera's gradual zooming in on Maria sitting on the fence. As the voice-over of Alexei makes clear, the family was constantly waiting for the father to come home from the war, which makes it plausible to claim that Maria is here waiting for her husband. The first occurrence of Bach's chorale prelude can therefore be understood as playing a dual role: it signals the overall emotional tone and concern of the film as a whole (and in doing so reveals to us the narrator's state of mind) while at the same time reflecting Maria's longing for her husband and, since he does not in fact seem to return, a sense of love lost. This account of the opening scene and the role of Bach's music in it gains further support if we consider the succeeding scene. This consists of a series of shots of Maria inside the dacha, which are accompanied on the soundtrack by a voice-over rendition of Arseny Tarkovsky's love poem "First Meetings."

As the poem is read, the camera focuses on Maria, who at the end of the poem is seen bursting into tears.[6] We may even envision a metadiegetic interpretation of the poem according to which Maria, recollecting the love that once existed between her and her husband, hears her husband's voice internally reciting the poem (cf. Sitney 2014a, 72). Later in the film we learn that the two have indeed gone separate ways (just as Alexei and Natalya have done, and Tarkovsky and his first wife, Irma Raush). From this perspective, "Das alte Jahr vergangen ist," as it appears at the beginning of the opening scene, can be understood as musically articulating Maria's intense longing for, and painful loss of, the deep and vibrant love expressed in the poem.

To further substantiate the previously mentioned reading, we may consider the second appearance of the Bach prelude later in the film. The brief scene in black and white where Maria levitates over the marital bed must be distinguished from the three dream-memory scenes (also in black and white) that feature Alexei's dreams of his early childhood. The "Levitation scene" is more aptly understood as a reverie or vision of Maria, following, as it does, immediately upon the close-up of her face after she has reluctantly complied with the request of the rich doctor's wife to behead a rooster. Accompanied by Bach's prelude, the scene begins with a brief shot of Maria's husband looking straight into the camera

Figure 3.1 Maria's vision of herself as levitating over the marital bed in *Mirror*
Source: Films Sans Frontières

before turning around and away from it. A sequence reminiscent of the Library scene in *Solaris* then shows us Maria hovering in mid-air above the bed, her hair splayed around her as if she were floating on water (Figure 3.1). She ponders why it is that she only thinks of her husband when she feels unwell, and then declares her love for him. The whole set-up of this scene – its black-and-white color scheme, the highly stylized *mise-en-scène*, the levitation – qualifies it as a reverie or vision of Maria (cf. Skakov 2012, 128), and the sense of love irretrievably lost becomes all the more poignant after the close-up of her almost demonic face in the preceding scene. Even more than in the film's opening, the slowly moving and chromatically saturated minor tonalities of the prelude emphasize Maria's intense longing for a love and an intimacy that lie irrecoverably in the past. In *Mirror*, the "Jahr" of "Das alte Jahr vergangen ist" is at once a lived and a recollected past that, however much one may long for and try to re-enliven it, is forever out of reach.

Love and Intimacy: *The Indian Queen*

In contrast to "Das alte Jahr vergangen ist," the two appearances of Purcell's music in *Mirror* are both closely connected to the film's narrator, and more specifically to the adolescent Alexei's longing for and thoughts about the red-haired girl with whom he is in love. Accordingly, instead of signifying or denoting the girl herself, the music from *The Indian Queen* is more accurately understood as articulating the nature or essence of Alexei's feelings for her. As I will argue in the last section of this chapter, the

Memories, Dreams and Mysteries 51

precision with which this music captures the experience of intimate and deeply felt love justifies an account of it as focalizing the young Alexei's interiority. Thus, rather than being a nondiegetic representation of his feelings or, as some writers would have it, simply a way of promoting "the aesthetic aspects of the film" (Mroz 2013, 123), the music should here be understood as constituting the young Alexei's interior world – and by implication the grown Alexei's remembrances of that world.

The first appearance of Purcell's music in the film comes just after the scene where Alexei's son Ignat, being alone at home, discovers a mysterious dark-haired woman in the living room. Toward the end of the scene, Ignat goes to answer a knock on the door, leading to a bewildering encounter with his grandmother Maria in which neither of the two recognizes the other. When he returns to the living room the dark-haired woman has enigmatically disappeared, the only evidence of her previous presence being a slowly disappearing heat mark from her cup on the table. As the boy stares confoundedly at the empty table, the phone rings. It is Alexei, who tells Ignat about the red-haired girl he was in love with at Ignat's age. The scene then shifts to a close-up of the adolescent Alexei leaning against a railing at an outdoor shooting range. We soon realize that he is looking at the red-haired girl, who is seen walking slowly through a wintery landscape, the crunching sound of her shoes in the snow dominating the soundtrack. Shortly thereafter, Purcell's music is introduced. It continues to play for 47 seconds before suddenly being interrupted by the loud sound of a gunshot. This prompts an abrupt, indeed violent, shift from Alexei's interior ruminations to the depressing atmosphere of the shooting range. In an instant, Alexei is wrenched away (and we with him) from his innermost feelings and returned to the gloomy and unfriendly reality of the shooting lessons. The intimacy and tenderness expressed by Purcell's music thus becomes all the more poignant by the sudden and ruthless intrusion of the hostile external world, established so effectively by the gunshot.

The second appearance of Purcell's music underscores one of the most moving scenes in the film. Like the scene at the shooting range, this scene takes place during World War Two when Alexei is around 12 or 13 years old. Having accompanied his mother to a well-to-do wife of a doctor, Alexei is asked to wait alone in one of the rooms while the two women discuss the price of the earrings Maria is about to sell. In the room, a large jug stands on a cupboard. Milk is seen dripping from the jug onto the floor, at which point Purcell's music begins. The music continues to play as Alexei sees a reflection of himself in a large mirror hanging on one of the walls. The camera begins to zoom in on Alexei's reflection and then shows us Alexei himself, seated on a chair in the middle of the room. This is followed by a brief shot of the red-haired girl warming her hands before a fireplace. As with Alexei just before, her appearance is mediated through the reflection of a mirror. As if returning Alexei's

52 *Memories, Dreams and Mysteries*

interior gaze, she turns her head and looks into the camera, which might suggest that the young Alexei's reverie is in fact a memory of a situation that actually took place, making the scene (understood from the grown Alexei's perspective) into a memory of a memory. The music stops as we see a close-up of one of the girl's hands in front of a burning log.

Once again, Purcell's music invests the scene with an atmosphere of intimacy and intense presence. However, as much as the scene is about Alexei's infatuation with the red-haired girl, it is also about Alexei discovering himself *through* the emotions he feels. In the words of Natasha Synessios, the scene represents "a personal revelation . . . a quiet stirring of the inner self" (Synessios 2001, 58). It is as if the music is working on two levels simultaneously, articulating Alexei's feelings from within while at the same time representing and clarifying what is clearly a crucial moment of awakening and self-recognition in the adolescent boy. Alexei is contemplating his reflection in the mirror, and the music – expressing and crystallizing with an almost otherworldly tenderness and precision the core of his innermost feelings – in turn reflects his growing awareness of himself. For us, and for Alexei, the music unlocks the most private and precious parts of his soul, and without it the scene would lose its character of a "personal revelation." The music from *The Indian Queen* is thus much more than a leitmotif denoting the red-haired girl or Alexei's love for her. It is a central co-contributor in the creation of those rare moments in the film where the main character is wholly transparent to himself, and where deeply felt intimacy and love (even though it does not seem to be reciprocated) enables him to experience an intensified self-presence and self-clarity. From the perspective of the "absent" narrator – that is, the grown Alexei – these moments seem to constitute his clearest and most distinct memories, memories that contrast sharply with the indefinable and electronically underscored dream-memories of the 5-year-old child (see next section).

Tranquility and Belonging: *Stabat Mater*

Unlike the music of Bach and Purcell, Pergolesi's music is heard only once in *Mirror*. The long excerpt from the composer's *Stabat Mater*, appearing 39 minutes and 56 seconds into the film, is taken from the final movement of the work, which is titled "Quando Corpus Morietur" ("when the body dies").[7] The music goes on for 2 minutes and 40 seconds and underscores two consecutive scenes, in this way connecting the film's second archival footage (following directly upon the sequence from the Spanish Civil War) of the Soviet balloon ascent in 1934 and the successful return to Moscow of the North Pole-crossing aeronaut Valeri Chkalov with the scene depicting the 12-year-old Alexei browsing through the Leonardo monograph.[8] For some reason, in the scholarly literature Pergolesi's music is almost exclusively mentioned with reference to the archival footage. In actual fact, however, the largest part of

Memories, Dreams and Mysteries   53

this extended musical passage occurs during Alexei's contemplation of Leonardo's images. This sequence is underscored in its entirety by Pergolesi's music, which first comes to a full stop in the ensuing scene as Natalya (in present time) calls out for Ignat to help her collect the things she has dropped on the floor.

As for the beginning of the Pergolesi excerpt, it does not coincide with the beginning of the documentary sequence, which, apart from the almost imperceptible sound of a human crowd in the background, commences in silence. The music does not begin until 13 seconds into the sequence, in connection with a shot of a slowly swelling giant balloon.[9] It then accompanies the footage of the ascending balloonists, imbuing the images with such tenderness and affection that the sequence is transformed into a sublime meditation on timeless beauty. The transformative and aestheticizing power of the music in this sequence is aptly described by Mroz when she writes that

> the music has an immediate transfigurative effect, changing an event of historical importance into a beautiful, slow balletic performance that brings out the rhythm of floating through its resonant, continuous string sounds.
>
> (Mroz 2013, 125)

However, the sequence can also be viewed as an elegy on the transience of human life. Whether or not it was a conscious decision on Tarkovsky's part, the title of *Stabat Mater*'s final movement, which accompanies this footage, appears curiously apt, in that the words "Quando Corpus Morietur" seem to allude to "the fact that the balloonists all died in the ascent" (Martin 2011, 125). Through Pergolesi's music, timeless beauty and death is inextricably interwoven in this sequence.

As the scene changes, Pergolesi's music continues to play on the soundtrack, now accompanying Alexei's contemplation of the Leonardo reproductions. The scene, which is reflected with almost exact precision at the beginning of *The Sacrifice* as Alexander browses through the art book given to him as a birthday present by Victor, is shot in such a way that we only see Alexei's hands as he turns the pages of the monograph. However, even though the spectator's attention is clearly directed toward the reproductions in the book, the scene seems to depict a moment of extraordinary concentration and serenity. Looking at Leonardo's timeless art and gently turning the pages of the book, Alexei is continuously enveloped by the buoyant and almost celestial character of Pergolesi's music, all of which creates an impression of the boy being embedded in a domain existing far beyond the everyday world with its constant conflicts and complex relationships, a domain of timeless beauty and eternal values. Thus understood, the scene is saturated by an atmosphere of tranquility and profound emotional equilibrium, an atmosphere already

54   *Memories, Dreams and Mysteries*

established by the peaceful and sublime images of the slowly drifting balloonists in the preceding newsreel footage and by the "transfigurative effect" of Pergolesi's music. By continuing to underscore the moving images as the scene changes, Pergolesi's music transfers the sense of an aestheticized and transfigured world in the newsreel footage and carries it over into Alexei's encounter with Leonardo's art. In direct correspondence with the scenes accompanied by Purcell's music, this scene can be seen as the grown Alexei's recollection and re-enlivening of a defining moment in his childhood, in this case one marked by an extraordinary presence and belonging.

Despair: *St. Matthew Passion* – "Und siehe da, der Vorhang im Tempel zerriß"

In what may be the most dramatic scene in the film, the father – in military uniform and having just returned on leave from the war – summons Alexei and his sister, who run to meet him. As the recitative "Und siehe da, der Vorhang im Tempel zerriß in zwei Stück" ("And behold, the curtain in the Temple was torn in two") from Bach's *St. Matthew Passion* is heard, the father embraces his two children. Far from depicting a happy reunion, however, the scene is rather one of grief and despair. In fact, the dismal tone is already established before the Bach recitative begins, when a brief passage of ominous, and electronically amplified, orchestral music is heard in tandem with a shot of Maria tearfully looking at her husband and children before turning around and away from them. We then see the father holding the children, his face expressing a combination of sorrow and unconditional affection. Alexei, clinging hard to his father's waist, is crying. Obviously, events must have taken a turn for which the young Alexei was not prepared. Running into the arms of his long-awaited father, it turns out that the father has returned to his family only to leave them again. Whatever expectations Alexei might have had for a happily reunited family are quickly frustrated and replaced with the insight that his father's absence will be permanent. (The father's absence from Alexei's childhood is confirmed in an earlier scene, where the grown Alexei responds to Natalya's claim that "you know only how to command" by saying "that's because I was brought up by women.") In a fitting reflection of the young Alexei's emotional turmoil, the Evangelist on the soundtrack sings:

> Und siehe da, der Vorhang im Tempel zerriss in zwei Stück von oben an bis unten aus; Und die Erde erbebete, und die Felsen zerrissen.[10]

However, this line from Matthew 27:51 is sometimes taken to confirm the salvation bestowed on mankind by Jesus' death: as he suffers on the

Memories, Dreams and Mysteries 55

cross and atones our sins, the curtain separating God from men is torn asunder, and through the sacrifice of Christ God moves out of the temple and becomes present in the world, available to all people. This is thus a moment of deliverance and hope as God is returned to mankind. Analogously, and in contrast to what I have just suggested, the return of Alexei's long-awaited father can be seen as a crucial moment of reconciliation and joy in the young adolescent's life.

Tarkovsky, however, seems to turn this crucial moment of reconciliation and joy into its direct opposite. As we have seen, the "reunion" is marked by despondency and despair. Moreover, as the recitative cadences, the scene shifts from the siblings and their father to a picture of Leonardo's *Portrait of Ginevra de' Benci* (1474–1478); at this point, the music climaxes in a brief outburst of electronic sound reminiscent of the reverberating electronic clusters heard in *Solaris* in connection with shots of the alien planet's surface. This is the only time in *Mirror* when classical and electronic music are combined. In line with my understanding of the role played by electronic music in the film (to be presented next), the intrusion of this alien sound world into the classical domain, from which it otherwise is meticulously kept apart, underscores the dramatic, almost violent way in which Alexei, deprived of his hope for a future life in which his father is again part of the family, is thrown into a reality so inconsistent with these hopes that it is virtually impossible for him to fathom it. In a split second, all the dreams the young boy may have nurtured about his father's return to the family are destroyed, and the exploding sense of confusion and despair that replaces it reverberates through the soundtrack in the form of a powerfully rumbling electronic thunder. Furthermore, not only Bach's music but also Leonardo's art, which in the "Pergolesi sequence" was associated with a strong sense of stillness and belonging, is enveloped by the sudden estrangement introduced by the unexpectedly appearing electronic sound cluster on the soundtrack. Seen from the perspective of the grown (and diseased) Alexei, this scene represents a recollection of an equally tragic and defining moment in the narrator's life. It is a retrospective realization that from this moment on, his father would be absent from his world, just as God was absent from the world of men before the death of Christ on the cross.

Reconciliation: *St. John Passion* – Opening Chorus

While the scenes accompanied by Purcell's *The Indian Queen*, Pergolesi's *Stabat Mater* and the recitative from the *St. Matthew Passion* can all be understood as recollections of situations that actually took place in Alexei's childhood, the film's final scene is much more ambiguous in this regard. Following the scene with Alexei on his sickbed releasing the

56 *Memories, Dreams and Mysteries*

small bird, it might perhaps be interpreted as a fusion of a memory and a dream-vision at the moment of death. It is a resplendent summer afternoon. The 5-year-old Alexei and his sister are being led by the old Maria (that is, the adult Alexei's mother) across a field, while in the more distant background a young version of Maria is seen standing, as if watching the old woman and the two small children. The scene is permeated by a simultaneously somber and idyllic atmosphere, a curious mix of bereavement and contentment that is further emphasized by the presence of the opening chorus to Bach's *St. John Passion* on the soundtrack. One can imagine Tarkovsky choosing the opening chorus to the *St. Matthew Passion* instead – or even more strikingly, the beginning of Mozart's *Requiem* – which would have given the scene a significantly more lugubrious and foreboding atmosphere than it has. Alternatively, one can envision the scene being accompanied by the concluding chorale in D Major ("Nun seid ihr wohl gerochen") of Part 6 of Bach's *Christmas Oratorio*, in which case the scene would have taken on a jubilant character that it now lacks (and which would have been conspicuously out of sync with the overall emotional tone of the film).[11] In other words, the specific character of *St. John Passion*'s opening movement is crucial for the atmosphere permeating the final scene of *Mirror*. While set in a minor mode (G minor), the steadily and gently moving 16-note figures in the violins and, in particular, the jubilantly ascending passages in the bass and soprano parts at bars 37 to 39 create an expression of rapprochement and elevated joy that transfers to the scene's images and imbues the ending of the film with a sense of contentment and reconciliation (Example 3.1).[12] At the same time, there is an air of solemn resignation and valediction flowing through the scene, as if the diseased narrator realizes that all the exuberant joy he once felt as a child is now summed up and re-imagined one last time in his dying consciousness.

The scene seems to blur the different time periods, which until now have been kept distinct, thereby opening it up to a multiplicity of interpretations. However, if we understand it as a compound of memory, dream and vision flowing from the ill narrator's consciousness – or perhaps even as a "postmortem vision" (Sitney 2014a, 91) – the scene can, despite being imbued with a sense of bereavement, be taken as accomplishing a rapprochement with not only a past that has continued to haunt the grown Alexei but also the present (perhaps the element of bereavement can even be seen as a prerequisite for this rapprochement). Being led by his mother as she is in the present, Alexei arrives in his dream-vision at an unconditional acceptance of her *as* his mother. He no longer feels the need to reject his strong ties to her, a rejection on which his (alleged) emancipation from her seems to have been built, and which has been continuously accompanied by strong feelings of guilt for how he has

Memories, Dreams and Mysteries 57

Example 3.1 Johann Sebastian Bach, *St. John Passion*: opening chorus mm. 37–39

treated her and other people close to him. This guilt-ridden character of the protagonist is commented on by Tarkovsky when he discusses *Mirror* in *Sculpting in Time*.

> I wanted to tell the story of the pain suffered by one man because he feels he cannot repay his family for all they have given him. He feels he hasn't loved them enough, and this idea torments him and will not let him be.
>
> (Tarkovsky 1986, 133–134)

Nevertheless, there seems to be some kind of reconciliation toward the film's end. The young Maria's presence in the final scene further emphasizes this theme of reconciliation. Not only is emotional concord attained with both versions of the mother, but Alexei's "vision" can also perhaps be understood as involving a rapprochement with his ex-wife Natalya (with whom he has twice been seen arguing during the film), in that Natalya and the young Maria look exactly alike. (They are played by the same actress, Margarita Terekhova.) In a thematic correspondence with the concluding scenes of *Solaris* and *Nostalghia*, this blurring of different persons and time periods in *Mirror*'s final scene seems at once to dissolve and mend the rift between an irreversibly lost past and a present permeated by repentance and guilt.[13] Unlike in *Solaris* and *Nostalghia*, however, this conflation of past and present is not reflected in a corresponding consolidation of musical dichotomies. In *Mirror*'s final scene, Bach's music reigns alone on the soundtrack, the words of the choir accentuating the

58   *Memories, Dreams and Mysteries*

transfiguration of the narrator's tortured and guilt-ridden interiority into an elevated state of reconciliation and perhaps even joy:

> Herr, unser Herrscher, dessen Ruhm
> In allen Landen herrlich ist!
> Zeig uns durch deine Passion,
> Dass du, der wahre Gottessohn,
> Zu aller Zeit,
> Auch in der größten Niedrigkeit,
> Verherrlicht worden bist!

Mirror, however, is a film that ends in silence. As Bach's music stops, the camera lingers for a while on the old woman and the two children, before slowly beginning to withdraw into the forest. The piping sound of the "simple child's pipe" (Synessios 2001, 57), which has been a recurring sonic feature throughout the film, is heard one last time as the camera tracks further into the trees, and we catch a few more glimpses of the three persons before the screen fades to black and the film is over. After the majestic opening chorus, the silence that follows seems replete with a quiet serenity, further underlining the impression that the narrator is finally at peace with himself.[14]

Moments of Incomprehensibility: Electronic Music

As with *Solaris*, and later *Stalker*, the electronic score for *Mirror* was prepared by Eduard Artemiev. While the distinctive quality of electronically produced sound is often less obvious than in the other two films, *Mirror*'s soundtrack features numerous instances of electronic music as well as electronically processed acoustic timbres and diegetic sounds, ranging from brief segments of a few seconds to extended sequences comprising several minutes. In this section, I concentrate on the parts of the electronic score that can be cogently defined as musical in character.[15] Most of these can be divided into three categories, in that the electronic music predominantly appears in connection with what at first sight may appear to be three unrelated themes: (1) dream-memories of early childhood; (2) encounters with unidentified and inexplicably appearing (and disappearing) characters; and (3) documentary footage from World War Two, the Cultural Revolution in China and the 1969 Sino-Soviet border conflict.[16] In what follows, I argue that the multiple instances of electronic music in *Mirror* are in fact closely linked to each other, as they can all be understood as sonic representations of experiences that in various ways lie beyond the reach of human understanding and comprehension. The electronic music thus functions as a "connective tissue," to borrow an expression from Claudia Gorbman (1987, 90), that ties these seemingly unrelated sequences to each other, and in doing so it participates in

Memories, Dreams and Mysteries   59

articulating a recurring topic in the film concerned with the more nebulous and elusive dimensions of human experience and existence, dimensions that sharply contrast with the familiar mental states and experiences portrayed in the scenes accompanied by classical music.

Dream-Memories of Early Childhood

In *Mirror*, electronic music appears in connection with two extended dream sequences. The first takes place about 16 minutes into the film, and the second (following the second argument between Alexei and Natalya in Alexei's flat) begins at 1:14:36.[17] Shot in black and white, both sequences are signaled as a combination of dreams and vaguely recollected memories of Alexei's early childhood. Or perhaps more accurately, they could be understood as Alexei's recollections of dreams involving memories of his early childhood. However we choose to describe them, both sequences are characterized by the strange logic and ethereal ambience typical of dreams. In fact, these dream sequences seem to have originated from Tarkovsky's own experiences. As reported by Natasha Synessios, when Tarkovsky several years later talked about the creation of *Mirror*, he described a recurring dream that had haunted him for a long time:

> I kept dreaming the same dream about the house where I was born. I dreamed of the house. And then as if I was walking into it, or rather, not into it but around it all the time. These dreams were terribly real, although I knew even then that I was only dreaming. And it was always the same dream, because it took part in the same place. I believed that this feeling carried some material sense, something very important, for why should such a dream pursue a man so?
>
> (quoted in Synessios 2001, 11)[18]

That Tarkovsky strived to recreate the content and atmosphere of his dream in the dream sequences of *Mirror* seems beyond argument. These sequences are closely interrelated, in that they all feature the same outdoor surroundings of Alexei's childhood dacha. The first sequence begins with a shot in color of the 5-year-old Alexei asleep in bed. Artemiev's electronic score, however, has already been introduced toward the end of the preceding scene. As we see a barn on fire, a low-frequency, reverberating and rocket-like electronic tone begins to resonate almost imperceptibly on the soundtrack, making it difficult to distinguish the music from the diegetic sound of the burning barn. This is a clear instance of a sound practice that Tarkovsky often uses in his films where

> a sound will fade in very gradually, often remaining at the border of audibility for so long that, as we begin to perceive it, we first question

if we have in fact heard anything and then wonder how long we have been hearing it.

(Truppin 1992, 237)

As an old man is shown running toward the barn, the music becomes progressively more prominent in the sound mix. The scene then shifts to a shot in color of the sleeping Alexei. He wakes and sits up in bed, after which the scene shifts again to a black-and-white shot of a forest. As the camera begins to track slowly to the left, the trees and bushes start to sway in a sudden gust of wind. Electronic music now completely dominates the soundtrack. A further change of scene returns us to a black-and-white shot of the sleeping boy. Again, he wakes up and utters the word "Papa," at which point (or just before) the electronic music stops.

In what can be described as a bridge into the second part of the film's first dream sequence, we see the boy climbing out of bed and walking up to the threshold of the adjacent room. The dream then continues with a shot of Alexei's mother sitting in front of a large basin washing her hair.[19] She rises, adopts a strangely stylized posture and "begins to make awkward flapping gestures with her arms" (Johnson and Petrie 1994, 118), while her face remains hidden behind her long, wet hair (Figure 3.2). At this point, the electronic music reappears in the form of a rumbling electronic tone cluster. A new shot reveals the room again, but this time without Alexei's mother. Large pieces of the ceiling begin falling slowly onto the drenched floor while the sound of a bell is heard beneath the electronic music. A deep male voice briefly appears, resembling more a ritualistic recitation than actual singing. We also hear a piping

Figure 3.2 Alexei's dream-vision of the mother in *Mirror*
Source: Films Sans Frontières

Example 3.2 Eduard Artemiev: music for *Mirror*.

sound – which has already appeared three times during the first part of this dream sequence and which Synessios, as we have seen, identifies as a "simple child's pipe"[20] – as well as the sound, heavily reverberated and strongly foregrounded, of dripping water. As Alexei's mother approaches a large mirror, she glimpses her reflection, but now as an old woman. At this point the electronic music fades out, leaving only the sound of dripping water on the soundtrack. The sound of the "simple child's pipe" then returns once more, leading over to the ensuing present-day scene where the grown Alexei talks to his mother on the phone.

Let us probe a bit deeper into the constitution and significance of the soundtrack in this extended dream sequence. After beginning with the rocket-like, reverberating electronic sound as the camera focuses on the burning barn, the first part of the dream sequence is then dominated by a 34-second long choral passage consisting of two female voices, one rising and the other falling in partly chromatic lines (Example 3.2). This choral passage, during which the "simple child's pipe" is heard twice, is introduced in connection with the first shot of the sleeping Alexei. It then continues to underscore the part of the dream depicting the wind blowing through the trees and bushes, until it comes to an end with the second shot of the sleeping Alexei. As Johnson and Petrie (1994, 118) point out, in *Mirror* "electronic music [constitutes] a recurring refrain [that] creates a sense of strangeness." In the sequence just described, the sense of strangeness is already inherent in the visuals themselves (the black-and-white scheme, the slow-motion-like pace of the camera, the mysterious gust of wind, etc.), but it is the slightly threatening and uncanny character of the music that turns the sequence into a representation of something utterly ungraspable and incomprehensible. The

62 *Memories, Dreams and Mysteries*

ethereal sound texture and, more importantly, the unstable tonality that results from the chromatically inflected voice-leading articulate a fleeting mental state that seems to elude every attempt to fully grasp it. Artemiev's music thus constitutes the very core of that sense of strangeness connected with Alexei's early childhood: a distant and remote life-world that can be accessed only through the lens of recurring dream-images, as if it forever must be experienced through a distorted mirror. If the classical music presents us with distinct and basically familiar mental states and emotions, the electronic music here expresses the radical otherness of experiences and situations occurring in a distant and all too vaguely recollected past, which appears as a foreign realm from which the film's narrator is irrevocably excluded. Thus, it is not only the dream-image itself that carries an ungraspable and incomprehensible component, but also the life-world of that very period in early childhood to which the dream-image refers.

The sense of strangeness is intensified in the second part of the dream sequence, and this intensification is evident both visually and aurally. Still black and white, the scene is characterized by a dreamy, almost funereal pace that is most evident in the shot where large chunks of the ceiling are falling like giant snowflakes to the floor. The feeling of a distorted dream-memory, however, is much stronger here than in the preceding part of the dream sequence, especially if we imagine Maria's stylized posture and the collapsing ceiling from the perspective of the 5-year-old Alexei. For all its poetic beauty, there is an air of dejection, even of a slight foreboding, over the scene, which in conjunction with the conspicuous absence of Maria's husband (who features only briefly in the scene's opening shot) creates an atmosphere of desertedness and alienation.[21] But it is Alexei rather than Maria who is the subject of this alienation. (Maria seems content enough as she walks through the desolated room.) Moreover, it is an alienation experienced above all by the grown Alexei, the "narrator" of the scene. As with the other dream sequences in *Mirror*, the present one may be understood as the grown Alexei's recollection of a dream-memory originating from the 5-year-old Alexei, in this case as the small child's attempt to make sense of witnessing a private situation characterized by intense intimacy, a situation of which the child is only a bystander and from which he is painfully excluded. As if to underscore this feeling of exclusion, the choral passage has now been replaced by a combination of foreboding vocal entries (the deep male voice), ringing bells and ominous electronic orchestral textures, occasionally punctuated by the piping sound of the "child's pipe," all of which gives this otherwise solemn and ceremonial scene a somewhat nightmarish tint.[22] Encircled by the music, it is as if the mother's private activities, indeed the mother herself, were transformed into something monstrous and alien in the little boy's mind.[23] Tarkovsky himself seems to have emphasized

Memories, Dreams and Mysteries   63

the uncanny character of the electronic music in *Mirror*, telling Artemiev that "he wanted a sound that would evoke a mood of childhood fears and nightmares" (Synessios 2001, 57). Interpreting the scene and the music's role in it along these lines leads us to construct it as a kind of trauma, one that consists precisely of the incomprehensibility of the experience – of the small child's utter inability to make sense of it. Following the shot of the grotesquely transformed mother, the room literally starts to fall apart, creating a sense of alarm and incomprehensibility that still reverberates in the grown Alexei's mind.

The film's second dream sequence, also in black and white, seems to be a direct reflection of Tarkovsky's own recurring dream as he recounted it several years after the completion of *Mirror*. The sequence begins with a shot of a glass vase containing what seems to be a broken watch, which coincides with the appearance of electronic music on the soundtrack. It then continues with the 5-year-old Alexei walking around the childhood dacha. Crossing a small field, he passes a large table on his way toward the house, which is dimly visible in the background. The music continues as the camera tracks to the left and starts to zoom in on the house. In an echo of the earlier dream sequence, we then hear the little boy utter the word "Mama," at which point the music stops. Even though the dream continues for a while (involving, among other things, another shot of trees and bushes bending in the wind), the music comes to a full stop here. Unlike the first dream sequence, this one contains no choral passages, only "instrumental" electronic music. Again, however, we are faced with the intangible and elusive logic of dreams, the present dream at once a repetition and an extension of the first dream. And again, the electronic music is a constitutive part of this incomprehensible and fleeting dream world, which seems to be the only access the grown Alexei has to a radically distant and largely forgotten early childhood. Thus understood, the music is a sonic articulation of those parts of "a person's interior world" (Tarkovsky 1986, 162) that cannot fully be comprehended and understood. Apart from just signifying or signaling this world, however, it is woven into the very fabric of it. In a sense, it *is* this world. If the electronic score removed from the soundtrack, the strangeness of this world – or more specifically, its alterity and fundamentally incomprehensible nature – would be significantly reduced.

Inexplicably Appearing and Disappearing Characters

A second way that electronic music is used to convey a sense of strangeness and alterity in *Mirror* is in connection with the inexplicable appearance and disappearance of characters whose identities are never revealed and whose relation to the overall narrative remains unclear. There is actually only one such scene in *Mirror*, namely the extended scene depicting

Ignat's encounter with a mysterious dark-haired woman and her maid in his father's flat.[24] The scene begins with Ignat helping his mother Natalya to collect some objects that she has dropped on the floor. While picking up some of the coins that have fallen out of Natalya's purse, Ignat receives a mild electric shock, and, as if to signal that something out of the ordinary is about to happen, a multilayered electronic sound mass begins to resonate on the soundtrack. In what appears to be some kind of déjà vu experience, Ignat tells his perplexed mother that "it is as if it had already happened," "but I've never been here before." When Natalya leaves the apartment, Ignat, believing that he is alone at home, discovers two strangers in the room next to the hallway: a dark-haired, middle-aged woman and her old servant. The dark-haired woman asks Ignat to read a passage from Pushkin's 1836 letter to Pyotr Chaadayev, in which the writer discusses Russia's special destiny and its historical significance as a country located between the Christian West and the Mongol East. Just as Ignat has finished his reading, the doorbell rings. It turns out to be Maria (his grandmother), who does not seem to recognize him, however, saying that she must have gotten the wrong address. Ignat, in turn, does not recognize her, and she leaves again. When Ignat turns back to the room he discovers that the dark-haired woman has mysteriously disappeared. The only evidence that she was there is a slowly evaporating heat mark from her cup on the table (Figure 3.3).

Most of this extended scene, which lasts for almost six minutes, is accompanied by electronic music. When the woman asks Ignat to "take the notebook from the third shelf in the bookcase," however, the music is momentarily silenced. It then resumes as he begins to read Pushkin's

Figure 3.3 Evaporating heat mark on the table left behind by the inexplicably disappearing woman in *Mirror*

Source: Films Sans Frontières

Memories, Dreams and Mysteries   65

letter, at which point a new variant of the electronically elaborated choral passage is heard, here built up of four successive diminished triads foregrounding the notes B, G#, G and Bb respectively. As Ignat continues to read, the music briefly disappears, but it soon returns in the form of an indefinable sound mass as the camera zooms in on the dark-haired woman, before disappearing again as he recites the final sentences of the letter. There is a knock on the door and the dark-haired woman tells Ignat to go and open it. The strangeness of the fact that Ignat and his grandmother do not seem to recognize each other is emphasized by a sudden crescendo in the music as Ignat opens the door, a dramatic intensification of the soundtrack that is further heightened by the music merging with diegetic sounds from the stairwell. However, the real musical climax comes at the very end of the scene, where electronically inflected orchestral textures and choral voices join in an ominously rising glissando strongly reminiscent of the upward-moving string crescendos used in countless horror movies to signal the presence of an acute threat. Here, however, it is closely coordinated with the shot of the heat mark on the table. The musical texture of this scene is extremely complex, but it can basically be described as a combination of electronically generated tone clusters and extended choral entrances, punctuated by occasional silences.

In this scene, the "strangeness" articulated by the electronic music is in full force. With telling precision, the electronic sound world is introduced at the exact moment when Ignat pulls back his hand from the coins that have given him the electric shock, in this way effecting an instant transfiguration of the everyday world into an unknown and enigmatic reality. Continuing to dominate the soundtrack as Ignat's mother leaves the apartment, the music heralds that something out of the ordinary is about to happen, only here the setting is not one of Alexei's dreams but an event taking place while Ignat is fully awake (and thus cannot plausibly be understood as a sequence recounted from the narrator's perspective). As to the inexplicable, and unexplained, appearance of the dark-haired woman, it is first signaled by the clinking sound of a teaspoon and a noticeable but brief intensification of the music. Correspondingly, her likewise inexplicable disappearance is accompanied by the powerful crescendo as the choral voices ascend through the vocal registers. The enigmatic appearance and disappearance of this woman, and by extension the uncanny atmosphere permeating the entire scene, is thus doubly emphasized: by the (almost) uninterrupted presence of electronic music and sound throughout the scene, as well as by the dynamic process – the alternation between climactic crescendos and more restrained passages – within this extended musical sequence.

The role played by the electronic score in this scene is both similar and dissimilar to how it functions in the dream sequences. In both cases, the music provides a sonic manifestation of an experience that cannot be

66 *Memories, Dreams and Mysteries*

accommodated within the confines of everyday human comprehension, and that therefore gives rise to a feeling of being in the presence of something radically other, something inherently incomprehensible. In the one instance the sense of alterity is represented by the elusive character of the dreams, in the other by the narratively undermotivated appearance of a possible supernatural being.[25] However, while the electronic music in the dream sequences can plausibly be understood as closely tied to the narrator's interior perspective, in the sense that it gives expression to the experiential quality or essence of the grown Alexei's frame of mind as he repeatedly recollects and re-experiences his dream-memories, this interpretation of the music's role is much less convincing when it comes to the scene with the mysterious woman. Portraying an extraordinary episode experienced by the young and fully awake Ignat, this scene cannot plausibly be understood as anyone's dreams or memories. Consequently, the music here takes on a more "objective" status, defining the sense of alterity and absolute strangeness saturating the entire situation rather than the qualitative state of Ignat's mind. In contrast to Alexei's confused and distorted dream-memories, Ignat's meeting with the mysterious woman is best understood not as a dream or a figment of Ignat's imagination, but as an enigmatic incident that actually takes place.

Documentary Sequences

If electronic music articulates the experiential reality or "feel" of an interior, subjective world in the dream sequences and a more objective atmosphere in the scene with the mysterious woman, it takes on yet another level of signification in the extended documentary sequence that appears about one hour into the film. As I will go on to argue, the electronic score is still closely connected with the theme of incomprehensibility, but here the focus has shifted from personal encounters and experiences to the incomprehensibility experienced when one is faced with human violence, fanaticism and destruction as manifested throughout modern history.

The sequence, which goes on for over six minutes, consists of a series of chronologically ordered newsreel footages, stretching from the Red Army crossing Lake Sivash in 1943 to the climax of the Sino-Soviet conflict in 1969. Inserted into these sequences are brief shots of the orphaned boy Asafiev, a character introduced in the preceding Shooting Range scene. Apart from a brief passage during the episode showing the crossing of Lake Sivash, where Arseny Tarkovsky's poem "Life, Life" is read in voice-over by the author, a combination of choral entrances, electronically generated sound and foreboding percussive rhythms underscore the whole sequence. The music is introduced by a series of repeated drum strokes on the timpani just before the documentary sequence begins as we are shown a brief close-up of the red-haired girl. When the scene changes to the crossing of Lake Sivash, we at first hear only the sound of

Memories, Dreams and Mysteries 67

the soldiers' footsteps as they walk across the shallow water. The drum strokes then return, and a few seconds later a C# diminished chord, sung by a combination of male and female voices and highlighting the diminished fifth, appears on the soundtrack (see also Egorova 1997, 237–238). This chord is repeated several times, continuously accompanied by the ongoing drum strokes, before it is echoed by an electronically generated "instrumental" chord, also a diminished C#. Both the "choir chord" and the "instrumental chord" are repeated a few times, after which the music fades out, making way for Arseny Tarkovsky's poem, which continues to be heard during the succeeding shot of Asafiev climbing a hill against a distinctly Bruegelesque background landscape (Figure 3.4).[26] The distinctive sound of artillery fire then takes us back to the newsreel footage and initiates a second round of electronic music. Celebrations in Moscow of the end of World War Two are followed by a shot of what is presented as the dead body of Hitler, which in turn is followed by images of fireworks lighting up the sky and a still of a man leaning against a wall. The soundtrack is here dominated by an electronic amplification of what seems to be a combination of exploding artillery and fireworks, over which a clearly distinguishable electronic soundscape is layered. The sequence continues with a shot of a mushroom cloud from an atomic bomb, reflected on the soundtrack by yet another outburst of roaring and rumbling electronic tone clusters. Again, there is a brief cut back to Asafiev. He looks straight into the camera with an expression of nausea and disgust on his face, as if he too had been witnessing the barbarities we have just seen. At this point, the "choir chord" reappears together with the drum strokes. When a bird lands on Asafiev's cap, the music intensifies, and as Asafiev raises his right arm and reaches for the bird, a sudden and vigorous crescendo is heard.[27] This leads into the final

Figure 3.4 The orphaned boy Asafiev climbing a hill against a distinctly Bruegelesque background landscape in *Mirror*

Source: Films Sans Frontières

68   *Memories, Dreams and Mysteries*

succession of newsreel footage, beginning with the Cultural Revolution in China. While the electronic music is in full force on the soundtrack, supported by frenzied tirades of timpani rolls, a series of shots show us a close-up of Chairman Mao's Little Red Book, young students carrying large placards of Mao, numerous busts of Mao in different sizes and a crowd of people waving with Mao's Little Red Book in front of the camera. The complex mix of shifting electronic sound textures and timpani strokes (now more slow-moving and staccato) continues as we move into the final newsreel sequence, consisting of footage from the 1969 Sino-Soviet conflict and showing Russian soldiers forming a chain to hold back an angry Chinese mob.

As several writers have pointed out, this extended sequence of newsreel footage constitutes a broader historical and political framework to the personal thoughts and reveries of the narrator, representing a collective memory that mirrors and contextualizes Alexei's private remembrances (see, for example, McSweeney 2015, 56). However, far from being an optimistic account of modern history, it offers a very dark and hopeless picture of human civilization. The world in which Alexei grows up and lives seems to be drenched in territorial conflicts, military aggression and fanatical nationalist propaganda and conformism. People celebrate the end of war, but the celebrations are merged with footage of bombs exploding and tanks rolling through the streets, suggesting that the exultant joy over a long-awaited peace is no more than a fleeting moment in a never-ending cycle of massacres, war and destruction. Anticipating one of the central themes in *The Sacrifice*, the shot of the exploding atomic bomb signals the real possibility of imminent global destruction. It is a world the madness and cruelty of which seem to be beyond human comprehension, a world filled with an inconceivable amount of malice, madness and suffering. For Tarkovsky, such a world must have seemed immensely intimidating, considering that when he was once asked what he most feared in life his answer was human violence.[28]

Through its close association with the eerie atmosphere saturating the dream sequences and the Pushkin scene, electronic music becomes increasingly linked with what may be termed the "theme of incomprehensibility" in the film, underscoring and strengthening a sense of being in the presence of something that one cannot fully fathom or grasp. In the one instance, this "something" is a radical alterity experienced in relation to fleeting and distorted dream-memories of a distant life-world, and in the other an indefinable and ominous ambiance that permeates an out-of-the-ordinary encounter with the inexplicable. Consequently, when we come to the documentary sequences, the strangeness (to use the word preferred by Johnson and Petrie) of this music is firmly established. So even if the unfathomable nature of the destructive forces exhibited in the archival footage is already apparent in the images themselves, it is their embeddedness in a sonic environment characterized by brooding electronic music, foreboding drum strokes and frenzied timpani rolls that brings the message home to us emotionally, namely that the mechanisms behind these cataclysmic forces elude our every attempt to understand and explain them, and that they accordingly lie beyond the power of human comprehension. It is through the music that the incomprehensibility of what we see becomes emotionally tangible and real. However, unlike the dream sequences and the Pushkin scene, which are concerned specifically with Alexei's and Ignat's experiences, the sense of incomprehensibility conveyed here is directed toward an objectively existing supra-individual world shared by and affecting humanity as a whole. In a sense, it is humanity itself that is the object of incomprehension here, or rather the ease with which people throughout history have been willing, again and again, to sacrifice their humanity and succumb to the depersonalizing forces of mass hysteria, aggression and war. Artemiev's music penetrates into the heart of the documentary sequences and brings forth the horrifying insight – in the narrator, the spectator, Asafiev, and Tarkovsky himself – not only that the collective madness of the human race eludes every attempt at rationalization and explanation, but also that humanity's meaningless drive to combat and destroy itself in the name of some higher cause will never come to an end.

Music, Diegesis and Dimensions of Human Experience in *Mirror*

The link in *Mirror* between electronic music and "being in the presence of something utterly incomprehensible" is consistent with how electronic music is used in *Solaris* and *Stalker*. The electronic music in *Solaris*, as we have seen, is closely tied to the enigmatic planet Solaris. And as I will argue in the next chapter, in *Stalker* it bears a special connection to the inscrutable and mysterious Zone. The role and function of electronic music in *Mirror* can thus be seen as forming part of an overall pattern within Tarkovsky's three films from the 1970s. However, and in comparison with *Solaris* in particular, there are also significant differences in how electronic music is used in *Mirror*, differences that above all concern the relationship between the electronic music and classical music. In *Mirror*, the dichotomy between these musical "worlds" or dimensions is much less pronounced than in *Solaris*. Watching *Mirror*, we search in vain for something corresponding to *Solaris*'s clear association of classical music with Earth and electronic music with a radically other life form (which is essentially what Solaris is, at least on a manifest level). Nevertheless, I would argue that in *Mirror*, too, there is a dichotomy between the two types of music, albeit of a subtler kind. This dichotomy could perhaps best be described in terms of dimensions of human experience. Thus, the classical music is connected with (memories of) life experiences that, because they are familiar and *nameable* human emotions and mental

70   *Memories, Dreams and Mysteries*

states, are recognizable in such a way that the character in question can "inhabit" and "feel at home" in them. The electronic music, on the other hand, is connected with feelings of estrangement and alienation in that it accompanies encounters with things (dreams, inexplicable presences, the impenetrable forces of human destruction) that transgress the limits of human experience and understanding, and that therefore are saturated with a sense of alterity and strangeness. In contrast to the feelings and states accompanied by classical music, there is no language for such feelings; they are essentially *unnamable*. When it comes to the role and function of music, the difference between *Mirror* and *Solaris* is thus not so much a difference in kind as a difference in how explicitly the dichotomy between classical and electronic music is articulated. In both films, classical music works as an anchoring force and existential "life-line" that places the characters within a recognizable emotional and phenomenological reality and so allows them to connect with their true sense of self. And in both films, electronic music signals the experiential dimensions that cannot be accommodated and made sense of within this phenomenological reality, in this way constituting the experiential outside of the known and inhabitable life-world represented by the firmly tonal music by Baroque composers such as Bach, Pergolesi and Purcell.

But if the two films construct a semiotically and structurally equivalent dichotomy between classical and electronic music, the observation that this dichotomy is much less clearly pronounced in *Mirror* raises the question of what consequences this has for our understanding of the diegetic status of the music in the film. In *Solaris*, the different interpretive constructions of the Bach prelude's diegetic status seemed to be largely independent from the film's basic Earth-Space dichotomy, in that they were all compatible with this dichotomy. But can the same be said about *Mirror*? Can the music's diegetic status be assessed independently of how we construct the semiotic significance of the different musical appearances in the film? To put this question in another way: given that *Mirror* is a film that in large part must be understood as depicting an interior world, a film unfolding from a consciousness behind the images, how does the music relate to this world? Tarkovsky himself seems to hint at an answer when he writes:

> In the autobiographical *Mirror* . . . music is often introduced as part of the material of life, of the author's spiritual experience, and thus as a vital element in the world of the film's lyrical hero.
>
> (Tarkovsky 1986, 158)

It is not entirely clear to whom the word "author" refers here. Is it Tarkovsky himself, the creator of the "autobiographical" film, or is it Alexei, the film's "lyrical hero"? However we are inclined to answer this question, it seems that Tarkovsky is here saying that music belongs to the same consciousness that produces the images; it is "a vital element in the world of the film's lyrical hero." But does this mean that Alexei should actually be understood as hearing the music? I suppose that much of the music in the film could be conceived of in this way, even if I do not find this view very compelling. Instead, I would suggest, in line with Guido Heldt's concept of internal focalization (derived from the work of Gérard Genette and Edward Branigan), that Alexei's interiority is focalized *through* or *via* the music, meaning that the music articulates and defines his state of mind (cf. Heldt 2013, 127–129). Thus, the music is not directly heard by Alexei; rather, it functions as a "representation or intimation" (Heldt 2013, 127) of his inner state. At the same time, and unlike more standard instances of nondiegetic music, Alexei's inner state is musically focalized from *within* this inner state itself. But it is not musically focalized *as* music (which would be tantamount to a more up-front metadiegetic reading); instead, the different feelings and atmospheres conveyed by the music articulate the *qualia* – the perceived subjective quality – of Alexei's memories and dreams. The music *is*, or is an essential part of, his inner state *as he experiences it*.

As should have become clear from the preceding pages, this way of conceptualizing the music's relation to the interior perspective of the film's narrator does seem convincing for most instances of music in the film. Thus, almost all occurrences of classical music can plausibly be construed as focalizing Alexei's mind, the only exception being the Bach chorale prelude accompanying the shot of the levitating Maria, which can perhaps more aptly be described as a vision emanating from the mother herself. As to the first playing of the chorale in connection with the film's opening credits, it too can be understood as an intimation of Alexei's interiority, as a musical (and, considering the title of the piece, textual) manifestation of the narrator's *Grundstimmung*, which sets the tone for most of what subsequently happens in the film. When we come to the electronic music, however, things become more complicated. Even though the dream-memory scenes can plausibly be construed in accordance with a focalization account, the documentary footage and the scene with the mysterious woman seem much more problematic in this regard. Perhaps some viewers would be prepared to accept a reading of the documentary footage according to which it depicts a view of the world as focalized through Alexei's tormented and mistrustful mind. However, a better way to conceive of the footage, and the music accompanying it, is as providing a historical framework to Alexei's personal ruminations and also to the convoluted relationships depicted in the present-day scenes. From this perspective, the music should not be conceived of as forming part of Alexei's interiority or subjective point of view, but rather as articulating the incomprehensibility of human destruction from the more abstract vantage point of the film itself.[29] As to the scene with the mysterious woman, it is even more obvious that we need to find an

72   *Memories, Dreams and Mysteries*

alternative account of the music's diegetic status, since here it becomes outright implausible to claim that we are situated within the interiority of the film's narrator. The scene is about Ignat's encounter with this enigmatic woman and thus recounts an experience that must be understood as lying outside the orbit of the "lyrical hero's" life-world. Instead, and as I have argued, the music takes on a more exterior and "objective" status here, underscoring and even constituting the otherworldliness, the sense of absolute strangeness, that characterizes the situation as a whole.

With *Mirror*, we have investigated what is arguably Tarkovsky's most complex and loosely structured film, with regard not only to its narrative construction but also to how music is put to use in the film. However, the dichotomous relation between classical and electronic music that was so obvious in *Solaris* is also evident in *Mirror*, even if articulated much more subtly. And, as we shall see in the next chapter, the dichotomy continues to play an important role in Tarkovsky's next feature film, *Stalker*, but now in a way that differs from both *Solaris* and *Mirror*.

Notes

1. See, for example, Tarkovsky (1986a, 134), Johnson and Petrie (1994, 118), Robinson (2006, 404–405), Sullivan (2012, 457) and Mroz (2013, 91).
2. In addition, the first documentary sequence in the film, from the Spanish Civil War, is accompanied by flamenco music. As I focus on classical and electronic music in this chapter, I will not discuss this sequence. For an extended account of the sequence, see Bird (2008, 137–138). See also Chapter 7 in this book.
3. For readers who are not familiar with *Mirror*, a detailed synopsis of the film that also identifies most occurrences of classical and electronic music is given in the appendix at the end of this book. Overviews of the film's structure are also provided by Johnson and Petrie (1994), Redwood (2010) and Martin (2011).
4. For an extended discussion of the complex key structure of "Das alte Jahr vergangen ist," see Temperley (2006).
5. This understanding of "Das alte Jahr vergangen ist" is in conflict with Sean Martin's interpretation of the piece and its role in the film. Also noting that the prelude "was intended for use at the New Year," Martin goes on to suggest, with reference to the prologue featuring the curing of the young stuttering boy, that "now that Tarkovsky could 'speak', what is to follow is a new beginning" (Martin 2011, 121).
6. See Skakov (2012, 110) for an English translation of the poem.
7. Often translated as "when my body dies."
8. Here I agree with Sean Martin's claim that this scene depicts Alexei and not Ignat. As Martin (2011, 215, note 125) points out, even though "most synopses of the film identify the boy as Ignat . . . a close examination of the costume – a tatty coat with a white collar – reveals that it is definitely the young Alexei." This claim is further supported by the fact that Alexei later in the film, in the scene where the homecoming father summons his children, is seen with the Leonardo monograph and wearing the very same coat.
9. Mroz (2013, 125) specifies that Pergolesi's music begins "at the third shot change."

Memories, Dreams and Mysteries 73

10. "And see, the curtain in the Temple was torn in two from top to bottom; and the earth shook and the rocks split."

11. See Gorbman (1987, 16–18) for a similar musical "commutation" on what she calls the "bicycling segment" from François Truffaut's *Jules and Jim* (1961).

12. In an account of the music's expressive character that is somewhat incongruent with the one just given, Robinson (2006, 199) writes that "the ending of *Mirror* . . . wouldn't be nearly as moving without those restless violins and clarinets [*sic!*] and voices which chase around in the air in Bach's *St. John Passion*." It is in particular the word "restless" with which I take issue here.

13. For a discussion of *Nostalghia* along these lines, see Chapter 5.

14. As I argue in Chapter 7, however, there is a strong ambiguity inherent in this silence.

15. Thus, an instance of electronically manipulated sound that I will not discuss is the one that occurs in connection with the malfunctioning shower tube at the end of the so-called Printing house scene. I believe this sequence is more plausibly described as a subtle elaboration of diegetic sound than an instance of electronic music. For a brief account of the sequence, see Mroz (2013, 124).

16. A few occurrences of electronic music fall somewhat outside this classification. One example is the sudden burst of electronic sound that merges with the last chord of the Bach recitative and which was discussed in the preceding section. Another example is a similar outburst of electronic sound appearing in connection with a brief shot of a large fire following directly upon the end of the Printing house scene. Even though I do not argue the point here, I believe that this latter instance too can be understood as a representation of incomprehensibility.

17. There are actually three dream sequences in *Mirror*. However, the third one, appearing toward the film's end, does not contain any electronic music. Instead, it is accompanied by Arseny Tarkovsky's reading of his poem "Eurydice."

18. The quote is from Tarkovsky's *Uroki rezhissury* (Lectures on Film Directing).

19. That this sequence is part of Alexei's dream is confirmed in the succeeding scene when the grown Alexei, talking to his mother on the phone, tells her that he just dreamt about her. Peter Green, among others, also describes the sequence as being part of Alexei's dream (Green 1993, 82; see also Truppin 1992, 242–243). P. Adams Sitney goes as far as saying that "the opening twenty minutes of the film can be seen retroactively as the very dream to which the narrator refers in a telephone call to his mother, in the first scene in his apartment in the present" (Sitney 2014a, 74).

20. Egorova (1997, 237) describes it as a "common toy pipe," while Fairweather (2012, 42) hears it as a "breathy panpipe."

21. Skakov (2012, 114) writes of Alexei's first dream that it "is gradually transformed into something uncanny," while Helena Bassil-Morozow describes the sequence where the mother washes her hair as "both poetic and terrifying" (Bassil-Morozow 2015, 196).

22. Fairweather (2012, 42) describes the sounds produced at the beginning of this sequence (when we see the mother washing her hair) as "akin to a metallic train or jet engine."

23. Mroz (2013, 107) similarly describes her appearance as "frightening and uncanny." In fact, the mother's appearance as she rises from the washbasin (her stylized posture, the long hair covering her face) is curiously reminiscent of the evil girl in Hideo Nakata's *Ringu* (1998); so much so that one may even conjecture that Verbinski was influenced by Tarkovsky's *Mirror*.

74   *Memories, Dreams and Mysteries*

24. The two characters reappear in the penultimate scene of the film, taking place in Alexei's flat, where they discuss the diseased Alexei's condition with a visiting doctor.
25. Nariman Skakov, for one, seems to think of the woman as a supernatural being, writing that "her manners and appearance testify that she belongs to a different age, perhaps to the nineteenth century. She may be a former pre-revolutionary owner of the flat who enters it as a ghost" (Skakov 2012, 120). The suggestion that the dark-haired woman is a supernatural being is problematized, however, by her reappearance in the film's penultimate scene.
26. Tarkovsky himself acknowledged the influence of Bruegel's paintings in the construction of this scene (see Gianvito 2006, 53).
27. When, in an interview with Philip Strick in 1981, Tarkovsky was asked if he "had a purpose in mind when arranging . . . that a bird should land on the boy's head," he replied: "My wife attracts birds. When we walk in the forest, birds fly close to her – she is like them, a part of nature. Some country people even call her a sorceress. Now, I know there is no malice in her at all, birds will never approach an evil being. In the film, the child has just misbehaved, so to show the audience he isn't some kind of delinquent, beyond hope, I illustrate with the bird a hint of his true nature" (Gianvito 2006, 72).
28. The interview is found in Michal Leszczylowski's documentary *Directed by Andrej Tarkovsky* (1988).
29. Speaking of "the vantage point of the film itself" may for some readers evoke Daniel Frampton's concept of filmind (see Frampton 2006). In the chapter on *Nostalghia*, I will discuss how a slightly revised version of Frampton's concept can function as a suggestive way to understand certain aspects of that film. With regard to *Mirror*, however, it seems to me that the concept is largely redundant, the filmind's thinking being indistinguishable from the thinking of the film's absent narrator Alexei, although scenes like the one just discussed might perhaps be understood as scenes where cinematic thinking is temporarily taken over by the filmind (see Chapter 7). Mai (2017) attempts a full-scale application of Frampton's concept to *Mirror*.

4   Beethoven Overcome
Transcendence and Utopia in *Stalker*

In a video clip available on YouTube, Eduard Artemiev reports that he once asked Tarkovsky why the director needed the combined sounds of classical music and passing trains recurring throughout *Stalker*. Tarkovsky's answer was that "often when a train rushes by or when you ride in a train . . . you would hear some music in the rhythmically organized sound rumble of the wheels," and it was this aural experience that he was interested in capturing.[1] Artemiev then goes on to say that for Tarkovsky, the recurring sonic compound of classical music and running trains "didn't have any meaning," and in particular it "didn't mean that civilization is rushing somewhere." Thus, far from seeking to invest these sounds with a figurative or symbolic meaning, Tarkovsky just wanted to exhibit a particular psychoacoustic phenomenon. Whether these statements should be taken as Artemiev directly quoting the director, or if they are rather to be understood as reflecting the composer's own view, this is the kind of answer one could very well expect from Tarkovsky, given his well-known skepticism toward symbolic readings of his films. I find this answer deeply unsatisfactory, even slightly magisterial in its attempt to control what things in the film do or do not mean. Consequently, in this chapter I will take the opposite approach, building my analysis of *Stalker* on the premise that not only is it plausible to claim that the pairing of classical music and the sound of trains *does* mean something, but what it can be taken to mean has precisely something to do with "civilization rushing somewhere."

The amalgamation of classical music and the rhythmic clicking of train wheels on the tracks forms an integrated and clearly identifiable sound image that recurs throughout the film – what I will refer to as the *sonic figure*. In developing my reading of *Stalker*, my argument revolves around the sonic figure as it appears in the film's final scene. The scene features a young girl causing glasses to slide on a table just by fixing her eyes on them, while a fragment of the "Ode to Joy" from the last movement of Beethoven's Ninth Symphony is briefly heard together with the sound of a passing train. As Vida T. Johnson and Graham Petrie point out, this scene is crucial, "as much of any interpretation of the

76   *Beethoven Overcome*

film depends on understanding what in fact happens here" (Johnson and Petrie 1994, 143). Although most critics and scholars agree about the open-ended nature of the scene, several commentators have nevertheless, explicitly or implicitly, attempted to understand its underlying meaning or message.[2] These readings, which range from affirmation of its enigmatic nature to an interpretation of Christian symbols, typically pay scant attention to what happens on the soundtrack, especially with Beethoven's music.[3] But the presence of this music is genuinely puzzling. What is it doing here? What is the relation, if any, between the "Ode to Joy" and the inexplicable actions performed by the Stalker's daughter, named Monkey? More specifically, how can we give a plausible reading of this decidedly *anti*-triumphant and noncelebratory scene, while taking into account the presence of arguably the most paradigmatic example of triumphant and celebratory music? Andrea Truppin suggests an answer when she writes that:

> In the last scene of *Stalker*, [the Stalker's little daughter] quietly and steadily moves glasses on a table with her gaze. One of the glasses falls. The sound of its rolling on the floor blends with the warning rattle of a window that heralds an approaching train. As the little girl sits quietly at the table, it begins to shake. The train roars by, obscenely blaring strains of orchestral music and filling the previously tranquil room with violence. The train noise dies away and the picture fades to black, but a soft rattling of windows remains as a reminder of the aural cataclysm that has just swept through. If the train's roar and its distorted music represent the destructive forces of Western civilization, the power of spirituality is represented by the small child, who calmly and gently moves the world.
>
> (Truppin 1992, 247–248)

In my view, this is a very rewarding way of viewing the last scene of *Stalker*, and much of what follows in this chapter can be seen as a further development of Truppin's brief account. The overall conclusion I work toward is that the scene reaffirms one of the central tenets of early Romantic aesthetics, namely the idea of transcendence. Moreover, I claim that this understanding of the scene has important consequences for our understanding of the film as a whole.

Stalker, Monkey and Beethoven: A Descriptive Preamble

Stalker, we may recall, is a film about three men – the Stalker, Writer and Professor – who travel into a derelict wasteland called the Zone. Purportedly transformed under mysterious circumstances in a not too distant past, the Zone is now considered a dangerous place for people to visit, and it has been put under strict surveillance with heavily armed

Beethoven Overcome 77

police guarding its borders. Led by the Stalker, a self-proclaimed spiritual guide who has visited the Zone several times and developed an intimate attachment to it, the three men's destination is a specific location inside the Zone – a room of which it is said that whoever enters it will have his innermost desires fulfilled. Professor and Writer, however, show a quite skeptical and at times even cynical attitude toward the whole enterprise. They repeatedly question the decisions made by the Stalker as he leads them forward, and the combination of scorn and fear with which they react to the Stalker and the Zone suggests that the trip is going to be a failure. And perhaps it is, for even though they eventually arrive at the mysterious room, both Writer and Professor, and also the Stalker himself, decline to enter it (at least as far as we can tell). Instead they end up sitting at the threshold of the room, and we do not know whether they are passively or perhaps raptly looking into it while the camera pulls back and gradually reveals the interior of the place to us, the spectators (cf. Söderbergh Widding 2006, 159).[1] In the scene that follows this hypnotic high point in the story, we find the three men once again in the bar where they met before leaving for the Zone. The Stalker's wife soon appears, after which the couple and their crippled daughter leave for home. The five scenes that follow the hypnotic ending in the Zone constitute a kind of coda, or epilogue. They comprise: (1) the return to the bar; (2) the Stalker and his family walking home with Monkey sitting on her father's shoulders; (3) a miserable and despairing Stalker being put to bed by his wife; (4) the wife's monologue; and (5) the final scene, where Monkey is telekinetically moving the glasses.

The final scene lasts exactly four minutes. As it begins, we see Monkey sitting alone at the table in front of a large window, silently reading a book. After a short while she closes the book, and we see her in profile as she sits in silence. Then suddenly, we hear her voice (in a voice-over) reciting a love poem, *I love your eyes, dear* (*Lyublyu glaza tvoi, moi drug*), by the nineteenth-century Russian writer Fyodor Tyutchev. As the last words of the poem are spoken, she briefly turns away from the camera to look out the window. But she soon turns her head again, this time toward the camera, and starts to look at the shortest of the three glasses on the table, half-filled with a dark liquid that looks like tea. At this point something quite extraordinary happens: the glass starts to move all by itself. We soon understand, though, that this is not really the case; it is Monkey who is moving the glass just by looking at it. She then turns her attention to the second glass – described by Johnson and Petrie (1994, 143) as "a jar containing a broken egg-shell" – and moves it in a diagonal line toward the left side of the table (from her perspective). Finally, as Monkey starts to move the third and tallest glass, she simultaneously lowers her head slowly toward the table and finally lays her head on the tabletop. With her gaze she moves the tall glass in a straight line toward the short end of the table until the glass falls off the edge. Surprisingly, the glass does

78 *Beethoven Overcome*

not break when it hits the floor, even though it looks extremely fragile.[5] After these supernatural acts, Monkey remains in this posture with her head resting on the table, while the camera slowly zooms in on her face. Just like the actions that have just occurred, her "blank and expressionless" face (Johnson and Petrie 1994, 144) appears to defy all explanation (Figure 4.1).

Let us consider what happens on the soundtrack during this sequence. Right from the beginning and through most of the scene, we hear birdsong. We also hear the sound of whistles from nearby trains. This is followed by Monkey reciting the poem, and when she starts to turn her attention to the glasses, we hear what is probably a boat's foghorn in the distance (the sounds of the whistle and the foghorn are heard again several times during the sliding of the glasses). When Monkey begins to move the first glass, we hear the dog that followed the Stalker from the Zone whimper nervously. Monkey hears it too, and briefly looks in the direction where the dog seems to be positioned. Then, just after the tall glass has fallen over the edge, we hear the sound of a train passing by. Shortly thereafter, the "Ode to Joy" from Beethoven's Ninth Symphony breaks in, and the rhythmic sound of the train must now share the auditory space with this music. (The passage used by Tarkovsky is from the finale, and is one that most audiences would be familiar with, namely the one that begins with the entrance of the full chorus at m. 213 in the *Alla Marcia* section.) Soon, however, both the music and the sound of the train fade away. For a few more seconds we see Monkey's face. The screen then goes into black and the film is over.

Figure 4.1 Monkey resting her head against the tabletop after having telekinetically moved the glasses in the last scene of *Stalker*

Source: Films Sans Frontières

Signifiers of Triumph and Progress

My reading of this scene takes as its point of departure Claudia Gorbman's statement that, in film, music "which calls attention to itself, swings away from the imaginary toward the symbolic" (Gorbman 1987, 6–7). In the Lacanian terminology Gorbman employs, we should understand this "swinging away" as a transition from the primarily preverbal and affective responses elicited by narrative underscoring to a more explicitly representational, emblematic and non-narrative function for the music. Despite its brief and fleeting appearance, the "Ode to Joy," as a piece of pre-existing and extremely well-known music, is obviously likely to "call attention to itself," even though this might not have been what Tarkovsky envisioned. Consistent with his answer to Artemiev's question about the reason for combining music with the sound of trains, Tarkovsky, on another occasion, expressed his intention that the classical music he used in *Stalker* must be barely discernable to the audience (Gianvito 2006, 51–52). But barely discernable is not the same as inaudible, and in the last scene Beethoven's music is distinctly noticeable to anyone who listens carefully. Moreover, the sharp contrast between this music and the visual image of the Stalker's daughter makes the music inherently unfit to fulfill the function of "imaginary" music, and instead opens it up to symbolic interpretations. As we will see, even Tarkovsky himself on occasion hinted at a symbolic understanding of it.

Now, given the open-ended nature of the last scene, there will obviously be many potentially interesting – though not equally convincing – answers to the question of how we should understand the simultaneous appearance of Beethoven's music and the sound of passing trains.[6] The answer I would like to explore in the following suggests that the sonic figure can plausibly be heard as a powerful symbol of the scientific revolutions, the political projects and the ideological struggles of modern history. As Esteban Buch has convincingly shown, the triumphant and ecstatic euphoria of the "Ode to Joy" is in itself deeply imbued with a history of symbolism and ideology. More specifically, Buch points out that "the *Ode to Joy*'s career as political music is bound up with that of the other ideals that underlie the history of the modern Western world" (Buch 2003, 263). This music would thus be one of the most obvious choices for a director who needed a sonic symbol of modern (Western) society. The claim that we can justifiably understand Beethoven's music as performing this role in the last scene of *Stalker* will gain further support when we take the second constituent of the sonic figure into account. The sound of running trains can clearly be imagined as one of the more entrenched symbols of modern history and civilization (cf. Beaumont and Freeman 2007; Aguiar 2008; Tsai 2018, 31). It is thus the sonic figure conceived of as a compound sound image that does the representational work in *Stalker*'s last scene, rather than its constituent parts considered

80   *Beethoven Overcome*

separately. Put differently, when the cultural, "extra-cinematic" codings (Snead 1994/2016, 38; see also Gorbman 1987, 13) of the constituent parts combine to form a larger integrated whole, there emerges a strong sonic symbol of modern civilization and its grand projects.

But there is clearly something else going on in this scene, for the symbolism of the sonic figure is not allowed to remain intact. Instead, the sonic figure is effectively recoded within the context of the scene in a way that fundamentally alters the impact of the music and also the sound of the train. These signifiers of triumph and progress become radically transfigured: heard alongside the magical actions and the vast and ineffable silence of the Stalker's daughter, they appear unfamiliar, strange, illusive – transformed into echoes of a pointless project already over. What is apparently real – our scientific progress, our grand political and ideological projects, the perceived teleology of human history, in short, the meanings of our jointly constructed "life-world" – becomes unreal. The steady visual focus on Monkey constructs an intensive presence around her, and this presence functions as a precondition for the possibility of perceiving the sonic figure in the way just mentioned. At the same time, it is *because* Monkey's actions and appearance can be experienced as so strongly contrasting with the known and common world indicated on the soundtrack that we can understand her as a signifier of transcendence. Hence, Monkey is presented to us as a representation of a different order of reality; through a combination of silence and unexplainable behavior, she demonstrates to us what, in the end, really matters when all the conceited and evanescent ambitions of humanity have been left behind. In short, what emerges in this scene is a statement about the, *sub specie aeternitatis*, very short-lived and ultimately futile collective construction of a shared, intelligible and recognizable world. In place of this constructed, illusory and signified world, another more permanent reality is asserted that does not rely on collective narratives and momentary signifying practices. This conception of a different and higher reality in *Stalker* has been aptly described by the Swedish film scholar Astrid Söderbergh Widding as an essentially mystical conception of what she terms an "absolute outside" (Söderbergh Widding 1992, 107).

The last scene of *Stalker* may thus be read a massive critique of modern history and civilization. In the sound of passing trains and in Beethoven's music, we can hear a faint and fading echo of the restless striving of humanity as it tries to make sense of, conquer and colonize the universe, without as well as within. The scene makes it clear, however, that this grand project is a failure, and that what is ultimately of importance is something very different, something that will forever elude and outlast the signifying practices represented in the soundtrack. The signifier of that unsignifiable something is of course Monkey, the Stalker's crippled daughter. The radical otherness represented by Monkey, whose appearance and magical actions can be taken as displaying the same evasion of

Beethoven Overcome 81

all signification and intelligibility as the Zone itself, is so obviously contrasted with the noisy train and the rallying cries of joy in Beethoven's music that we are almost forced to experience soundtrack and film image as opposites, even antagonists.[7]

Signifiers Beyond Intelligibility

Let us call the proposal that the sonic figure represents modern civilization *the basic claim*. The idea that this sonic figure is radically transfigured in the film's final scene can then be called *the specific claim*. How can these claims be further grounded? With regard to the basic claim, we can start by considering how the final scene relates to *Stalker* as a whole, that is, ask what connection exists between Monkey and the Zone. This would open up the possibility of understanding the former in terms of the latter, which, in turn, would make the suggested symbolism of Beethoven's music and the sound of the train even more apparent. For starters, we must ask: what is the Zone? At the very beginning of the film we get to know that the origin of the Zone is uncertain. It might have been caused by a meteorite or by a visit of alien creatures – but no one really knows. Furthermore, the place is regarded with what seems to be an inconsistent mixture of reverence and utmost suspicion; on the one hand, it is described as a "miracle," but on the other hand, an immediate decision is made to send government troops there. After the mysterious disappearance of these troops, the entire area is sealed off and armed police are called in to guard its borders. What we basically know about the Zone, then, is not very much: it is a mysterious, supposedly dangerous and, at any rate, highly protected area with an unknown origin.

There has been no shortage of suggestions about the meaning of the Zone, and what it represents or symbolizes.[8] As Slavoj Žižek points out:

> For an ex-citizen of the defunct Soviet Union, the notion of a forbidden zone gives rise to (at least) five associations: the Zone is (1) Gulag, i.e. a separated prison territory; (2) a territory poisoned or otherwise rendered uninhabitable by some technological (biochemical, nuclear . . .) catastrophe, like Chernobyl; (3) the secluded domain in which the *nomenklatura* lives; (4) foreign territory to which access is prohibited (like the enclosed West Berlin in the midst of the GDR); (5) a territory where a meteorite struck (like Tunguska in Siberia).
>
> (Žižek 1999, 227)

Žižek believes, however, that there is ultimately no right answer to the question of the "true meaning" of the Zone; what is important is rather "the very indeterminacy of what lies beyond the limit" (Žižek 1999, 227).[9] Instead of trying to determine what the Zone actually represents, we

82 *Beethoven Overcome*

must acknowledge that we cannot and should not strive to specify its meaning. In this respect, Žižek is in full agreement with Tarkovsky, who remarked that

> people have often asked me what the Zone is, and what it symbolizes, and have put forward wild conjectures on the subject. I'm reduced to a state of fury and despair by such questions. The Zone doesn't symbolize anything, any more than anything else does in my films.
>
> (Tarkovsky 1986, 200)

Despite such protestations, it is hard to imagine that audiences could watch *Stalker* without speculating on the meaning and purpose of the Zone, or at least using it as a foil or placeholder for such meanings. Whatever the function or significance of the Zone, our experience of it will most certainly stand in striking contrast to the noisy trains and the half-hysterical chorus of the last scene, just as our experience of Monkey will most likely be perceived in contrast to these soundtrack phenomena. That the Zone, like the Stalker's daughter, is pervaded by a profound silence can hardly escape anyone who has watched *Stalker*. The importance of this characteristic becomes explicitly evident when the three protagonists have finally arrived in the Zone after the long ride on the motorized railway trolley. The first thing the Stalker comments upon is the immense silence that pervades the place: "Here we are, home at last. How quiet it is. This is the quietest place in the world. You'll see for yourselves."[10]

On one level, the connection between Monkey and the Zone is obvious, for it is clear in the film (as it is in the novel, *Roadside Picnic*, on which the film is based)[11] that the Zone affects certain people in a special way, and that Monkey's poor health as well as her extraordinary powers are in some sense caused by the Zone's radiation and her father's frequent excursions into it. But beyond this causal link, a connection is also established by subtle relationships pertaining to the image- and soundtrack – a connection that not only binds Monkey very closely to the Zone, but even suggests that she in some respects can be regarded as a direct *extension* of the Zone. This connection was envisioned by Tarkovsky. Not only does the girl display the same radical otherness as the Zone, but the director links the two visually and sonically in very concrete, albeit subtle, ways. Firstly, and most obviously, the only scenes shot in color outside the Zone are the two toward the end of the film in which Monkey appears. As Peter Green (1993, 105) has noted, we are somehow supposed to understand the girl's appearance as a reflection or an embodiment of the Zone. Secondly, there is a conspicuous musical connection between Monkey and the Zone: Eduard Artemiev's electronic music, which has hitherto been connected almost exclusively[12] with the three men's experiences inside the Zone, reappears toward the end of the film in the scene where the

Stalker is carrying his daughter home on his shoulders. Now the entrance of this music is unmistakably associated with Monkey, as we hear it while the camera focuses on a close-up of her face. Finally, Johnson and Petrie point out a very specific connection between Monkey and the Zone, in that the "rich golden texture of the daughter's headscarf" echoes the colors, the "subtle shades of gold and red," of the room itself (Johnson and Petrie 1994, 153).

The close connection between Monkey and the Zone makes sense in the larger context of the film, for these two "signifiers beyond intelligibility" can be seen to contrast sharply with a central theme recurring throughout *Stalker*, what might be termed the theme of "fear and denial." The state-sanctioned decision to seal off the Zone is perhaps the most obvious representative of this theme (a decision whose paradoxical nature should not go unnoticed, since it actually participates in constituting the Zone). But the theme also surfaces explicitly during the three men's ride on the railway trolley into the Zone. At the beginning of this extended sequence, Writer inquiries into the possibility that the police can catch up with them, to which the Stalker answers that no one will follow them, since "they fear it [the Zone] like the plague." The word "they" here is laden with ambiguities, for even though it most obviously refers to the police guarding the Zone's border, on a broader level it can be taken to refer to all of us, to humanity as a whole. Finally, a more subtle version of the theme can be found in the sometimes rather infantile behavior and reactions of Professor and Writer as the Stalker leads them: the unwarranted skepticism they exhibit toward the Stalker and the Zone, their unwillingness to follow the Stalker's advice, their perpetual discussions and quibbles, their decision not to enter the mysterious room, etc. Taken together, all this suspicion toward the Zone (on the part of the state, the police, Professor and Writer) can be seen as expressing the attitude of humanity writ large – the latter aligned with Beethoven's music and the sound of trains in the context of the last scene. Indeed, these seemingly unrelated moments in the film are simply different ways of displaying the same idea: the failure of humanity, or at least modern civilization, to accommodate and acknowledge the presence of something that is as ungraspable as it is important to human life.

Musical Dichotomies Between East and West

A closer look at the choice and appearance of classical music in the film, and how this music relates to the film's electronic score, will further substantiate the previously mentioned considerations. As is typical for Tarkovsky, classical music occurs in the film at dramatically and structurally important points: at the very beginning (when the Stalker and his family are still asleep); when we as viewers have been allowed to enter the room said to constitute the heart of the Zone; and finally at the very end, in

84   *Beethoven Overcome*

the scene that is the focus of this chapter. These occurrences of classical music, at important nodes of the narrative, are always coupled with the sound of running trains, linking the two types of sound inextricably to one another (and further substantiating the idea of a recurring sonic figure in the film). Seen from a narrative rather than a strictly temporal perspective, classical music thus functions as an important marker that articulates the different sections of the story. At the beginning of the film, when we see the Stalker and his family sleeping in the antiquated bedroom, we should perhaps speak of classical music in quotation marks, for what we hear is *La Marseillaise* (soon to be followed in one of the next scenes by an almost imperceptible fragment of music from Wagner's *Tannhäuser*). In the two other scenes, however, it is classical music proper that we hear: Ravel's *Bolero* in the Room; and Beethoven's "Ode to Joy" in the final scene. Artemiev's recollections notwithstanding, the consistent pairing of this type of music with the sounds of trains – and the resulting occurrence of the sonic figure at structurally and dramatically important points – did *not* follow a merely formal impulse on the director's part. This is clear from the fact that Tarkovsky himself seems at times to have conceived of the music in terms of its symbolic function. Thus, when asked in an interview with Tonino Guerra about the presence of classical music in the film, Tarkovsky said that he had wanted to use "music that is more or less popular, that expresses the movement of the masses, the theme of humanity's social destiny" (Gianvito 2006, 52). For Tarkovsky, "humanity's *social* destiny" is to be found in "the movement of the masses," which could here reasonably be understood as connoting the grand projects of modern Western civilization in the name of the Enlightenment ideals, as expressed by *La Marseillaise* (originally conceived of as a revolutionary "Chant de guerre") and by Beethoven's music.[13] And, of course, similar beliefs in continual historical and political progress were a central pillar of the Marxist and ultimately Hegelian-derived state policy of Soviet Russia (and other communist countries) where the "Ode to Joy" played an extremely important role as the official "gospel of a classless world" (Buch 2003, 4).[14]

Tarkovsky's talk of "humanity's social destiny" could, however, also be understood to refer to the more destructive forces unleashed by the rapid development of technology in the post-Enlightenment world. These forces would more accurately be expressed by the persistent rhythmical figure, the constantly shifting instrumentation and the gradually growing crescendo of the *Bolero*, whose combination of musical parameters not only brings about an ever-increasing intensity of the melodic line, but also implies the inevitable and arguably destructive climax of the piece. Certainly, one of the more striking aspects of the *Bolero* is its inexorable and quasi-mechanical way of proceeding toward this climax. The piece is like a giant orchestral clockwork that finally breaks, and it may well serve as a symbol for the seeming unstoppable and ultimately destructive

Beethoven Overcome 85

course of modern history.[15] In *Stalker*, this impression is clearly strengthened when we hear the *Bolero* while the camera focuses on a dead fish covered with oil, together with parts of the bomb that the Professor has thrown into the Room – an unmistakable image of a damaged world.[16] In any case, Tarkovsky's comment supports the impression that certain works of Western classical music are closely tied to a central characteristic of post-Enlightenment modern society: an increasingly systematized urge to know, to control and to administer the world in all its aspects.

The symbolic function of the sonic figure becomes even more apparent when we consider the relation between Beethoven's music and what is sometimes called the "Stalker theme." Even though it appears in its entirety only three times (all other occurrences of electronic music in the film function more as allusions to this theme),[17] this simple little tune is indispensable to the film's emotional impact. It importantly occurs during the lengthy dream-like sequence in the Zone as the camera pans over a water-drenched "black-and-white ceramic tiled floor" (Riley 2017, 23), successively revealing a series of deteriorating objects; in Johnson and Petrie's words,

> a syringe, a bowl, a glass dish with a goldfish swimming inside, rocks, a mirror, a metal box containing coins and a plunger, a fragment of Jan Van Eyck's Ghent altarpiece with coins lying on it, a rusting pistol, a coiled spring, paper, a torn calendar, a clockwork mechanism, and other detritus.
>
> (Johnson and Petrie 1994, 145)

Regarding the other two occurrences of the theme – in connection with the opening credits and the scene where the Stalker carries his daughter home on his shoulders – they constitute the only instances of electronic music outside the Zone. When asked by Guerra about this theme, Tarkovsky responded:

> I think the theme will be Far Eastern, a kind of Zen music, where the principle is concentration rather than description. The main musical theme will have to be, on the one hand, purged of all emotion, and on the other, of all thought and programmatic intent. It must express its truth about the world around us in an autonomous way. It must be self-contained.
>
> (Gianvito 2006, 52)

Tarkovsky's idea of the Stalker theme thus stands in sharp contrast to his thoughts about Beethoven's music and classical music more generally in the film. While the latter represents "the movement of the masses" as well as an unhealthy individualism,[18] the Stalker theme is associated with what the director perceived to be traditional (if stereotypical) Eastern

86 *Beethoven Overcome*

values and ways of life (and, it would seem, more specifically with the quiet and peaceful life of the followers of Zen Buddhism). In Tarkovsky's view, then, these different kinds of music effectively establish a dichotomy between East and West. This dichotomy consists in the fundamental discrepancy between the focus on the self or ego and its continued existence (even after the earthly life) in the West, and the erasure of the ego in Eastern philosophy and religion. It is based on the difference between Western affirmation of the individual and her/his development, self-realization and strivings, and the rejection of the individual in Eastern thought with the consequent search to "purge" this illusory substance of "all emotion . . . thought and programmatic intent." It is a contrast between, on the one hand, a teleological conception of history (both the life-history of the individual human being and the grand History of Humanity) and, on the other, a wish to transcend and expunge history altogether. In the words of Tarkovsky himself:

> Compare Eastern and Western music. The West is forever shouting: "This is me! Look at me! Listen to me suffering, loving! How unhappy I am! How happy! I! Mine! Me!" In the Eastern tradition they never utter a word about themselves. The person is totally absorbed into God, Nature, Time; finding himself in everything; discovering everything in himself. Think of Taoist music.
>
> (Tarkovsky 1986, 240)

The fixation on the ego that Tarkovsky here attributes to Western classical music is not incompatible with the symbolic meaning of Beethoven's music and classical music more generally in *Stalker*. On the contrary, with such somewhat simplistic expressions as "the West is forever shouting" and "humanity's social destiny," Tarkovsky emphasizes that Western individualism is of a piece with the grand projects of modern civilization. Artemiev's electronic score represents an attitude toward the self and the world that is completely at odds with these ideals.

The musical characteristics of the "Ode to Joy" and the Stalker theme clearly underscore this dichotomy. In contrast to the exuberance of Beethoven's music and Schiller's words of exultation, the Stalker theme is a slow, simple and serene little tune consisting of four short phrases (Example 4.1). Notwithstanding the purported "Eastern" quality of the theme, the melodic outline of the first phrase – which starts on E♭, rises a fifth to B♭, and then slowly descends to E♭ again via A♭ and G♭ – reveals that the tune resembles and may actually be based on a medieval chant, according to Artemiev a "fourteenth or even twelfth century" setting of the medieval prose text *Pulcherrima Rosa*.[19] The melodic line, rendered on a wooden flute, is set against a dronelike sonic background in which the timbre of traditional Eastern instruments like the *tar* and the *tampura* is electronically manipulated, giving the music an air of strangeness,

Example 4.1 "Stalker's theme." Adapted from *Stalker* (1979). Composer: Eduard Artemiev.

perhaps even otherworldliness, that arguably could not have been accomplished with acoustic sounds only.[20] The resulting music stands in sharp contrast to the "Ode to Joy." It seems to suspend or even dissolve all motion and directionality as it weightlessly rests in itself and perpetually returns to itself. The meditative quality of this music is intimately connected with the mysterious Zone and – given the close relation between the two – with Monkey. In this way, we are supposed to experience it as articulating the same ineffable truth about our existence as do the Zone and the Stalker's daughter.

In *Stalker*, then, the spiritual integrity of the main theme bears out the seeming illusion of Beethoven's music. Conceived on "the principle of concentration" (which in fact is one of the factors of the "Eightfold Path" in Buddhist teachings), the Stalker theme, resting like an enlightened Buddha in its self-sufficiency, "express[es] the truth about the world around it." The incompatibility of this music with the "Ode to Joy" relegates the latter (and its cousin, *La Marseillaise*) into the category of humanity's grand illusions. Ultimately, it is the *contrast* between classical and electronic music that signifies. With specific regard to Beethoven's music, it is the dialectically established meaning of this music that, in the last scene of *Stalker*, turns it into a signifier of all the spiritual failures of modern civilization; the glorious "Ode to Joy" becomes an aural representation of the "spiritual emptiness of contemporary society" (Johnson and Petrie 1994, 146).

Transcending the Ninth

My reading of the last scene of *Stalker* suggests that the film as a whole can be understood as affirming a highly ideologically charged conception of what is of ultimate value in human life. Although my main purpose in this last section is to show that this conception is characteristic of the utopian aesthetics of early Romanticism, I will also claim that *Stalker* manifests a central conviction of twentieth-century Christian existentialism.[21]

88   *Beethoven Overcome*

Given the importance of sound in Tarkovsky's films, one of the more striking aspects of *Stalker* is the recurring sound of trains coupled with music, what I have called the sonic figure. I submit that we can view these recurring sound patterns and the scenes in which they appear as important interpretive keys to the film as a whole, so that they function as what Lawrence Kramer has called "hermeneutic windows." For Kramer, the most powerful hermeneutic window is the *structural trope*, which he defines as "a structural procedure, capable of various practical realizations, that also functions as a typical expressive act within a certain cultural/historical framework" (Kramer 1990, 6). Such structural tropes "can evolve from any aspect of communicative exchange: style, rhetoric, representation, and so on" (Kramer 1990, 10). One specific structural trope (among several) is the phenomenon he terms *expressive doubling*. Expressive doubling is "a form of *repetition* in which alternative versions of the same pattern define a cardinal difference in perspective" (Kramer 1990, 22; my emphasis). He elaborates:

> Expressive doubling is a process that submits a well-defined *Gestalt* to reinterpretation and revaluation. More particularly, it exemplifies what Jacques Derrida calls the logic of the supplement, that is, the completion of something that at first seems complete in itself. The initial term of an expressive doubling is always presented as a totality: in our examples, as a scene, a fictional world, a musical section, a musical movement. The supplemental term of an expressive doubling is an extra, a discontinuity, that displaces – but does not nullify – the original term. When the two terms are considered together, the effect is compelling, hermeneutically provocative; each term energizes the other as if a spark had leapt between them.
>
> (Kramer 1990, 24)

The practice of expressive doubling is inherently bound up with utopian and quasi-religious ideals that belong firmly within the early Romantic aesthetics of the late eighteenth and early nineteenth centuries (see Kramer 1990, 30). This kind of structural trope typically enacts a progression "from the actual to the ideal," and we can identify this progression in a particular work of art precisely because

> the terms of an expressive doubling form a hierarchy; one term represents a freer, happier, or more enlightened condition than the other. Or, to be more exact, one term represents the transposition of the other to a higher or deeper plane, a more brilliant or profound register.
>
> (Kramer 1990, 30)

In what follows, I aim to show that such Romantic utopian ideals are enacted in *Stalker* by illustrating how the iteration of the sonic figure amounts to an expressive doubling in the film. In doing this, I will focus on its first and last appearance.

Fundamentally, the structural trope at work here consists in the iteration of the sonic figure within new scenic contexts, the result of which is that it gradually comes to take on a significantly different meaning with each new appearance. Depending on the specific details of the relevant scenes, as well as on where in the narrative it occurs, the signification and function of the sonic figure alters. This transformation of the sonic figure in turn acts as a constitutive component within the scenes, contributing each time to a significant "difference in perspective." Thus, the "initial" and "supplemental" terms in the scenes connected through expressive doubling comprise both soundtrack and image track. As mentioned, the sonic figure first appears at the very beginning of the film, in the scene where the Stalker and his family are still in bed. In my reading, the *manifest* symbolic or representational meaning of the *Marseillaise*-plus-train sound pattern is the same as that of the "Ode to Joy"-plus-train sound pattern in the final scene: in both cases, the sonic figure can plausibly be taken to represent the "grand projects" of modern civilization (this corresponds to what I referred to earlier as "the basic claim"). What has changed is the visual setting and the explanatory matrix in which music and the diegetic sound of the train are embedded, and this has important consequences for how the manifest meaning of the sonic figure is perspectivized and assessed in the two scenes.

In the earlier scene, the relative misery and poverty of the family's everyday life are accentuated by the sepia tint, which also emphasizes the archaic character of the bedroom and suggests, initially, a setting that might be closer to an earlier stage of the Industrial Revolution (Figure 4.2). Watching the family asleep in the bedroom, we get the impression

Figure 4.2 Black-and-white shot of the family's bedroom at the beginning of *Stalker*
Source: Films Sans Frontières

90   *Beethoven Overcome*

of witnessing not only the beginning of a day in their life like any other, but also a replaying of the beginning of a period in modern history. What is more, the portrayal of drab everyday life and the absence of mystery are further emphasized by the rather mundane fact that the glass on the bedside table starts to shake as a result of the train approaching. We do not witness anything of Monkey's supernatural powers, since she is asleep during the whole scene. In the final scene things are different: the whole scene is in color; no natural connection is established between the sound of the train and the moving of the glasses; and Monkey, of course, is very much awake and becomes the main actor.[22] Now the cultural associations of Beethoven's music and the sound of the train are effectively recoded, turning two of the master signifiers of modern civilization's technological, political and ideological triumphs into powerful representations of the transitory and ultimately meaningless dimension of those triumphs (what I earlier referred to as "the specific claim"). This final scene can thus be viewed as a troping of the earlier scene. It thereby confirms the sought-after "progress from the actual to the ideal," which, in addition to the "fear and denial theme," can be seen as constituting a second central theme in the film.[23] In the earlier scene, the sonic figure may be experienced as an intrusion, as a threat from a surrounding world preoccupied with the human collective and therefore indifferent to the joys and sufferings of individuals. Symbolizing the impersonal and supra-individual forces that drive human history, it effectively highlights the vulnerability and isolation of the family. In the final scene, this threat has been neutralized; the sonic figure has lost its force and instead becomes something to be transcended. It now serves merely as a background, a faint echo of a world from which an escape or transcendence into a higher and more ideal mode of existence becomes a real possibility.

In Chapter 2, I suggested that Tarkovsky's conception of art resembled a kind of *Kunstreligion*. As pointed out by Carl Dahlhaus (1989), the ideals behind this "art-religion" can be found most clearly expressed in the early Romantic aesthetics represented by such writers as Karl Philipp Moritz, Wilhelm Heinrich Wackenroder, Ludwig Tieck and E. T. A. Hoffmann. Assuming that Tarkovsky's conception of art is a fundamentally Romantic one, the claim that *Stalker* expresses utopian ideals closely tied to early Romantic aesthetics is not far-fetched. Despite the fact that Tarkovsky himself rejected that assumption, and despite the director's place in a distinctively Russian intellectual and spiritual tradition, it is hard not to notice the blend of idealist and Romantic conceptions that permeates his notion of art. For example, Tarkovsky confidently asserted that "art . . . is an instrument for knowing [the world] in the course of man's journey towards what is called 'absolute truth'" (Tarkovsky 1986, 37). Partly as a result of this idealism, he was convinced that the proper and ultimate function of art is to help us live a life in sincere truthfulness. Accordingly, the responsibility that befalls the artist is "to prepare a person for death,

Beethoven Overcome 91

to plough and harrow his soul, rendering it capable of turning to good" (Tarkovsky 1986, 43). The essence of Tarkovsky's *Kunstreligion*, then, is that art and the experience of art are intrinsically connected to deep existential, spiritual and "eternal" truths.

This almost eschatological conception of art surfaces explicitly in Tarkovsky's relationship with Bach's music. Rejecting most of the art and music of Western civilization (especially the music of the Post-Baroque and post-Classical eras), Tarkovsky nevertheless made an important exception for Bach, asserting in an interview with V. Ishimov and R. Shejko that the truth and sincerity of his music resulted from its enabling a "relationship with God [that] is absolutely outside of civilization" (Gianvito 2006, 141). Such statements can clearly be interpreted as expressing what is basically a Romantic view of art, and indeed of Bach. Mark Evan Bonds captures this view succinctly when noting that the central belief of early Romantic aesthetics is "the belief that the arts . . . can provide refuge from the failed world of social and political life" (Bonds 1997, 397), a belief that, in turn, is directly premised on the possibility of experiencing the work of art as "a vehicle by which to sense the realm of the spiritual and the infinite" (Bonds 1997, 420). Contrary to Beethoven's Ninth, at least as it is treated in the film, *Stalker* itself can be understood as inviting just such an experience. The is because the critique of musical works like Beethoven's Ninth in *Stalker*, and by extension the whole of modern civilization, takes place within an artwork that itself, in the manner of Tarkovsky's Bach, aspires to be "a vehicle" through which the audience can catch a glimpse of what it would be like to live a (purely spiritual) life "absolutely outside of civilization."

How, then, are we to understand the utopian ideal of the film? I suggest that the subtle change in perspective enacted by the expressive doubling of the sonic figure makes a rather specific claim about how we should live in and relate to the world. The transfiguration in the last scene places the Stalker's daughter firmly outside of civilization; her relation to the sonic icons of modern civilization expresses in a radical way the possibility of overcoming and transcending the illusory ideals of that civilization. At the same time, Monkey is in an obvious sense a part of the world in which she lives: she has a body, she is sitting in a room, she is reading from a book, she has a mother and a father and so on. Just like the Zone itself, she simultaneously belongs and does not belong to the world. Seen in this way, civilization is overcome from inside the world, not from outside. The appearance of the sonic figure, the image of the Stalker's daughter, the mysterious Zone to which she is so intimately connected, and ultimately the film as a whole project a utopian existential ideal. They affirm a crucial difference between, on the one hand, accepting our constructed world as a given and, on the other hand, finding a way of living in the world in which we, in some important sense, no longer belong to it. In doing this, *Stalker* not only enacts one of the central characteristics of

92 *Beethoven Overcome*

early Romantic aesthetic ideology but also echoes the bringing together of the "transcendent . . . [and] the this-worldly" (Cobb 1962, chap. 9) found in the Christian existentialist hermeneutics of such twentieth-century German theologians like Rudolf Bultmann. The idea that life can be lived to its fullest only when we radically withdraw from and rise above the trivialities of everyday life might very well be what Tarkovsky had in mind when, in an interview in Stockholm in 1985, he said that in *Stalker* he was above all "interested in the problem of inner freedom."[24] In *Stalker*, the music of Beethoven (as well as *La Marseillaise* and the music of Wagner and Ravel) and the train on the soundtrack represent all the grand strivings of modern civilization toward emancipation, but they are also symbols of its bondage. It is precisely those strivings – and the way they restrict our lives and self-understanding in accordance with collective standards determined by that civilization – that Tarkovsky would view as the greatest obstacle to our inner freedom and, hence, are what he would have us transcend.

I do not mean to deny that up to a certain point such an emancipatory project is possible. Perhaps it is even necessary for our well-being. Still, it is here, I think, that Tarkovsky's own illusory idealism ultimately exposes itself: in the unrealistic and uncompromising extent to which a quasi-Romantic and existentialist utopia is pursued in the film. It is true that the Stalker, Professor and Writer probably never enter the mysterious room at the center of the Zone. It is also true that the Stalker's return home is marked by disappointment and despair. And all this would suggest that the quest is a failure and that the ideal life sought for is perhaps forever out of reach. The last scene, however, sets things right again, and the shortcomings of the father are redressed by the tranquil but intense presence of the daughter, who, through a mixture of enigmatic silence and supernatural powers, restores the promise of total transcendence for us. But total transcendence is not an option for historically, socially and culturally situated finite beings. *Stalker* might offer the false promise that we can escape from and step outside of history and civilization. In an ideological reversal of the classical music that it criticizes, the film can be viewed as itself enacting the illusion that it is possible for us to cleanse our inner being of the socially and culturally determined aspects, that, for good and bad, make us who we are.

Notes

1. The clip can be found at www.youtube.com/watch?v=xjVT7MlE5rY (accessed 2019-05-17).
2. See, for example, Turovskaya (1989, 115), Green (1993, 105–106), Johnson and Petrie (1994, 143–145), Golstein (2008, 204) and Martin (2011, 149). By contrast, Jeremy Mark Robinson says of the last scene that "the symbolism is unclear" and that it therefore "could mean whatever one likes, really" (Robinson 2006, 464). In response to Robinson, I would say that the symbolism

Beethoven Overcome 93

is open rather than unclear and, furthermore, that this openness does not license total interpretive freedom. The scene can be made sense of in several different ways, to be sure, but it does not follow from this that it "could mean whatever one likes."

3. One of the most imaginative, and at the same time problematic, readings of this scene is that of the French critic Barthélemy Amengual in *Dossier Positif*. Amengual divides the scene into a backtracking camera movement, pulling away from the girl and gradually revealing the large table at which she is seated, and a reversal of this camera movement, zooming in on the girl's face. In Amengual's Christian reading, the movement of the three glasses on the table forms a cross-like pattern that symbolizes the cross: "L'enfant est infirme, l'innocence est crucifiée." The poor health of the girl (one consequence of the Stalker's excursions into the Zone is that she cannot walk) is interpreted as the crucifixion of innocence. In this spirit, he associates the three glasses on the table with the holy Trinity. Yet for Amengual, the sheer beauty of the scene also shows that in a world where evil, violence, ugliness and death will never go away, the hope and longing for the good will still persist, affirmed and preserved in and through art – "Le mal, la violence, la laideur et la mort perdurent mais le foi, l'espérance, le désir du bien eux aussi demeurent, réaffirmés, auvegardés dans et part l'art" (Amengual 1988, 33). As Johnson and Petrie point out, Amengual's reading rests on a description of the scene that on several points is incorrect (Johnson and Petrie 1994, 145).

4. The fact that the film in a sense places us, the audience, inside the room may somewhat paradoxically suggest that the journey has not been a failure. From this perspective, the extended scene (it lasts almost five minutes) may be understood as inviting us to reflect upon what *our* innermost desires are.

5. As I see it, Johnson and Petrie here incorrectly describe the glass as "thick" (Johnson and Petrie 1994, 143).

6. Regarding the diegetic status of these soundtrack phenomena, it seems obvious that the train should be understood as an instance of diegetic sound. Whether or not the music should also be understood as diegetic is a more complex question. In the earlier quote, Truppin seems to take for granted that it should, but this view is complicated by the fact that when the sonic figure is heard in the extended scene depicting the mysterious room (where the classical music heard is Ravel's *Bolero*) neither the music nor the sound of the train can be diegetic, since the scene takes place at the heart of the Zone, far away from any railway that is in use (I am grateful to Steven Reale for pointing this out to me). Smith (2007, 44) considers several possibilities with regard to *La Marseillaise* (which he incorrectly identifies as "Beethoven's music") in the post-credit scene: "Is this [music] a dream of one of the figures in the bed? Does it hold symbolic meaning that will be revealed later? Or can it just be understood literally as a diegetic sound connected to the train?"

7. The last scene of *Stalker* bears certain affinities with the ending of Hans-Jürgen Syberberg's *Hitler: A Film from Germany* (1977), in which we see a young girl draped in celluloid while fragments of the finale of Beethoven's Ninth Symphony play on the soundtrack. Caryl Flinn (2000, 125–126) discusses the scene from Syberberg's film but does not mention Tarkovsky's *Stalker*.

8. One of the most interesting suggestions is offered by Robert Bird, who writes that "in many respects the Zone is simply the demarcated area within which an event can occur, akin to the screen in cinema. . . . The Zone is where one goes to see one's innermost desires. It is, in short, the cinema" (Bird quoted in Foster 2010, 308). Elaborating on this idea, Foster (2010, 318) proposes that "the Zone . . . is a space of thought that engages the viewer in cinematic thinking procedures."

94 *Beethoven Overcome*

9. Operating within his Lacanian framework, Žižek goes on to say that "the Zone is the void that sustains desire . . . a pure structural void constituted/ defined by a symbolic barrier: beyond this barrier, in the Zone, there is nothing and/or exactly the same thing as outside the Zone" (Žižek 1999, 227).

10. The screenplay gives a rather different version of this passage, rendered as a conversation between the three men: "Stalker: 'Right, we're home!' Writer: 'Phew, at last.' Professor: 'It's so quiet . . .' Stalker: 'The quietest place on earth. There's nobody to make any noise'" (Tarkovsky 1999, 389).

11. See Arkady Strugatsky and Boris Strugatsky (2000).

12. "Almost exclusively" because electronic music is actually heard already in the opening scene as the credits appear (I return to this later).

13. Esteban Buch points out that Schiller's 1785 poem *An die Freude* "quickly [became] an Enlightenment manifesto" (Buch 2003, 1). As to the close connection between Beethoven's music and *La Marseillaise*, Buch states that "towards the end of the nineteenth century, there were those who went so far as to call the 'Ode to Joy' the 'Marseillaise of Mankind'" (Buch 2003, 6).

14. Regarding *La Marseillaise*, Orlando Figes has pointed out its importance in relation to the 1917 October Revolution in Russia, writing that it "became the national anthem of the revolution" (Figes 1997, 355).

15. Nicholas Reyland, in his discussion of the significance of Zbigniew Preisner's *Bolero* for Krzysztof Kieslowski's film *Three Colors: Red* (1994), draws attention to the multilayered cultural tradition of the bolero as both dance form and musical form (see Reyland 2012b, 167–171).

16. As to the narrative role of the *Bolero*, one can note that it marks the transition from the Zone back to the bar and the everyday world, just as the gradually emerging electronic music during the journey on the railway trolley marks the crossing between the everyday world and the Zone (for a similar view of how sound works in the trolley sequence, see Totaro 2007).

17. The altered soundtrack of the new 5.1 Dolby version of the film that was issued by the Russian Cinema Counsel in 2001 features numerous occurrences of the theme, including a distinctly synthesizer-produced version of the melody heard over the clicking of the railway trolley's wheels during the three men's ride into the Zone (a brief discussion of this sequence is provided in Chapter 1). For a detailed account of the confusion that followed in connection with the release of the new 5.1 version, see the posts on *Nostalghia.com* in 2002 (especially January 29 and 30, March 20, April 24 and 28, May 1, August 9 and October 15). URL: www.nostalghia.com/TheNews2002. html (accessed 2019-05-17).

18. Tarkovsky associated much Western classical music with what he saw as a repellent and unhealthy individualism: "Take for example the music of Wagner or, I don't know, Beethoven – that's an unending monologue about oneself: look how poor I am, all in rags, how miserable, what [a] Job I am, how unhappy, how I suffer – like nobody else – I suffer like the antique Prometheus . . . and here is how I love, and here is how I. . . . You understand? I, I, I, I, I." See Jerzy Illg and Leonard Neuger, "I'm Interested in the Problem of Inner Freedom" (interview with Andrei Tarkovsky in Stockholm 1985), *Nostalghia.com*. URL: www.nostalghia.com/TheTopics/Stalker.html (accessed 2019-05-17).

19. Artemiev in interview. URL: www.youtube.com/watch?v=xjVT7MlE5rY (accessed 2019-05-17). As Artemiev also reports in the interview, *Pulcherrima Rosa* was a prose text devoted to Virgin Mary. See also Egorova (1997, 250). Sean Martin describes the melody as "an amalgam of plainchant and Indian music" (Martin 2011, 31).

20. Unlike *Solaris* and *Mirror*, where Artemiev used the ANS synthesizer, the electronic processing of acoustic instrumental timbres in *Stalker* was achieved

Beethoven Overcome 95

on a SYNTHI-100 synthesizer. As Egorova (1997, 251) remarks, the timbre of "the old transverse flute" is also manipulated by electronic means. In the case of the flute, however, these manipulations are for the most part barely noticeable. In the interview referenced in the previous footnote, Artemiev may actually provide an explanation for this, saying that Tarkovsky wanted the Stalker theme to be a "structural combination of East and West" while at the same time "those two rivers would never converge." Thus, by letting the flute (a Western instrument) retain much of its acoustic timbre, it could at the same time be combined with and kept separate from the more electronically inflected sounds of the tar and the tampura.

21. Such an interpretive aim would surely have outraged Tarkovsky, who strenuously rejected that either his films or his conception of art had anything to do with Romanticism (let alone Christian existentialism), and who once said that "whenever I hear the word 'Romanticism' I get frightened" (see Illg and Neuger, "I'm Interested in the Problem of Inner Freedom" at *Nostalghia.com*).

22. A further difference between the two scenes is that the high-angle shot of the sleeping family in the earlier scene has been replaced in the last scene with an eye-level shot of Monkey.

23. Clearly, one can understand the film overall as a quest for an ideal life. The whole point of the journey into the Zone is, in this reading, to transgress the limit between the actual and the ideal in order to access a more enlightened condition and a higher, truer mode of existence.

24. See Illg and Neuger, "I'm Interested in the Problem of Inner Freedom" at *Nostalghia.com*. This idea also comes up in the interview with Ishimov and Shejko, where Tarkovsky says that "the entire point of human existence consists in using the time allotted to you to take at least one step away from the level upon which you were born up to a higher level. This is the meaning of life" (Gianvito 2006, 152).

5 Musical Offerings, Soothing Sounds and Sacrificial Acts

Managing the Nostalgia of *Nostalghia*

In common parlance, "to be nostalgic" means, roughly, to be in a state of mind where a recollection of a past and positively charged life-event, or a place or person associated with such an event, gives rise to feelings of longing and bittersweet contentment. We tend to regard nostalgia as a basically agreeable emotion, which, while it may be tinted with a sense of loss, involves a pleasurable re-imagining of a cherished earlier moment in our lives. When we turn to the dictionary definitions, however, the picture becomes rather more complex. The *Oxford English Dictionary*, for example, gives two broad definitions of nostalgia. The first one centrally incorporates the notion of a particular *place*, describing nostalgia as "an acute longing for familiar surroundings." This definition is explicitly tied to the historical understanding of nostalgia as a "medical condition," an acute and severe homesickness that in the seventeenth and eighteenth centuries was believed to afflict soldiers who had been away from their homeland for too long. The second definition emphasizes the *temporal* dimension of nostalgia, characterizing it as a "sentimental longing for or regretful memory of a period of the past, especially one in an individual's own lifetime."[1] Taken together, the two definitions demarcate a mental state or condition in which far more is at stake than just a pleasant and soothing reverie over a happy memory. According to Svetlana Boym, nostalgia is an inherently problematic and potentially dangerous phenomenon, one that is nurtured by a "longing for continuity in a fragmented world" and that "inevitably reappears as a defense mechanism in a time of accelerated rhythms of life and historical upheavals" (Boym 2001, XIV). The danger of nostalgia consists in its tendency "to confuse the actual home and the imaginary one," thus harboring "the promise to rebuild the ideal home that lies at the core of many powerful ideologies of today, tempting us to relinquish critical thinking for emotional bonding" (Boym 2001, XVI). But the danger also lies in the fact that nostalgia easily "goes beyond individual psychology" and develops into a collectively shared utopian yearning for a perfect state

Soothing Sounds and Sacrificial Acts   97

of affairs. In this capacity, it is essentially concerned with the temporal rather than the spatial:

> At first glance, nostalgia is a longing for a place, but actually it is a yearning for a different time – the time of our childhood, the slower rhythms of our dreams. In a broader sense, nostalgia is rebellion against the modern idea of time, the time of history and progress. The nostalgic desires to obliterate history and turn it into private or collective mythology, to revisit time like space, refusing to surrender to the irreversibility of time that plagues the human condition.
>
> (Boym 2001, XV)

Maybe this "yearning for a different time" is at its strongest when human beings are forced into exile. Under such circumstances, nostalgia may indeed turn into a utopian obsession with an idealized past and a romanticized homeland, an obsession that, while its goal is a sense of absolute belonging, seems to achieve the very opposite, in that it combines a refusal to live in the present with fantasies of a perfect place and time that has little or no counterpart in reality (cf. Oushakine 2007, 452).

Nostalghia was the first film Tarkovsky made outside of the Soviet Union. It was shot in Italy in autumn 1982 and was completed in spring 1983. On July 10, 1984, approximately one year after he had completed *Nostalghia*, at a press conference in Milan, Tarkovsky declared his intention not to return to Russia. This decision had probably been brewing for a long time, but it seems that the decisive factor was Tarkovsky's belief that the Soviet authorities, through director Sergei Bondarchuk, had gone to great lengths to make sure that his film did not receive the *Palme d'Or* at the 1983 Cannes Film Festival (Tarkovsky 2012, 735). Whatever the truth behind this assumption, it must have been an extremely difficult decision for Tarkovsky, given that his wife and young son were not allowed to leave Russia to join him. Moreover, on several occasions Tarkovsky described his feeling of displacement and alienation while working in Italy, and when he first watched the complete material filmed for *Nostalghia* he was astonished by how accurately the (not yet edited) film captured the mood he often experienced during filming:

> I have to say that when I first saw all the material shot for the film I was startled to find it was a spectacle of unrelieved gloom. The material was completely homogeneous, both in its mood and in the state of mind imprinted on it. This was not something I had set out to achieve: what was symptomatic and unique about the phenomenon before me was the fact that, irrespective of my own specific theatrical intentions, the camera was obeying first and foremost my inner state during filming. I had been worn down by my separation from my

98   *Soothing Sounds and Sacrificial Acts*

family and from the way of life I was used to, by working under quite
unfamiliar conditions, even by using a foreign language.

(Tarkovsky 1986, 203–204)

Not surprisingly, then, along with *Mirror*, *Nostalghia* has been regarded as
Tarkovsky's most autobiographical film, with the fate of the film's main
character in certain respects mirroring the situation and state of mind
of the director.

Music and Nostalgia in *Nostalghia*

Nostalghia revolves around a dejected Russian intellectual who travels
across a gloomy Tuscan landscape to research the life of an obscure
eighteenth-century composer by the name of Pavel Sosnovsky.[2] In this
somber and visually refined film, the presence of music is pared down
to a minimum. Apart from recurring bits of Russian folk song, a brief
passage of Chinese music and an almost imperceptible fragment of what
Johnson and Petrie (1994, 165) describe as "middle eastern music,"[3]
the soundtrack of *Nostalghia* comprises in total four musical passages:
two short fragments from Beethoven's Ninth Symphony and two brief
excerpts from Giuseppe Verdi's *Requiem*. These musical passages are
closely, if not obviously, connected to central themes and characters of
the film. The two male protagonists – Andrei Gorchakov (the Russian
intellectual and poet-musicologist at the center of the narrative) and the
Italian "madman" Domenico – are both haunted by a deep and recurring
nostalgia for their pasts, a nostalgia that mirrors the disorientation and
loss of coherence that characterizes their present. Their acts of apparently pointless self-sacrifice at the end of the film are both closely linked
to classical music – Andrei's with Verdi's *Requiem*, and Domenico's with
Beethoven's "Ode to Joy."[4]

In Tarkovsky's hands, the condition of nostalgia becomes a complex
and ambiguous phenomenon. On the one hand, it is depicted as a compulsive preoccupation with an idealized homeland and an unattainable
past that besets the film's main character – an obsession that successively
draws him into an ever-more vicious existential circle, in that the fantasies and dreams he nurtures to escape his present sense of loss and
displacement have the rather opposite effect of driving him even deeper
into despair and alienation. On the other hand, for both Domenico and
Andrei, it manifests as an acute concern about the suffering of mankind,
which eventually leads to their spectacular acts of self-sacrifice. However,
while Andrei and Domenico (the latter in particular) are obviously driven
by the conviction that the wrong-doings and sufferings of humanity can
be redeemed by their acts of self-sacrifice, I suggest that what *ultimately*
drives them is a need to break free from their own personal isolation and
reconnect with a more authentic way of life that seems irredeemably out

Soothing Sounds and Sacrificial Acts 99

of reach. A genuinely compassionate attitude can instead be found in the way the film itself relates to its characters, a notion that will be fleshed out in the following with the help of Daniel Frampton's concept of "filmind."

In this chapter, I argue that classical music – that of Beethoven and Verdi – plays an important part in the film's multifaceted construal of nostalgia. Far from being clearly discernible, however, its involvement is both subtle and complex. While classical music can justifiably be interpreted as an emotional and symbolic resource employed by the film's characters in their attempts to cope with a growing sense of isolation and displacement, it can also plausibly be understood as an expression of grief and compassion issuing from the more abstract vantage point of the filmind, and in this latter sense as being directed *toward* the characters and their fates. As will become clear from my argument, although the relation between Domenico and Beethoven's music is by no means uncomplicated in this regard, it is above all Verdi's music that, by virtue of its position and placement in the film, creates the most challenging ambiguities. Taking the different possible diegetic locations of Beethoven's and Verdi's music into consideration, the chapter aims to clarify the ways in which music interacts with and partakes in the multilayered examination of nostalgia, displacement, existential alienation and the call for redemption that is at the center of *Nostalghia*. I begin the next section by discussing the relation between Domenico and Beethoven's music. I then discuss the role of Verdi's music in the film, considering first the connection between this music and the metadiegetic reveries of Andrei, and then how it can be interpreted as an expression of the filmind's thinking.

The Triumphant Music of Failed Self-Sacrifice: Domenico's Beethoven

Although Andrei Gorchakov must be regarded as the central character of *Nostalghia*, Domenico is far from a peripheral figure. Not only is he an intriguing character in his own right, but as the narrative unfolds it also becomes increasingly clear that he will play a decisive role in the fatal turn that Andrei's life will take toward the end of the film. Influenced by Domenico's conviction that the deplorable present state of the world can only be redeemed by an act of radical self-sacrifice, Andrei postpones his journey back to Russia and instead returns to the thermal baths of Bagno Vignoni. Here he fulfills Domenico's request expressed earlier in the film that he carry a lit candle across the grand basin at the center of the village.

Domenico's reputation as a madman is based on events earlier in his life. We learn that he spent a long period in a mental asylum after keeping his family locked up in a house for seven years, apparently in order to protect them from what he believed to be imminent global destruction. In a poignant flashback sequence (shot in black and white), we

100 *Soothing Sounds and Sacrificial Acts*

witness the dramatic rescue of Domenico's family by the police. With his family taken away, Domenico seems to have receded more deeply into his apocalyptic fantasies, and is now planning a spectacular event at the Piazza del Campidoglio in Rome, where he will sacrifice himself for the greater good of humanity by burning himself to death – a plan that is realized near the end of the film.

Beethoven's Ninth Symphony is linked to Domenico at two different moments in *Nostalghia*. It first appears shortly after Domenico has granted Andrei entrance into his dilapidated house. What we hear at this point is the choral passage that begins with the words "Ihr stürzt nieder, Millionen? Ahnest du den Schöpfer, Welt?" ("Do you fall down, you millions? Do you sense the Creator, world?"), which forms part of the *Andante maestoso* section about two thirds into the fourth and final movement. The passage culminates in one of the movement's several variations of the "Ode to Joy" theme, of which we hear only a few seconds before the music is suddenly cut off. That we are supposed to understand the music as diegetic here becomes clear from Andrei's reaction as he turns around with an expression of mild surprise as the piece abruptly stops. This impression is further confirmed by Domenico who solemnly proclaims "Allora, hai sentito? È Beethoven!" ("Well, did you hear? It's Beethoven!")

Judging from Domenico's elevated tone of voice, it is evident that he has some kind of special relation to Beethoven's music. The complexity of this relation is bound up with the complexity of the music's diegetic status. Despite being acknowledged by Andrei and Domenico, its location within the diegetic space of the scene is not straightforward. During most of the scene we may actually perceive it as nondiegetic underscore; before Andrei's reaction and Domenico's announcement, there are no clues to suggest that the music is originating from a source inside the house.[5] This impression is strengthened by the fact that the music not only is strongly foregrounded on the soundtrack but also dominates the soundtrack at the expense of all other sounds. The scene thus displays a clear deviation from standard sonic representations of diegetic music, which typically align the volume and sound quality in accordance with established cinematic conventions of how diegetically produced music should sound. In other words, Beethoven's music does not conform to "the aural fidelity we would normally expect from realistic diegetic sound" (Heldt 2013, 93). Because of this we may, even on repeated viewings, be inclined to perceive the music as nondiegetic, despite knowing that it eventually will be anchored in the film's fictional space. Understanding it as nondiegetic, we may become more alert to the possibility that it should perhaps be interpreted as a commentary on Domenico's character and situation. In short, the perception that Beethoven's music cannot be described as unproblematically diegetic, but may also be experienced as a piece of nondiegetic underscore, amplifies an already complex interpretive situation. If its presence

Soothing Sounds and Sacrificial Acts 101

in the scene is already difficult to account for on a diegetic reading (why is Domenico playing Beethoven's music for Andrei?), it becomes even more so when we understand the music as nondiegetic.[6]

Furthermore, there may be other options here than just choosing between manifestly diegetic and nondiegetic readings. For example, by being so strongly foregrounded in the soundtrack – and by implication in the viewer's audiovisual experience – Beethoven's music comes to penetrate and envelop the space of Domenico's house to such a degree that it can plausibly be construed as a piece of background music existing *inside* the fictional world. That is, up until the moment it stops, it may be experienced as a kind of musical underscore that permeates the diegetic space without Andrei or Domenico necessarily noticing or even hearing it, in this way functioning approximately as what Ben Winters has termed "intra-diegetic" music (Winters 2010). As yet another alternative to manifestly diegetic and nondiegetic readings we can envision that Andrei has here entered what, following Robynn Stilwell, could be called Domenico's "metadiegetic lair" (Stilwell 2007, 199). In this perspective, Domenico is posed as the visually absent but psychologically foregrounded subject into whose musically rendered grandiloquent fantasies both Andrei and the film's audience are drawn. Functioning like a sonic force field, the music helps to delineate and demarcate Domenico's physical and mental world, setting it off from an external reality with which he seems to have cut all ties. We may conjecture that despite its acknowledged diegetic status "the music is symbolically metadiegetic . . . while musically it is functioning like nondiegetic underscore" (Stilwell 2007, 199). The upshot of all these options is that up until its diegetic disclosure, the relation of this music to the scene's fictional space is inherently ambiguous, existing, as Stilwell would say, in a kind of "fantastical gap" between stable diegetic states (Stilwell 2007, 186).[7] This cine-ontological complexity can be understood as an important factor in the intimate connection that is established between Domenico and the music of Beethoven. Domenico confirms the importance of Beethoven's music at the same time as this music pervades, encapsulates and demarcates his domestic space to such an extent that we may actually experience it as an integral part not only of this space, but of Domenico himself. Thomas Redwood goes even further, suggesting that "perhaps the music was not audible to Gorchakov, its diegetic source belonging somewhere in Domenico's subjectivity" (Redwood 2010, 188). This might be an overinterpretation, however, since Andrei clearly reacts to the music stopping. In any case, by working on several diegetic levels simultaneously, Beethoven's music enters into the very constitution of the madman's confused interiority, and so becomes inextricably interwoven with his somewhat distorted self-image and his rather pessimistic view of the world and the people inhabiting it.

But why this close relationship between Domenico and Beethoven's music? An answer to this question emerges when we look more closely

102 *Soothing Sounds and Sacrificial Acts*

at the second appearance of Beethoven's music in the film. The second excerpt from Beethoven's Ninth in *Nostalghia* is the most well-known passage of the symphony, namely the "Ode to Joy" theme, as it appears in full chorus at measure 213 in the *Alla Marcia* section of the final movement. It is thus the same part from the finale that Tarkovsky used in *Stalker*. And, as in *Stalker*, it occurs here toward the end of the film when Domenico – having delivered his exalted speech in Rome about the wrong path taken by humanity and the necessity of returning to "the main foundations of life" (a phrase clearly alluding to Schiller's words "Do you sense the Creator, world?") – sets himself on fire. Domenico's spectacular and deadly performance is witnessed by a small group of people, most of whom seem rather disinterested, and some of whom look conspicuously like patients from a mental asylum. In this scene, the music is unambiguously diegetic. Having ended his speech, Domenico asks for the music to be put on, and after some initial technical problems it begins to resonate from the loudspeakers. After only a few seconds, however, the tape recorder malfunctions, turning Domenico's dramatic performance into a kind of tragic charade. In an act of heroic self-sacrifice and accompanied by the triumphant music of the "Ode to Joy," the burning Domenico throws himself from the statue of Marcus Aurelius on which he has been standing while holding his speech. As he hits the ground, the music starts to skip and repeat (sounding more like a broken car engine than a supreme expression of pure joy) and immediately after comes to a full stop. Considering this music's importance to Domenico, already established on its first appearance at his house, the unsuccessful playing of it at this crucial moment underscores the failure of his meticulously planned martyrdom, and perhaps can even be seen as ridiculing his somewhat outrageous conviction that such an act, beyond being a mere protest, could actually make a difference in redeeming humanity from the "wrong course" it has taken. In the words of Vida T. Johnson and Graham Petrie, "the breakdown of the music as Domenico dies underlines the fact that what was intended as a solemn and triumphant affirmation of faith has degenerated into something uncomfortably and embarrassingly close to farce" (Johnson and Petrie 1994, 170).[8]

Deprived of the music that was meant to underscore his sacrificial act, the screaming Domenico – engulfed in flames – ends his life crawling around on the ground while calling out for his dog Zoe (Figure 5.1). In the absence of his family, this dog is presumably all he has left in this world, something that is already suggested when Andrei visits his home and Domenico shows strong signs of distress when the dog is temporarily absent. His desperate calling out for Zoe at these final moments of his life suggests that the elevated ideals he has so fully embraced – and boosted with the aid of Beethoven's music – are in fact empty generalizations, the purpose of which is to help him escape the alienation at the center of his own life. Living in almost-complete existential isolation after the loss

Figure 5.1 Domenico in flames calling out for his dog Zoe toward the end of *Nostalghia*
Source: Films Sans Frontières

of his family, Domenico's obsession with Beethoven's exuberant and celebratory music betrays a profound longing for communion and contact with other people and with life itself. While Domenico is manifestly and intensely preoccupied with the notion that humanity must be redeemed from its wrong-doing, and in this spirit calls for a "return to the main foundations of life" in the name of the ideals of universal brotherhood and communion expressed by Beethoven's music and Schiller's poem, what he above all seeks is a way out of his own alienated condition. Like Andrei, he is plagued by a state of deep and consuming nostalgia. But unlike Andrei, who revels in dreams and fantasies of his beloved homeland, Domenico's nostalgia – to the extent that his obsession with the shortcomings of humanity allows him to be conscious of it – is essentially temporal in character, nurtured by an impossible longing after an (imagined) intimacy and closeness lying irretrievably in the past.[9]

Domenico's failed performance signals the collapse, and perhaps ultimate illusoriness, of the ideals connoted by Beethoven's music and Schiller's poem. The remedy to Domenico's profound existential quarantine and displacement does not lie in the abstract ideals of universal brotherhood or a collective return to "the main foundations of life." Indeed, the technical break-down that puts an end to Beethoven's music at the peak of Domenico's spectacular self-sacrifice underscores the inevitable failure of the "madman's" attempt to escape his personal isolation through this excessive engagement with the failures of humanity as a whole. In *Nostalghia*, the shattered Ninth Symphony functions as a kind

104   *Soothing Sounds and Sacrificial Acts*

of distorted musical offering that, while clearly intended to elevate and transfigure the poor Italian's heroic self-immolation into a universally valid statement, instead comes to parallel and reflect his broken interiority. Rather than expressing human emancipation and joy, it takes on the appearance of a false consciousness, a flawed ideology, that the deeply unhappy Domenico has internalized in order to protect himself from a threat far greater than humanity's supposed wrong turns – the full awareness of his own alienation and his inability to break out of it. The cinematic deconstruction of the "Ode to Joy" toward the end of the film makes it clear that this self-deception cannot be maintained; instead of a final grand statement crowned by Beethoven's triumphant music, the dying Domenico calls out in anguish for his dog. But, of course, to some extent Domenico's Beethoven is everyone's Beethoven. On the assumption that Domenico's relation to Beethoven's music should be assigned a broader significance, the appearance and deconstruction of the Ninth Symphony in *Nostalghia* may more generally be understood as a subtle but powerful denunciation of what Tarkovsky regarded as a deeply questionable tendency in modern (Western) culture, namely its undue emphasis on and celebration of abstract ideals and collective values at the expense of interpersonal relationships and individual life experience. From this perspective, *Nostalghia* can be seen as continuing the critique of post-Enlightenment civilization that I argued was a central concern in *Stalker*. In both films, Beethoven's Ninth Symphony stands at the center of this critique.

Metadiegetic Reveries and the Contemplating Filmind: Andrei and Verdi

If Domenico more or less self-consciously weaves Beethoven's music into his distorted self-image and his desperate quasi-heroic act, Andrei's relation to Verdi's music is somewhat more complex. Although the music is closely related to the main character, there are no clear indications in *Nostalghia* that Andrei intentionally invokes or interacts with Verdi's *Requiem*. Instead, the piece may initially be felt to function more like nondiegetic musical commentary – though what it is commenting on and why may not be immediately obvious. As a starting point, however, we can safely assume that the choice to include a mass for the dead in the film could hardly have been a random decision on Tarkovsky's part.

The *Requiem* first appears at the very beginning of the film, before we have made acquaintance with the main character. As the opening credits roll over the screen, we are shown a beautiful Russian landscape encased in mist. In the midst of this scenery, we see Andrei's family walk across a meadow toward a lake or a river (Figure 5.2). What is not immediately obvious is that the little group – four people and a dog (and further down the slope a white horse) – are placed in front of the family's dacha,

Soothing Sounds and Sacrificial Acts 105

Figure 5.2 Andrei's family, a dog and a horse at the beginning of *Nostalghia*
Source: Films Sans Frontières

which means that the spectator sees them from the perspective of the dacha, where Andrei himself would presumably be positioned. On the soundtrack, Verdi's *Requiem* is preceded by a passage from the traditional Russian folk song *Oi Vi Kumusciki*.[10] The folk song then reappears, but this time *alongside* Verdi's music, creating the overall impression that the two musical pieces are layered upon each other rather than one following the other. As Julia Sushytska points out, "already at the beginning of the movie, Verdi's 'Requiem' and Russian folk songs form a strange, unheard of harmony" (Sushytska 2015, 40). Even more than forming a harmony, however, we can claim that the two musics are so closely linked as to merge into one composite musical gestalt. The second appearance of the *Requiem* occurs in the film's penultimate scene, where it underscores the fatal outcome of Andrei's decision to comply with Domenico's request. This passage then leads into the concluding scene, where *Oi Vi Kumusciki* returns to accompany a shot of Andrei and his (or is it Domenico's?) dog sitting in front of the Russian dacha, which is now framed in a Tuscan setting, placed inside the ruins of San Galgano Abbey, a thirteenth-century gothic church located a few kilometers southwest of Siena.[11] In contrast to its occurrence at the beginning of the film, here the *Requiem* precedes the brief passages from *Oi Vi Kumusciki*.

In what follows, I will approach Verdi's *Requiem* as it appears in *Nostalghia* from two different perspectives. I will first explore it as a metadiegetic phenomenon, i.e. as something emanating from Andrei's state of mind. I will also, however, investigate its significance from the more

106 *Soothing Sounds and Sacrificial Acts*

abstract vantage point of the filmind. This dual perspective will help me to more fully capture Tarkovsky's multilayered understanding of nostalgia and the relation between this complex phenomenon and Verdi's music in the film.

A metadiegetic understanding of Verdi's music originates from the observation that the opening and concluding scenes of *Nostalghia* are closely related to other scenes throughout the film. To begin with, fragments of folk song similar to those of the opening and closing scenes are actually heard several times during the course of the film, mostly in connection with the black-and-white dream (or dream-like) sequences portraying Andrei's inner visions of and longing for his beloved Russia and for his family.[12] There is thus a musical affiliation between the film's opening and closing scenes and the scenes concerned with Andrei's recurring metadiegetic reveries. But the opening and closing scenes are also connected visually and thematically to these other scenes in that they depict the same people and the same Russian countryside that occur in Andrei's reveries (cf. Burns 2011, 104). We can therefore plausibly imagine the scenes at the film's beginning and end as also being part of or emanating from Andrei's interior, and consequently we can imagine the music in these scenes as constituting an integral part of Andrei's intense nostalgia.

Deeply plagued by his memories and his geographic displacement, Andrei demonstrates many of the signs of severe homesickness traditionally associated with the concept of nostalgia.[13] If we assume that the opening and closing scenes can plausibly be imagined in conjunction with the rest of Andrei's recurring nostalgic reveries, Verdi's *Requiem* can be interpreted as an expression of Andrei's despondent state of mind. More specifically, the *Requiem* can be construed as an acknowledgement on the protagonist's part that something deep inside of him prevents his return to his homeland and that as a consequence he is doomed to end his days in isolation and exile. Thus understood, the *Requiem* itself is focalized from within the main character's subjectivity. In conjunction with the folk song fragments – in which the nostalgia of the film's title seems to be particularly densely encoded – the *Requiem* comes to define the Russian's state of mind (not only for us, but also *for himself*) as he simultaneously invokes the memory of his former life and yields to the insight that his inability to return to it is also his inability to go on living. As pointed out at the beginning of this section, a requiem is a mass for the dead, and this particular requiem, by Italian composer *par excellence*, is a clear indication that, for Andrei, Italy has become synonymous with death.

In this reading, the concluding scenes can be understood as reinforcing the insight expressed in the opening scene. With Andrei lacking the strength to return to his earlier life, all that remains for him in Italy is increasing existential estrangement and, ultimately, physical expiration. In the film's penultimate scene, Andrei carries out his promise to Domenico and walks with a lit candle in his hand through the drained pool of St. Catherine in Bagno Vignoni.[14] Domenico has previously made several failed attempts to complete this symbolic act. Unlike Domenico, Andrei is successful, but only at the cost of his own life. Reaching the opposite side of the pool with the candle still burning, Andrei suffers a heart attack and dies. With this outcome, the symbolic act transfigures into a peculiar form of self-sacrifice that can perhaps be seen as a compensation for Domenico's failed performance in Rome. We may imagine, though, that Andrei remains conscious for a while and that the film's concluding scene reveals his final thoughts in life. In so doing it may actually take on an extra layer of signification, as it reveals a newfound insight of the dying Andrei, namely that he has finally achieved some kind of reconciliation between the memories haunting him and the alienation of his present exiled condition. Although the two musics are not combined at the end of the film, Verdi's music is closely associated with the melodic fragments of the Russian folk song, just as it was in the opening scene. But now, this intermingling of Italy and Russia is taken to a new level as we witness Andrei's vision of himself in front of his Russian dacha, which itself is located inside the roofless Italian gothic church (Figure 5.3). For Tarkovsky, the scene should be understood as expressing

> [a] new wholeness in which the Tuscan hills and the Russian countryside come together indissolubly; [Andrei] is conscious of them as inherently his own, merged into his being and blood, but at the same time reality is enjoining him to separate these things by returning to Russia. And so Gorchakov dies in this new world where those things come together naturally and of themselves.
>
> (Tarkovsky 1986, 216)[15]

Figure 5.3 Andrei in front of the family dacha inside San Galgano Abbey in the end scene of *Nostalghia*
Source: Films Sans Frontières

108 *Soothing Sounds and Sacrificial Acts*

From this perspective, and envisioned as flowing from Andrei's mind, the words of the *requiem aeternam* section of Verdi's music – which read "Give them eternal peace, oh Lord" – take on an added import in relation to the opening scene. If in the opening scene they are most plausibly understood as an expression of Andrei's appeal for desperately needed redemption, the fact that the *Requiem* precedes the Russian folk song at the film's end signals that the tension between Italy and Russia, between existential alienation and the ineradicable "longing for an inner home,"[16] may finally have been overcome. In other words, if "eternal peace" is *asked* for at the beginning of the film, at the film's end it is *given*. In the final scene, the visual synthesis on the image track combines with the sole presence of *Oi Vi Kumusciki* on the soundtrack to suggest the possibility that Andrei has finally attained a state of spiritual equilibrium, that his seemingly incurable nostalgia and deep existential alienation may perhaps have been redeemed by his peculiar self-sacrificial act, an act of genuine altruism performed out of a sense of duty to Domenico. But it seems that something else, something much more radical, is needed to set Andrei free: he must die. Just as how, at the conclusion of Wagner's *Tristan und Isolde*, Isolde's *Liebestot* is needed for the work to reach its dramatic and constantly deferred musical resolution, Andrei's expiration at the end of *Nostalghia* is necessary if he is to attain true reconciliation and inner peace. Thus, Andrei reaches the insight that only in death is perfect harmony possible; only in death can his nostalgic desires for wholeness be satisfied.

Whether or not one is inclined to accept the previously mentioned metadiegetic reading, there is another way to conceive of Verdi's *Requiem* in *Nostalghia*, one in which it is seen as issuing not from the mind of Andrei but rather from the film itself. Thinking about films as embodying a kind of consciousness is at the core of Daniel Frampton's concept of "filmind." For Frampton, the filmind is essentially "just the film" (Frampton 2006, 74), but it is the film imagined or thought of as an "organic intelligence," which is to say "a 'film-being' thinking about the characters and subjects in the film" (Frampton 2006, 7). According to Frampton, "the filmind and the film-world are one and the same," which implies that "the film-world does not organize itself independently of the filmind" (Frampton 2006, 75). The term "film-world" should here not be taken in the limited sense as referring to the diegetic reality of the film. Instead, as Philipp Schmerheim writes, the film-world "should be understood as an organic whole in which *all parts* [of a film] interrelate with each other, and which also causes such an impression on a film spectator" (Schmerheim 2006, 111; emphasis added). It follows that all music in film, regardless of its diegetic status, is a part of this all-encompassing film world.

By expressing itself through Verdi's music, the filmind, already at the outset of the film, reacts with sorrow and compassion to the fates and foreseen deaths of *both* Andrei and Domenico. At this point, however,

Soothing Sounds and Sacrificial Acts   109

I would like to introduce a modification to Frampton's concept, which I feel is less able to capture those elements of the film that more closely relate to the main characters' visions and actions. As I see it, we do not have to strictly apply Frampton's idea that the filmind is coextensive with everything that appears and happens in a film, i.e. that it pantheistically "*is* its objects and characters" (Frampton 2006, 79; emphasis in original). Instead, we can attribute to the filmind those elements of a film that we believe most aptly can be understood as an expression of its thinking. The *Requiem*, being much more loosely tied to Andrei's reveries than the extracts from *Oi Vi Kumusciki*, is more amenable to being imagined as a kind of filmic thinking than those fragments. To flesh out this thought in more detail, we can invoke Jerrold Levinson's theory of musical expressiveness. According to this theory, to hear a musical passage as expressive, one should "first be imagining a persona for it, and second, be imagining this persona to have the power to achieve in unmediated fashion an outpouring of sound that normally requires . . . the intermediary of musical instruments" (Levinson 1990, 339). With regard to the opening and closing scenes of *Nostalghia*, the idea of a particular persona *behind* the music may further an understanding of the *Requiem* in which the filmind more strongly comes to express a personal and deeply felt concern with the film's characters, which in turn may lead us to experience the filmind's presence more intensely. In contrast, making sense of the expressive intention behind *Oi Vi Kumusciki* requires neither the concept of filmind nor the idea of an imagined persona. In other words, though we may conceive of the *Requiem* as issuing from the filmind's thinking, i.e. as being expressed by a filmind persona, we may still feel that *Oi Vi Kumusciki* is more plausibly experienced as a metadiegetic phenomenon closely tied to Andrei's interiority. The upshot of all this is a "mixed reading" of the two musics' diegetic locations that combines them into a composite musical whole and fuses their subjective outlooks and expressive perspectives. This intermingling of Andrei's thinking and the thinking of the filmind thus results in a diegetically complex musical gestalt through which Andrei's longing for an idealized but unobtainable past becomes, simultaneously, an insignia of his nostalgia and a premonition of death articulated by the filmind persona.

In "choosing" Verdi's *Requiem*, the filmind persona alerts the viewer to the theme of death. However, this should not be taken simply as a forewarning of Andrei's and Domenico's actual deaths at the end of the film. More importantly, it can be taken as the filmind's reaction to their present life situations, which are characterized by existential and emotional sterility, as the two men are incapable of establishing a deeper connection with other people and are unable to live in the present.[17] In Andrei's case, this incapacity grows directly out of his continuous and compulsive reimaginings of an increasingly idealized past and a homeland that in an important sense no longer are his and to which, judging from his decision

110   *Soothing Sounds and Sacrificial Acts*

at the end of the film to cancel his trip to the airport (and back to Russia), he might never have had any serious intention to return. (I will return to this aspect of the film in the final section of this chapter.)

However, by expressing itself through Verdi's *Requiem*, the filmind persona does more than just react to the fates of Andrei and Domenico. As previously mentioned, it is the *requiem aeternam* section of the *Requiem* that Tarkovsky uses. The first words of the text, in Latin, are *Requiem aeternam dona eis Domine*; that is, "Give them eternal peace, oh Lord." By expressing itself with these words, the filmind persona is in fact issuing a plea for redemption; it is praying for the haunted and unhappy characters at the center of the film. Thus understood, the *Requiem* is an entreaty on the filmind's part for Andrei and Domenico to be released from their sufferings. It is at this point that a further dimension of the concept of nostalgia is revealed, a dimension seldom mentioned in connection with Tarkovsky's film. In praying for the protagonists' salvation, the filmind persona displays a compassion that Tarkovsky himself saw as closely connected to the Russian understanding of the word nostalgia. Describing the condition of nostalgia both as a "deadly form of homesickness" (Hara 2016, 6) and, more radically, as "a profound alienation from the world . . . a global yearning for the wholeness of existence" (Tarkovsky 1986, 204–205), he seems *also*, and perhaps somewhat idiosyncratically, to have understood the term in a wider, more altruistic sense:

> [F]or us [Russians] nostalgia is not a gentle and benevolent emotion. . . . For us it is a sort of deadly disease, a mortal illness, a profound *compassion* that binds us not so much with our own privation, our longing, our separation, but rather with the suffering of others, a *passionate empathy*.[18]

And in another formulation:

> The Russian term is difficult to translate: it could be compassion, but it's even stronger than that. It's identifying oneself with the suffering of another man, in a passionate way.
>
> (Gianvito 2006, 80)

In this latter quote, Tarkovsky is explicitly discussing Andrei's relation to Domenico, and in particular Andrei's decision to comply with Domenico's request that he carry the candle Domenico has given him across the thermal bath of Bagno Vignoni. I would suggest, however, that Andrei's compassionate identification with Domenico also reflects how the filmind persona relates to its characters by its use of Verdi's *Requiem*. And this has a further consequence. If Jeremy Barham (2014, 228–229) is correct in his suggestion that we reconceive the filmind as an amalgamation of, on the one hand, what Jerrold Levinson calls the implicit fictional

Soothing Sounds and Sacrificial Acts   111

presenter and, on the other, the responsive viewing subject – that is, of poietic and esthesic principles – then we should realize that as spectators we are also deeply implicated in this compassionate stance toward the characters.[19] Indeed, much the same thing happens in *The Sacrifice* (1986), though with the help of the aria "Erbarme dich" from Bach's *St. Matthew Passion*. Just as with the *requiem aeternam* in *Nostalghia*, Bach's aria in *The Sacrifice* appears at the very beginning and end of the film. And just as in *Nostalghia*, in *The Sacrifice*, we may envision a filmind persona meditating over and bemoaning the destiny of the increasingly confused and ill-fated protagonist (though I will explore a different approach in Chapter 6). Again, the filmind being partly constituted by our own reactions, our proper response is not only to observe the compassion it expresses but also to feel it ourselves, to *live* it through the film and its music. How *deep* we should go into this emotional identification with the characters' suffering is, however, a difficult question, and one I will return to later in this chapter.

I have argued for a twofold interpretation of Verdi's *Requiem* as it appears in *Nostalghia*: that it can be experienced as issuing from the interiority of the film's main character or, alternatively, that it can be envisioned as a compassionate prayer emerging from an imagined filmind persona. It might indeed be difficult to keep both these perspectives in one's mind at the same time, but it does not follow from this that they should be seen as ruling each other out. Rather, by complementing each other, they together enable a richer understanding of the film and the role played in it by Verdi's music, just like the dual interpretation of the Bach chorale prelude in Chapter 2 enabled a richer understanding of *Solaris*. Admittedly, in stressing one of these perspectives, we will direct our attention to some of the possible meanings of the concept of nostalgia at the expense of others. However, by acknowledging the plausibility of both perspectives, and by allowing ourselves to switch between them in our viewing of and thinking about the film, we can attain a deeper and more comprehensive understanding of the film's multilayered exploration of nostalgia as well as how Verdi's *Requiem* is implicated in the construction and expression of this nostalgia.

The nostalgia in Tarkovsky's film is not only an impossible longing for loved-but-lost objects such as one's homeland or family but also a loss of, an alienation from, one's own self (cf. Tarkovsky 1986, 204). In other words, the nostalgia of *Nostalghia* encompasses all the trappings of homesickness in its traditional sense as well as a "yearning for the wholeness of existence." More than this, however, it also involves a deep compassion for the suffering of others, a compassion expressed by Andrei's and Domenico's sacrificial acts *and* by the filmind in its reaction to the film's characters. I have shown in this section that Verdi's music is compatible with all these senses of nostalgia, and I have further claimed that it invites the viewer to take active part in the conceptual and emotional

112   *Soothing Sounds and Sacrificial Acts*

exploration of this complex and multifaceted phenomenon. Whether felt as issuing from the film's main character himself or from the diegetically more remote position of a filmind persona, Tarkovsky's Verdi implicates us all; it unites director, spectator, filmind and film character in a shared compassionate contemplation of the inescapability of existential alienation and our ineradicable longing for wholeness.

Resisting the Nostalgia of *Nostalghia*

Still, there seems to be something not altogether right about unconditionally participating in this compassionate contemplation, for by doing so we perhaps become too implicated in the nostalgia permeating the film. Putting it another way, we might ask: where does this nostalgic "yearning for the wholeness of existence" lead us to in the end? As we have seen, the film seems to be very clear on this point: when left to grow unchecked, the desire for closure and fulfillment that is the mark of severe nostalgia leads to isolation and death. Andrei wants to mend himself, while Domenico – who has come to believe that his peculiar attempt to save his own family was an indefensibly egoistic enterprise ("prima ero egoista") – wants to mend the world. But to the extent that they succeed in accomplishing these goals, it is at the cost of their own lives. Viewing the sacrificial acts they perform as expressions of spiritual integrity, as Tarkovsky himself was inclined to do (Tarkovsky 1986, 205–206), seems to be a half-truth at best. These acts are fueled by desperation; they are carried out by persons who have already lost or given up everything, persons who in different ways and for different reasons are driven into an ever more devastating psychic quarantine. How is spiritual integrity possible under such circumstances? And what, one might ask, are they sacrificing? Unlike Alexander in *The Sacrifice*, who, as we shall see in the next chapter, actually gives up the things he loves, Andrei and Domenico have already lost or forsaken all that they hold dear *before* they engage in their final sacrificial acts. These are acts that are *triggered* by the alienated states they are in, and that are performed for the primary purpose of finding a way out of an increasingly paralyzing state of estrangement and despair, to break the vicious circle of nostalgia. In this sense, they should be understood less as altruistic sacrificial deeds and more as final and drastic attempts at self-salvation.

Nostalgia, as Tarkovsky depicts it, does not only lead to death but is also ultimately incompatible with life itself. In Tarkovsky's words, it is a "deadly disease," and the entire film can in a sense be seen as a direct reflection of Verdi's *Requiem*, as a kind of requiem over the characters' inability to go on living. Significantly, a crucial difference between Andrei and people living in real exile (as Tarkovsky himself was soon to do) is that Andrei is free to return to his family and to Russia. Yet he chooses not to. Instead, he dies carrying out his promise to Domenico. This in itself may be an

Soothing Sounds and Sacrificial Acts   113

important decision, since by honoring Domenico's request Andrei is in fact for the first time in the film acting out of a sense of duty to another human being. But one gets the strong impression that even if he had survived the exhausting walk through the emptied pool of St. Catherine, he still would not have returned home. Such is the nature of Andrei's extreme nostalgia that returning to his homeland and his family would be just as incompatible with his compulsive dream fantasies as staying in Italy. Home no longer exists; it has been replaced by the "ideal home" (Boym 2001, XVI) constructed out of Andrei's nostalgic reveries. Andrei is tormented by longing for his beloved homeland, and yet the one thing he is not ready to do is to return. Such a decision would mean having to abandon his nostalgia, and this he cannot do. Going home would have been a life-affirming act; it would have meant resuming his *real* life. But Andrei seems to reach the conclusion that, just like his compatriot Sosnovsky, he is incapable of such a life-affirming act and that reuniting with his family will not save him. By choosing to remain in his condition of nostalgia, he chooses death.

The nostalgia of *Nostalghia* is a paradoxical phenomenon, for it does not really want what it most yearns for. In obsessively returning to the object of its affection, it comes to reject the very object itself. It does not want the real thing, only the imaginatively constructed reflection of it. To protect that reflection, the real thing must be denied. Like a parent who is incapable of establishing a deep relationship with her grown-up child because she cannot let go of the primordial bond that once existed between her and the small child, Andrei distances himself from his real-world relationships for the sake of the nostalgic dreams of these relationships. His yearning for "the wholeness of existence" is built on an idealized version of his family and homeland. Whether conceived of as flowing from the filmind or from Andrei's interiority, the combination of Verdi's *Requiem* and the Russian folk song is the musical embodiment of this nostalgia, and as such becomes synonymous with Andrei's inability or unwillingness to resume his real life in Russia. Given that music is one of the most effective means for arousing our emotions, the *Requiem* and the Russian folk song can thus be understood as paradigmatic expressions of the soothing lure of nostalgia. Together they constitute a gloomy but powerful version of the song of the sirens, one that urges the addressee to leave everything behind and find rest in sublime resignation. The weary Andrei cannot resist the lure of nostalgia, but perhaps we as spectators should. The beginning of Verdi's *Requiem* is an immensely beautiful piece of music, and in *Nostalghia* its beauty is further magnified by the breathtaking visual splendor of the film's dream sequences. The film thus becomes a "beautified longing for unity" (Skakov 2012, 190), or rather, it vacillates throughout between displaying this longing and turning into an aestheticized celebration of it. To the extent that nostalgia is beautified in *Nostalghia*, the spectator is faced with the choice

114　*Soothing Sounds and Sacrificial Acts*

of whether or how much she should allow herself to be drawn into the film's aesthetic and emotional ambit. The recurring claim among scholars and critics that Tarkovsky's films should be felt rather than analyzed thus takes on a special urgency with regard to *Nostalghia*. Unreserved emotional surrender to the film's remarkable aesthetic appeal may in fact be tantamount to an indiscriminate acceptance of life-denying nostalgia. The film's final scene is particularly problematic in this regard, since its extreme beauty may arouse a strong sense of fulfillment and catharsis at the same time as it arguably can be understood as the ultimate expression of a self-serving and alienating nostalgia. The scene is all about the dying Andrei's reconciliation with himself; like the end of *Mirror*, it depicts an experience of rapprochement at the moment of death. But it is also the irreversible step into complete resignation, a final and radical withdrawal into a hermetically sealed interiority, the crowning end state of a process of "distancing oneself from perceiving the present by escaping into existence in an idealized imagined space" (Skakov 2012, 168). No matter how liberating the final scene may be, the fact remains that Andrei dies alone in this foreign country, far from the people he loves.

As we saw in the previous chapter, Tarkovsky described Western Post-Baroque music on occasion in rather negative terms, criticizing what he saw as its shamelessly self-centered and obsessively melodramatic expressiveness. From this perspective the expressive discrepancy between Beethoven's and Verdi's music conceals a more fundamental common denominator. While the "Ode to Joy" is an exultant celebration of life and the *Requiem* a solemn meditation on death, and in this sense the two pieces stand as diametrically opposed musical statements, they are united in Tarkovsky's view by their preoccupation with the joys and sufferings of the human self. Thus, Western music is "forever shouting: 'This is me! Look at me! Listen to me suffering, loving! How unhappy I am! How happy! I! Mine! Me!'" (Tarkovsky 1986, 240). Perhaps, then, it is the Chinese music in the film that offers the most proper response to the misfortunes of Andrei and Domenico. The General, a guest at the hotel of Bagno Vignoni and also one of the bathers seen in the basin upon Domenico's first appearance in the film, claims that this music "beats Verdi any time" and promptly describes it as "the voice of God, of nature." These last words are echoed by Tarkovsky in his diary in an entry from February 8, 1983, where he describes Eastern music – the music of "China, Japan, India" – as a "complete fusion with God, with Nature" (Tarkovsky 2012, 704; my translation).[20] The Chinese music in *Nostalghia*, despite being initially strongly foregrounded on the soundtrack, is clearly diegetic in character, since we are informed that the General listens to it in his hotel room. It is introduced shortly after we have witnessed Eugenia's tempestuous break-up with Andrei. While Eugenia is seen standing in the hotel corridor reading a copy of the letter by Sosnovsky that Andrei had previously handed her, the camera

Soothing Sounds and Sacrificial Acts   115

tracks slowly back to reveal Andrei, who is busy stopping a nosebleed. Playing throughout the scene, the music functions as "anempathetic" diegetic sound (cf. Chion 1994, 8–9; see also Stilwell 2007, 190–191), distinctly indifferent to what is going on between the two characters and to Andrei's state of mind. In other words, the emotional investment in the main character's subjectivity that characterizes the *Requiem* and the Russian folk song is completely lacking here. The General's music is similarly not implicated in Domenico's grandiose sacrificial plans in the way that Beethoven's music is. Instead, the position of the Chinese music is more akin to that of a detached observer; though registering the intense suffering of the characters, it does not respond by taking that suffering upon itself. To suggest that we take up this position as spectators might seem insensitive and cold-hearted, but given what has been said earlier, such a viewing approach may not be altogether inappropriate. *Nostalghia* is a deeply moving film, and I presume that most people who have experienced its immense beauty would prefer to remain receptive to its aesthetic and emotional impact. As I claimed previously, we do not just want to watch the film; we want to *live* it. Yet one's emotional identification with the film's characters should perhaps be tempered by a more neutral and dispassionate approach modeled after the calm detachment of the General's Chinese music. To put it another way, if compassionate involvement in the fate of the film's characters is an appropriate way to respond to the film, true compassion may not mean to share in and duplicate their suffering in ourselves, but rather to approach and acknowledge it in the same way we would approach and acknowledge the pain and suffering of someone close to us in our actual life. And here the sober but respectful impartiality recommended by the Chinese music may be preferable to the emotionally suffused empathy expressed by the beautiful *Requiem* and the touching *Oi Vi Kumusciki*. So, the conclusion reached at the end of the previous section needs to be revised somewhat: we are all implicated in a compassionate contemplation of deep nostalgia, but the nature of that compassion is not necessarily the same for the characters who undergo the experience and the spectator who witnesses it.

Notes

1. "nostalgia, n." *OED Online*, Oxford University Press, March 2019. www.oed.com/view/Entry/128472 (accessed 2019-05-17.)
2. The real-life model of Sosnovsky is the Ukrainian eighteenth-century composer Maxym Berezovsky (ca. 1745–1777). Like the film's main character, and like Tarkovsky himself, Berezovsky seems to have developed severe nostalgia for his homeland during his extended stay in Italy. See also Skakov (2012, 167).
3. Later in their book, Johnson and Petrie specify this description when they speak of this music as "the strangely discordant 'Turkish' music" (Johnson and Petrie 1994, 200). The music, occurring during one of the film's

116 *Soothing Sounds and Sacrificial Acts*

many dream sequences, is genuinely difficult to identify, however. At certain moments it sounds almost like a classical tango à la Carlos Gardel.

4. A third central character in the film is Eugenia, a translator helping Andrei with his research on Sosnovsky. Since she is not connected with the film's music in the explicit way Andrei and Domenico are, I will have less to say about her presence in the film.

5. Thomas Redwood (2010, 188) makes a similar point. See also Quandt (2008, 278).

6. In hindsight, of course, we may justifiably conjecture that Domenico's playing of Beethoven's music is part of his planning of the performance in Rome, in which the music will centrally feature (more on this later). But at this point in the film, we do not have access to this information.

7. Jeff Smith argues that in cases such as these, there is in fact only an apparent ambiguity. The music is diegetic the whole time, even though this is not immediately revealed to us (see Smith 2009). In a strict sense this may be true, but this does not mean that we cannot experience the music as ambiguous. As Giorgio Biancorosso notes, "an ambiguity that is finally solved is no less ambiguous for that" (Biancorosso 2009, 11).

8. A somewhat different perspective is taken by Sitney, who claims that "Domenico's fanatical behavior translates that of the Old Believers in seventeenth- and eighteenth-century Russia, who resisted liturgical reform by taking to the forests and often committing suicide in the conviction that the Last Days had come. Thousands of them burned themselves to death, convinced that the cleansing fire was the holiest form of salvation in the face of the Antichrist" (2014b, 234).

9. Hara (2016, 14) expresses a similar view when he says that "Domenico is a character whose actions in the present are constantly haunted by his memory of the past."

10. I rely here on the "Trivia Page" at *Nostalghia.com*, according to which "the Russian folk song heard in *Nostalghia* is called *Oi Vi Kumusciki.*" See URL: www.nostalghia.com/TheTopics/Tarkovsky_Trivia.html (accessed 2019-05-17). A more common spelling of the song's title seems to be "Kumushki." As far as I can tell, the first verse of the song goes like this: "Oh, godmothers, godmothers; Be godparents, be loving; Be godparents, be loving; Love me."

11. See "Locations of *Nostalghia*" at *Nostalghia.com*. URL: http://nostalghia.com/ThePhotos/Nostalghia_Locations.html (accessed 2019-05-17).

12. Interestingly, in comparison with *Stalker* the color scheme in *Nostalghia* seems to be reversed. While in the earlier film the scenes shot in color are associated with the mysterious Zone (the black-and-white and sepia-tinted sequences being reserved for the more mundane life outside the Zone), in *Nostalghia* Andrei's recurring entrances into his intense interior states are consistently displayed in black and white, with color being reserved for the more "objective" happenings revolving around his encounters with Eugenia and Domenico (see also Martin 2011, 160–161).

13. See Hara (2016, 7) for a fuller elaboration of this point.

14. To be precise, this is the third scene from the end, because a brief sequence featuring Andrei's little son intervenes between this scene and the final scene at San Galgano Abbey.

15. See also Sushytska (2015, 41).

16. "To Journey Within" (Gideon Bachmann in conversation with Tarkovsky). At *Nostalghia.com*. URL: http://nostalghia.com/TheTopics/Gideon_Bachmann.html (accessed 2019-05-17).

17. Johnson and Petrie describe Andrei as being "unable – or unwilling – to overcome his understandable loneliness and homesickness to the extent

Soothing Sounds and Sacrificial Acts   117

of making meaningful contact with other human beings. His dreams and memories are self-enclosed, circular, and repetitive, and seem to be used as an excuse for avoiding any commitment to his existing reality" (Johnson and Petrie 1994, 160).

18. Natalia Aspesi, "The Gentle Emotion That Is a Mortal Illness for Us Russians" (Interview with Andrei Tarkovsky in Cannes 1983) at *Nostalghia.com*. URL: www.nostalghia.com/TheTopics/Tarkovsky_Aspesi-1983.html (accessed 2019-05-17). Emphasis added.

19. I should note that this explication of the concept of filmind is in conflict with Frampton's own understanding. According to Frampton, the filmind is "not a human mind. It is another kind of mind, its [the film's] own mind, a new mind" (Frampton 2006, 73).

20. Translated from Swedish. I have used the Swedish edition of Tarkovsky's diaries because it is generally considered to be the most comprehensive and accurate to date.

6 The Voice of Truth

Liminal Music, Spiritual Authenticity and Gradual Awakening in *The Sacrifice*

In the concluding chapter of *Sculpting in Time*, Tarkovsky's voice is no longer so much that of the director and film theorist. Instead, he speaks more from the position of a philosopher or cultural critic, and in a somewhat prophetic tone delivers what can only be described as a very pessimistic diagnosis of modern civilization. According to Tarkovsky, contemporary people (in the 1980s) are above all governed by petty material needs, and he repeatedly laments the "fact" that we are becoming increasingly unable to recognize the true spiritual values of human life. In our contemporary consumerist culture,

> we are witnessing the decline of the spiritual while the material long ago developed into an organism with its own bloodstream, and became the basis of our lives, paralysed and riddled with sclerosis.
> (Tarkovsky 1986, 234–235)

Such bodily metaphors indicate the extent to which Tarkovsky perceived modern civilization to be saturated with what, in Marxist terms, could be described as false consciousness. But Tarkovsky's truth and his remedy for humanity's current existential crisis are very different from those of Marxist thinkers. For Tarkovsky, rather than the emancipation of oppressed social classes, it is the spiritual self-realization of the individual that should be in focus. In fact, Tarkovsky reckons Marxist communism among the ideological systems that have prevented modern man from realizing his full spiritual potential (see Tarkovsky 1986, 235–236).[1] Both in the capitalist West and in communist Russia, "the rift between the material and the spiritual has been growing," the common denominator of these two geopolitical spheres being that they both force us to "live in a world governed by ideas which other people have evolved, and we either have to conform to the standards of these ideas or else alienate ourselves from them and contradict them" (Tarkovsky 1986, 233). To achieve true spiritual awakening, a radical rejection of materialist values and entrenched societal and ideological norms is needed. In order to perceive the voice of truth and obtain true inner freedom, one must distance oneself from

The Voice of Truth   119

the collectively shared standards and the insubstantial way of life of a mendacious society. Such radical measures are taken again and again by characters in Tarkovsky's films: Andrei in *Andrei Rublev*, Kelvin in *Solaris*, the Stalker in *Stalker*, Domenico in *Nostalghia* and, of course, Alexander in *The Sacrifice*.

The importance of spiritual truth and the necessity of taking radical measures to achieve it are also commented upon in the chapter on *The Sacrifice*, the penultimate chapter of *Sculpting in Time*. Tarkovsky writes that in making the film, he was "interested above all in the character who is capable of sacrificing himself and his way of life," a character ready to act in a manner that "refutes the laws of a materialistic worldview" (Tarkovsky 1986, 217). The space that such a person inhabits "becomes a rare, distinctive point of contrast to the empirical concepts of our experience, an area where reality . . . is all the more strongly present" (Tarkovsky 1986, 217). The "reality" Tarkovsky refers to here clearly has little to do with the empirical and socially constructed reality of our everyday world. Rather, it is a spiritual condition or dimension that can only be reached by turning one's back on the taken-for-granted norms at the heart of contemporary culture and society. Although we have banned this spiritual dimension from our lives, Tarkovsky's predilection for terms like "God," "the eternal," "the infinite," "the absolute" and "absolute spiritual truth" indicates that he thinks of it as an objective, if largely unacknowledged, presence in the world. The voice of spiritual truth is continuously present around and within us, but we have forgotten how to listen to and act in accordance with it. In Tarkovsky's own words: "Our feelings remain untouched by the supremely important messages that could change our lives" (Tarkovsky 1986, 228).

In this chapter, I argue that the herding calls heard regularly throughout *The Sacrifice* represent precisely the kind of true spirituality that Tarkovsky claims is lacking in the modern world. Furthermore, this representational meaning is inextricably linked to the complex diegetic status of the herding calls, an issue I will consider more closely in the next section. Based on the conclusions reached in this section, the main part of the chapter then develops a narrative interpretation of the film in which the herding calls play a central role. I call it a *narrative* interpretation because I will argue that these recurring musical fragments are essentially involved in the main character's gradual spiritual awakening. This spiritual awakening is reflected both in the changing relation between the herding calls and Alexander's consciousness and in how the herding calls relate to the film's diegesis. While in their first appearances the calls are best described as unacknowledged and diegetically ambiguous, by the film's end they have become firmly instantiated in the characters' empirical reality. During the course of the narrative, Alexander thus becomes increasingly aware of the voice of truth, and as he learns to listen to it he is also prepared to let it guide his course of action, ultimately leading to

120 *The Voice of Truth*

his radical act of self-sacrifice in the light of an ongoing nuclear disaster (whether real or imagined).

The Liminal Voice of Truth: The Herding Calls as Transcendental Diegetic Music

In *The Sacrifice*, Swedish herding calls, or *kulning*, occur both in connection with dream sequences and in scenes where the characters are fully awake.[2] Even though kulning is nowadays an integral part of the Swedish folk music scene and is performed almost exclusively by professionally trained singers, it originally developed in rural parts of Sweden as a way of gathering herds of cattle that often could be spread over a large geographical area.[3] This occupation was traditionally associated with women, and professional performances of kulning today are without exception carried out by female musicians.[4] Not surprisingly, then, all instances of kulning in *The Sacrifice* are performed by a female voice.

As with the sonic figure in *Stalker*, we might ask what these recurring appearances of traditional Swedish song are doing here, what they mean and what they contribute to our understanding of the film. The standard Tarkovskian answer would probably be that they do not mean anything; indeed, that inquiring into their symbolic or representational value is to overlook the deeper emotional and aesthetic impact they have in the film. However, from a hermeneutical perspective these are important and potentially very rewarding questions. It is perhaps not coincidental, as we attempt to understand the herding calls, that the technique of kulning was developed as a way of summoning the cattle and bringing them safely back to the farm. Without this practice, the animals would get lost in the terrain and eventually would have wandered so far off that they could not find their way back home again. Analogously, the herding calls in the film can be understood as the voice of God or the voice of Conscience (or something similar), summoning a humanity that has lost its way in order to bring it back to its existential home. But whether or not we opt for religious terminology in our description of the calls, it is not at all far-fetched to interpret them as the voice of a higher spiritual truth addressing each and every one of us: that is, as a plea for a return to a more spiritual and authentic way of life.

I believe that this is a highly plausible way of understanding the herding calls in the film. And it connects in interesting ways with questions about the music's diegetic status. As with the Bach chorale prelude in *Solaris*, this diegetic status can undoubtedly be construed in different ways, depending on the interpretive framework we bring to the film. Nevertheless, the standard categories of diegetic, nondiegetic and metadiegetic music seem peculiarly unfit to account for how this music relates to the film's fictional world. Apart from the very last scene, a diegetic account would fail to capture the impression that the music often seems to originate from a point outside of the diegesis. A nondiegetic account, on the other hand, would have a problem explaining the recurring scenes where characters are obviously reacting to the music. And while a metadiegetic description would probably work for some of the instances (especially the more explicit dream sequences), it would fail to capture the sense in which this music appears to have an objective presence independent of the characters' mental life.

The problem with the diegetic status of the herding calls in *The Sacrifice* is that they simultaneously seem to belong and not belong to the film's diegesis. As off-screen sounds that continually evade any concrete grounding within diegetic space, their relation to this space becomes inherently indeterminable. Thus, we cannot conclusively establish whether they "derive from the fictional world [or] if they emanate from another off screen space dimension" (Söderbergh Widding 2006, 152), and in this sense the voice producing them is a clear instance of what Michel Chion has termed the cinematic acousmetre (Chion 1994, 129–131). Given this ambiguous status, I suggest that a fruitful way to conceive of the herding calls is to describe them as residing somewhere along the boundary of the diegesis, which keeps the possibility open that they in fact belong to the diegesis. But they do so in a very special way. I will coin the expression *transcendental diegetic music* to capture the sense in which the herding calls can be understood as being part of the diegesis while at the same time entering the *empirical reality* of the characters from a position outside it. This understanding is in line with Chion's description of the herding calls in his book *Audio-Vision: Sound on Screen*:

> In Tarkovsky's final film, *The Sacrifice*, one can hear sounds that already seem to come from the other side, as if they're heard by an immaterial ear, liberated from the hurly-burly of our human world. Sung by sweet young human voices, they seem to be calling to us, resonating in a limpid atmosphere.
>
> (Chion 1994, 123)

As transcendental diegetic music, the calls participate in constituting an *enlarged* diegesis containing a non-empirical dimension only partly accessible to the characters: a liminal space beyond the "hurly-burly" of the human world that, even if largely unacknowledged, is constantly present throughout the film. This understanding is in line with Tarkovsky's notion of the artistic film image. For Tarkovsky, to the extent that the film image constitutes a true artistic representation, it points beyond itself, in that it "stretches out into infinity and leads to the absolute" (Tarkovsky 1986, 104). Similarly, the herding calls can be understood as ambiguous sonic entities that, by not being tied to an identifiable sound source, radically expand the diegesis and occasionally even transcend it, in this way opening it up to an "invisible spiritual world" (Truppin 1992, 236)

122   *The Voice of Truth*

that only with difficulty can be contained within a coherent conception of what constitutes a filmic diegesis. As Andrea Truppin notes, this way of using sound and music "plunges the audience into a never fully resolved struggle to believe in the diegesis, much as the film's characters struggle with their own ability to have faith" (Truppin 1992, 235).

From the previously mentioned considerations, it is clear that the representational meaning we ascribe to the herding calls cannot easily be detached from the way we determine their diegetic status. The possibility of experiencing them as transcendental diegetic music – that is, as a kind of liminal music located at the intersection between the characters' empirical reality and an "invisible spiritual world" – is what makes plausible the claim that they represent the voice of spiritual truth. It is precisely because they can be experienced as existing beyond or apart from the empirical reality of the characters that we can understand them as a manifestation of what Tarkovsky, with his mix of Romantic and Hegelian terminology, calls "the absolute" (see Tarkovsky 1986, 37–39). The liminal voice of spiritual truth is the voice of absolute truth, and it is summoning the characters in the diegesis to acknowledge it and live according to its standards. The tragedy of *The Sacrifice* is that most of the characters seem completely unable to hear the herdswoman's calling.[5] But one of them, Alexander, begins to listen to it and as a result is led to undertake a series of actions that appear utterly incomprehensible to his less enlightened family and friends (cf. Skakov 2012, 197).

A Process of Gradual Awakening: Listening to the Voice of Truth

The Sacrifice begins with an extended shot of Leonardo da Vinci's painting *Adoration of the Magi* (1481). As the opening credits roll over the screen, the painting is meticulously examined to the accompaniment of the aria "Erbarme dich, mein Gott" from Johann Sebastian Bach's *St. Matthew Passion* (BWV 244). With these two works, Tarkovsky signals from the very outset that his final film will revolve around questions of spiritual and existential truth. As pointed out several times in previous chapters, in Tarkovsky's artistic universe Leonardo and Bach stand out as the two chief representatives of a spiritually authentic art.[6] In using Leonardo and Bach, Tarkovsky thus sets the standard for his own film and makes clear his intention to create a work of art that aspires to the same level of artistic truthfulness as the art of his two masters (cf. Jones 2007, 195).[7] To be sure, *The Sacrifice* is not the first of Tarkovsky's films to feature both Leonardo's art and Bach's music, but this is the first time they appear together at the very beginning of a film. Moreover, the aria from the *St. Matthew Passion* can here be seen as performing a role similar to that of Verdi's *Requiem* at the beginning of *Nostalghia*. As Gunnar J. Gunnarsson points out – and is obvious already from the title of the piece – the "Erbarme Dich" aria "is a prayer of mercy" (Gunnarsson 2006, 249) and as such can be understood as articulating the same theme of redemption introduced at the outset of the earlier film by the first words of the *Requiem*, which read "Give them eternal peace, oh Lord." However, while my argument in the previous chapter was that the *Requiem* in *Nostalghia* could plausibly be understood as a lamentation over the fates of Andrei and Domenico, the "Erbarme Dich" of *The Sacrifice* is an expression of grief that targets the disintegration of spiritual values in contemporary society as a whole. Gunnarsson continues:

> The fact that Tarkovsky uses this aria both at the beginning and end of *The Sacrifice* is intriguing. The prayer of mercy is sung in the *Passion* when Peter has denied Jesus three times and goes out and weeps upon hearing the rooster crow. In Tarkovsky's understanding, modern man has denied God in his materialism and brought spiritual death upon himself.
>
> (Gunnarsson 2006, 249)

The extended credit sequence goes on for five minutes and is then followed by a similarly extended opening scene in which Alexander – a retired actor who now devotes his time to writing essays and giving lectures on aesthetics – is seen planting a barren tree by the sea together with his temporarily mute son (usually called "Little Man" in the literature[8]). The scene also introduces postman and retired history teacher Otto who, as I will return to later, is the only character other than Alexander that seems to have the ability to perceive the herding calls. In the narrative interpretation that follows, I examine the numerous occurrences of herding calls in *The Sacrifice* under six separate headings, each section corresponding to what I consider to be a cohesive segment of the film. I discuss the segments in the order they occur, with the aim of revealing a narrative process in which the herding calls go from being completely ignored or unrecognized to being increasingly acknowledged by Alexander (and Otto), and finally are realized as concrete diegetic music in the characters' empirical world.

"Words, Words, Words"

As Alexander and his son prop up the dead tree, Otto approaches on his bicycle. Otto congratulates Alexander on his birthday, reads him a birthday telegram and, as if for no reason, asks Alexander about his relationship with God. "I'm afraid it's nonexistent," Alexander answers. Otto expresses concern for Alexander's mental condition, saying that Alexander is always so gloomy and sad. The important thing, he continues, is "not to expect anything": "Take me, for example. For my entire life I've been waiting for something; it's as if I've spent my life at a railway station,

124   *The Voice of Truth*

waiting for something real." He then changes the subject and begins to speculate about Nietzsche's theory of the eternal return and the importance of having faith, concluding that "if I have faith that something will be a certain way, it will be that way." When Otto eventually leaves, declaring that he needs to find a present for Alexander's birthday dinner later that evening, Alexander and Little Man walk into a nearby grove where they encounter Alexander's wife Adelaide and the doctor, Victor, a close friend of the family. Before long, however, father and son are left alone again, and Alexander begins to recount the story of how he and his wife found the house where they now live. But he soon digresses into a long monologue about the flaws of modern civilization, echoing many of the thoughts Tarkovsky himself expresses in *Sculpting in Time*: humanity continuously inflicts violence upon itself and upon nature; we cherish comfort and a high material standard as the most important values; every result of scientific progress is immediately turned into something evil. In short, our entire civilization is built on sin, and there is a terrifying imbalance between our material development and our lack of spiritual growth. It is during this monologue that the herding calls make their first appearance, and they continue to accompany Alexander's speculations until he suddenly interrupts himself, having discovered that Little Man has disappeared. When his son runs into him from another direction, Alexander is startled and unintentionally pushes the boy so hard that he falls to the ground and starts to bleed from his nose. At this point, a loud thunderclap is heard and the music abruptly stops.

In his monologue, Alexander deplores the spiritual impoverishment of our modern civilization and even claims that it is beyond rescue. He complains that people everywhere are doing nothing but talking, and he summarizes this regrettable state of affairs with a quote from *Hamlet*: "Words, words, words!" The world is brimming with petty-minded dreams, viciousness and empty chatter, but no one seems to care, no one really *does* anything about it.[9] Alexander says that he is infinitely tired of all this talk, but to his own disgust he realizes that he has been babbling away himself, and self-dismissively he exclaims: "Why do I talk so much!" While Alexander engages in these pessimistic and self-deprecating ruminations, the herding calls are clearly noticeable in the background, but he takes no notice of them. Caught up in his own verbiage, he seems oblivious to the spiritual presence around him. Of course, at this point in the film we might simply assume that the herding calls constitute a kind of non-diegetic music and, consequently, that Alexander is not really supposed to hear them. But later in the film he *does* hear them, and since, with the exception of the film's final scene, there is no discernible difference in acoustic form and sound quality between the first and later occurrences of the herding calls, the claim that they could be described as traditional nondiegetic music at the beginning of the film would require additional interpretive support to be convincing, and it is unclear to what extent

The Voice of Truth   125

such interpretive support could be provided.[10] They clearly seem to be present in diegetic space, though at the same time they linger at the threshold of the empirical reality of this space, calling for and insisting on Alexander's attention. Put differently, the herdswoman's voice issuing the calls is a voice that simultaneously belongs and does not belong to this empirical reality, for just as "the tracking shot of the camera through the trees suggests an *alien presence*, [so] does the mysterious sound of [this] female voice" (Bird 2008, 217; my emphasis).

Sitting with his back against a tree and deeply immersed in his conjectures about the condition of the world, Alexander eventually arrives at the conclusion that modern civilization has gone astray as a result of its materialistic way of life and its rejection of true spirituality. But he is not yet ready to open himself up to that spirituality. As transcendental diegetic music, the "alien" voice of spiritual truth penetrates the space around him and demands his attention, but in his desperate tirades against the emotional and spiritual bankruptcy of contemporary society, he is unable to hear it. Or maybe some unconscious part of him is actually responding to the music, but just as for Otto in a later scene, it is as if the encounter with the voice of truth is so overpowering that he is incapable of bearing it. And so he faints.

"What Is Happening to Me?"

After the unintended collision with his son, Alexander takes a few stumbling steps forward, leans up against a tree and then whispers the words "Oh God, what is happening to me?" He collapses and falls to the ground, at which point the herding calls return and the scene changes. In black and white we see an empty street, littered with debris, leading up to the entrance of a dark tunnel flanked on either side by steep stairs (Figure 6.1).[11] A demolished car comes into the frame as the camera begins to backtrack in a high-level shot over the street. More debris appears (broken chairs, plastic bags, an empty cement sack), littering a pedestrian crossing, until finally a large plate of glass comes into view. In the glass, the surrounding buildings and a small segment of the gray sky are reflected.

Following as it does directly upon Alexander's blackout, this short scene can be viewed as depicting a delirious vision caused by the collapse. At the same time, it also seems to anticipate the nuclear disaster soon to be unleashed, as a kind of prophetic vision. During the entire scene, the herdswoman's voice is continuously present, strengthening the impression that Alexander is experiencing "a clear premonition of some extraordinary event" (Skakov 2012, 194). And given that the scene can plausibly be understood as a representation of the unconscious Alexander's oracular hallucinations, it is reasonable to claim that in some sense he is also hearing the calls. Clearly, he is not yet ready or able to

Figure 6.1 A delirious anticipation of nuclear disaster in *The Sacrifice*
Source: Films Sans Frontières

acknowledge them while in a fully wakeful state. Nevertheless, in relation to the preceding scene, a significant change has occurred, namely that the herdswoman's voice has now established itself as a presence in Alexander's mind, even if only as a faint echo at the very periphery of his consciousness. In contrast to the previous scene – where Alexander, deeply involved in his apocalyptic fantasies, appeared to be completely ignorant of the music – the delirious prophecy following his blackout constitutes a first sign that he is prepared to listen and open himself up to the voice of true spirituality. Thus understood, the brief hallucinatory scene can simultaneously be viewed as both a prophetic vision of an approaching nuclear conflict and the portrayal of a first encounter with the voice of truth. And herein also lies the seed of Alexander's self-sacrificial acts later in the film, which are driven by the dual insight that the world is about to come to an end and that the only thing that can prevent it is a spiritually authentic and completely unselfish act of sacrifice.

Otto

As previously mentioned, apart from Alexander, the only other character who is visibly affected by the herding calls is Otto. He is a collector of inexplicable but, he claims, true events, and by his own admission he has gathered no less than 284 such occurrences. Otto's first encounter with the herdswoman's voice occurs when he is recounting one of these

The Voice of Truth   127

stories. To Victor, Adelaide and Adelaide's daughter Marta, he tells the story of a widow who lived in Königsberg with her 18-year-old son before the war. When war broke out and the young man was inducted into the army, mother and son decided to visit a photography studio to have a photo taken of themselves. At this point in Otto's story, the herdswoman's voice is briefly heard, and in what appears to be a direct response to it, Otto abruptly interrupts himself in the middle of a sentence. Victor, Adelaide and Marta, on the other hand, do not seem to hear it and, after a moment's silence, Otto resumes his story. The son was sent to the front and was killed only a few days later. Perhaps as a consequence of this devastating news, the woman forgot about the photo and never went to the studio to pick it up. Many years later, she visited a studio in another town to have her picture taken. When she received the developed photograph, however, she discovered that she was not alone in the picture. Next to her in the photo was her 18-year-old son.

Leaning against the doorframe to the kitchen, Otto recounts the last part of his story with great seriousness. Victor is skeptical, however, and asks Otto if he is making fun of them. Otto assures him that he is not and that he has collected ample evidence that everything he has just told them is true. As he turns around and walks slowly into the adjacent living room, he concludes that "we are all blind, none of us is able to see anything." Otto's claim here can be interpreted in the light of his claim earlier in the film that "if I have faith that something will be a certain way, it will be that way." Our blindness is thus connected to, or perhaps is a consequence of, our inability to have faith, and Victor's skepticism is just one example of this inability. In addition, the claim that "we are all blind" takes on an extra layer of signification in the present scene in that it can be seen as a direct reflection of the fact that none of the people in the room show any sign of hearing the herdswoman's calls. In his conversation with Alexander in the film's opening scene, Otto had stated that we are all "waiting for something real, something important." But as long as we close our eyes and ears to this "real" thing, we will wait in vain.

Otto the postman, though, seems to have the ability to see and hear. When he has entered the living room, the herding calls are heard again. And now there is no question whether he notices them. He turns around slowly, utters a brief "Huh?" and listens attentively. Unlike Alexander's first encounter with the herdswoman's voice, Otto is able to hear it while fully awake. But just as with Alexander, this encounter affects him so strongly, is so overwhelming, that he is unable to listen further. As if being hit by some invisible force, he spins around and then falls to the floor unconscious. When he wakes up a few moments later, he looks into Victor and Adelaide's faces and says "Now, what could this be? What do you think?" He crawls across the floor, creeps up into a chair and in a somewhat dispassionate tone of voice answers his own question: "It was just an evil angel that touched me."

128 *The Voice of Truth*

If Victor and Adelaide lack the capacity to hear the herdswoman's voice, Alexander has taken the first steps toward acknowledging its presence in the world. At this point in the narrative, however, only Otto seems to have the ability to perceive the herding calls while fully awake. This is not coincidental. As a collector of supernatural and inexplicable events, Otto clearly distinguishes himself from the other characters in the film by his readiness to accept a spiritual dimension that transcends empirical reality. As Peter Green remarks, Otto "is the key to the supernatural world of this film" (Green 1993, 130).[12] Furthermore, by convincing the tormented Alexander that the only way to save the world from nuclear disaster is for Alexander to visit the family's maid Maria and sleep with her, Otto induces Alexander to perform his first act of sacrifice.[13] Also, as I will return to in the next section, it is in the company of Otto that Alexander is first able to hear the herdswoman's voice in a fully awake state. In leading Alexander out of his paralyzed despair and in making him aware of a higher spiritual presence in the world, Otto simultaneously takes on the appearance of a Virgilian figure and a messenger of spiritual truths. This latter aspect is further reinforced by the fact that Otto's stated profession is that of a postman, a deliverer of letters. Finally, Otto is the only one who seems to have the prophetic ability to foresee what course of action is needed to reverse and rectify the disastrous situation they have ended up in, once again distinguishing himself from the other characters.

"What Was That?"

There has been some discussion among critics and scholars about whether the nuclear catastrophe at the center of the film actually takes place or if it is rather supposed to be understood as part of Alexander's dream. How one is inclined to answer this question depends on where in the film one thinks that Alexander's dream begins (an issue to which I will return in the final section of this chapter). In any case, when Alexander realizes that a nuclear war has broken out, he withdraws to his study and begins to pray. He begs God to save his family and friends and put an end to the ongoing disaster. He offers to give up everything that binds him to this life if God will only set things right again: he will abandon his family, destroy his home, part with his son. He will become mute, never speak to anyone ever again. These are not empty words; before the film is over, Alexander will have fulfilled his promise to God.

After having made his vows, the exhausted Alexander crawls up onto the sofa and falls asleep. The herding calls return, this time accompanying what is obviously one of Alexander's dreams. In a black-and-white shot, Marta is seen removing her dress, and a few moments later we see her walking naked through a large bedroom. Alexander, who appears to be watching her, flees down a long corridor. The dream then changes to

The Voice of Truth   129

a view of Alexander in front of an abandoned house. His feet sink into the drenched ground as he pulls something out of the mud before the scene changes again and we see him standing in a snow-covered landscape dominated by large trees. Alexander sees the naked feet of his son and cries out to him. But the boy, instead of going to his father, turns around and runs away. The camera does not follow the boy's flight but moves instead over the drenched ground, eventually revealing a nearby barn and a door slamming wide open in the strong wind. The sound of jet fighters is heard on the soundtrack (a sound that recurs several times in the film). At this point Alexander wakes up. Throughout the whole sequence, the herding calls have appeared at regular intervals, implying that Alexander is still only able to hear them in his dreams.

As Alexander gets up from the sofa, he hears a light tapping on the window glass. Otto has come to give him an important message. Through the window, he tells Alexander that there is still time to put things right again; one last opportunity is available to them. Entering the room, he repeats several times that Alexander "must go to Maria." Alexander is confused and asks Otto to express himself more clearly. What is he supposed to do? Which Maria is the postman talking about? Otto clarifies that he must go to the family's maid Maria and persuade her to sleep with him. If he does this, everything will go back to the way it was in the morning, before the catastrophe struck. This is because, Otto explains, Maria has special abilities. He has gathered evidence that she is a witch, though "in the good sense," he adds. In the midst of the two men's conversation, they are suddenly interrupted by the herdswoman's voice. Otto looks at Alexander, points to the window and whispers, "did you hear that?" Alexander listens attentively and answers, "hear what?" When the voice is heard again, Otto repeats his question: "what was that?" Now Alexander hears it, too. Perplexed, he sits down on the floor beside Otto and says, "I don't know, I really don't know, I think it sounded like music." After a moment's silence, Otto again repeats that Alexander must go to Maria, and then he leaves the house the same way he came.

From the perspective of the present interpretive approach, this is clearly an important turning point in the film's narrative. For the first time, Alexander is able to clearly recognize the mysterious voice while fully awake, and given the representational meaning we have ascribed to this voice, we can say that it is at this very moment that Alexander becomes capable of reaching beyond the empirical diegesis and acknowledging the existence of a higher and more authentic spiritual dimension. It is not only Alexander's relation to the herding calls that has changed. Like Alexander, Otto too fell unconscious during his first encounter with them, but is now able to listen to them without being struck to the ground. Although the two men are now able to perceive the herdswoman's voice, it is difficult to determine to what extent they understand its nature or significance. As soon as they have recognized it, they seem to forget about it again,

130   *The Voice of Truth*

continuing their dialogue as if the extraordinary event they have just aurally witnessed were merely another everyday incident. Even so, the fact that the herdswoman's voice has now become an acknowledged presence in their consciousness implies the occurrence of a fundamental change in their relation to it. For Alexander, as we shall see in the next section, this newly acquired ability to hear the herdswoman's voice will play a decisive role in his decision to heed Otto's exhortation that he visit Maria.

Maria

Before leaving, Otto informs Alexander that he has placed a ladder against the balcony rail so that Alexander can slip out of the house unseen. He urges Alexander not to take the car, but instead to use the bicycle that Otto has left for him by the boathouse. Outside, the rest of the family has gathered for an evening dinner. Stepping out on the balcony, Alexander hesitates for a while before climbing down the ladder. Careful not to draw any attention to himself, he sneaks up to the bicycle and then slowly withdraws from the house. When the scene changes to a long shot of a small, winding road, Alexander becomes visible in the far distance, slowly approaching on his bicycle. Suddenly he loses control over the bike, tumbles into a small puddle and incurs an injury on his knee. As he gets up again, the herdswoman's voice is briefly heard. It is almost as if it were urging him to go on and not give up at this crucial moment. Alexander, however, acts as if he has not noticed it, and instead of continuing on his way, he turns around and starts to lead the bicycle toward his own house (cf. Skakov 2012, 209). But a few moments later the voice calls out to him again, this time in a more demanding tone. And now Alexander does indeed seem to hear it, for in direct response he turns his bike around again and proceeds toward Maria's home. Even more than before, it becomes clear at this point that the herdswoman's voice is not just another fixture of the characters' empirical reality, but must be understood instead as the articulation of a spiritual truth struggling to make itself known to the characters. And when they begin to listen to it, as does Alexander, they also begin to act in accordance with it, more or less consciously allowing it to become their moral and spiritual compass. The course of action that Alexander is about to take, the series of sacrificial acts that he is about to perform, may appear pointless and absurd to many viewers. But within the universe and logic of this film, they are guided by an absolute spiritual necessity, a necessity embodied and encoded in the repeatedly occurring herding calls.

Arriving at Maria's house, Alexander begins to knock insistently on her door. Maria opens it and lets him in. Unable to explain the purpose of his visit, Alexander sits down at the table in silence. Maria inquires whether something has happened at home, to which Alexander, alluding to the ongoing catastrophe, responds by asking her if she has a TV.

She says that her TV stopped functioning earlier that evening and then notices that his hands are dirty. Alexander washes his hands, sits down at a small harmonium and begins to play an organ prelude (an adapted version for the film of BWV539). By his own admission, he learned to play it as a child and his mother loved it. Alexander then recounts the story of when, as a young man, he visited his sickly mother and worked in her garden for several weeks. He wanted to make the dilapidated garden beautiful so that his mother could enjoy it, but when he was done, he realized that he had completely destroyed its natural, overgrown beauty. Alexander is interrupted by three strokes from an old pendulum clock and, with a panic-stricken expression on his face, proclaims "it's three o'clock, we won't make it." He walks over to Maria, sits down beside her on the bed and begs her to love him, to save him, to save them all. When the confused woman tells him that he should go home to his family, Alexander pulls a gun out of his pocket and points it to his head. Sensing the profundity of Alexander's desperation, Maria, presumably out of a sheer compassion, begins to kiss him passionately.

In a distinctly Tarkovskian sequence, the loving couple levitates over Maria's bed while the herding calls are heard again (Figure 6.2). This time, however, they appear together with another kind of music, namely the Japanese shakuhachi flute music heard earlier in the film when Alexander switched on his home stereo. That this music is strongly associated with the character of Alexander is further underlined by the yin-yang symbol on the back of his favorite kimono, the planting of the Japanese tree

Figure 6.2 Alexander and Maria levitating over Maria's bed in *The Sacrifice*
Source: Films Sans Frontières

132 *The Voice of Truth*

at the beginning of the film and Marta's comment that he has become obsessed with Japan. According to Julia Shpinitskaya, the combination of Swedish kulning and Japanese flute music here constitutes "a polyphonic sound space," and she views the two kinds of music as referring to the characters of Maria and Alexander respectively (see Shpinitskaya 2014). While the notion of a polyphonic sound space is an attractive one, I find Shpinitskaya's claim that the herdswoman's voice should be seen as a "representation of the mysterious Maria" to be somewhat undermotivated.[14] Instead, I want to view the merging of the two musical worlds in this scene and the sequences that follow as an affirmation of Alexander's newly acquired ability to link his empirical self with a higher spiritual reality. Borrowing terminology from Kierkegaard, we might say that at this point the timeliness of the Japanese music (it is timely in the sense that it functions as an expression of Alexander's self-image) is fully integrated with the eternal or infinite truth represented by the herding calls. Thus understood, Alexander's first sacrifice (making love with Maria) constitutes yet another step toward spiritual self-realization.

After Alexander and Maria's levitation, the contrapuntal combination of Swedish and Japanese folk music continues to be heard during what undoubtedly is a series of delirious dream images: another black-and-white shot of the tunnel entrance and city street, now filled with people running around and jostling each other in panic; Alexander and Maria (dressed as Adelaide) resting under a tree; a brief glimpse of Leonardo's *Adoration of the Magi*; and Marta running naked through a corridor chasing a pair of roosters. It may, however, be an understatement to speak of a contrapuntal combination, because the herding calls and the Japanese flute merge so inextricably that they are more aptly described as forming a musical unity, a unity that corresponds to and at the same time articulates the coalescence of Alexander's empirical self and a higher spiritual truth. Eventually the herding calls fade away, but the Japanese flute continues to play as we return to Alexander's studio, where he is seen lying on his sofa. He gets up, bumps his left knee on the writing desk and limps to the stereo with a groaning sound and turns the flute music off. The electricity, which had previously been cut off, has now been restored, and Alexander makes a call to his editor to test that the phone is working. Thus, even though it might be virtually impossible to determine where in the film Alexander's dream actually begins, this is clearly the moment when he wakes up.

Diegetic Instantiation

Alexander's second sacrifice, the burning down of the family house, is accompanied by the Japanese flute music. In fact, Alexander himself turns the music on, as if he wanted it to underscore the dramatic events that are about to take place (Figure 6.3). As the house burns, the family

Figure 6.3 Near the end of *The Sacrifice* Alexander turns the shakuhachi flute music on after having set fire to his house
Source: Films Sans Frontières

comes rushing back from their walk by the sea. They try to get Alexander into an ambulance (oddly occurring at just the right moment), and after several failed attempts he enters it voluntarily and the ambulance drives away. Maria seizes Otto's bike and begins to pedal in the opposite direction. At this point, there is a cut to the film's final scene, which begins with a shot of Little Man at the seashore, the barren Japanese tree that he planted with his father clearly visible in the background. The boy is carrying heavy buckets of water. Slowly, he moves the buckets closer to the tree. Maria arrives on the bike, passing a flock of cows that graze peacefully in a nearby field. The ambulance becomes visible further down the road and Maria and the little boy watch as it passes by. Maria leaves again and the little boy begins to water the tree, an act that Tarkovsky himself interpreted as "a symbol of faith" (Tarkovsky 1986, 224).[15] When he is done, he lies down beneath the tree and with fragile voice utters his first words in the film: "'In the beginning was the Word'; why is that, papa?"

From the opening of this scene to the moment when the boy begins to water the dead tree, the herdswoman's voice is present. But in this final appearance in the film, its relation to the empirical reality of the characters has significantly changed. It no longer has the character of transcendental diegetic music, of a liminal voice originating from the boundary of the diegesis. Instead, it seems to come from a person in the immediate surroundings; aurally and acoustically, it is equal to the other diegetic sounds in the scene. In other words, the herdswoman's voice is here clearly presented as diegetic music, and "for the first time the viewer

134 *The Voice of Truth*

sees its possible source: there is a flock of cows with a shepherd nearby" (Skakov 2012, 214). From the perspective of the narrative interpretation developed in this chapter, this is highly significant. Understood as the voice of spiritual truth, the diegetic instantiation of the herding calls signals that Alexander's spiritual transformation and his sacrificial acts have not been in vain. On the contrary, they have enabled the voice of spiritual truth to enter the film's empirical reality, to materialize as diegetic music proper. And this diegetic instantiation means that it is now present in the world for everyone who cares to listen to it. The questions remains, however, whether people will let themselves be summoned by its calls.

As the final scene draws to its close, the camera focuses on the dead tree and slowly begins to pan upwards. On the soundtrack, the herding calls overlap for a brief moment with the second and final appearance of the "Erbarme dich" aria, which is reminiscent of the overlap between the Russian folk song and Verdi's *Requiem* at the beginning of *Nostalghia*. Here the overlap may be taken as further emphasizing the presence of an eternal truth – of what Tarkovsky interchangeably calls the "infinite" and the "absolute" – as the diegetically instantiated herding calls merge with the nondiegetic music of the one composer whose "relationship with God is absolutely outside of civilization" (Gianvito 2006, 141). In this perspective, *The Sacrifice* is a film that ends on an optimistic note;[16] it is a film that allows into the world precisely that spirituality that Tarkovsky, in *Sculpting in Time*, claims is lacking in modern civilization.

Interpretive Glitches: Narrative Ambiguities in *The Sacrifice*

Most writers on *The Sacrifice* agree that the film is highly ambiguous with regard to when Alexander's dream begins.[17] According to Johnson and Petrie, "the clues we are given . . . could place almost any scene as the starting point." From this they draw the conclusion that

> it is possible to interpret all the major "events" of the film – Otto's visit to Alexander's study, Alexander's visit to Maria, the miraculous reversal and elimination of the seemingly imminent nuclear catastrophe – as at one and the same time real *and* imaginary.
>
> (Johnson and Petrie 1994, 177–178)

In a similar vein, Terence McSweeney notes that *The Sacrifice* is Tarkovsky's "most dream-imbued text, to the extent that the audience is entirely unsure of what is dream and what is reality" (McSweeney 2015, 151), while Sean Martin writes that "the film takes place in a world which seems to be simultaneously a dream and also real" (Martin 2011, 171). Thomas Redwood, though agreeing that the spectator is cued "towards mutually exclusive inferences," in that she can "comprehend the entire

The Voice of Truth 135

narrative . . . as a dream and/or as reality" (Redwood 2010, 202), goes even further, arguing that in the final analysis the film's narrative composition is not only ambiguous but essentially unintelligible. According to Redwood, there is "no logical sense to be found in this film. As a narrative, *The Sacrifice* is explicitly incoherent, chaotic and incomprehensible" (Redwood 2010, 201).

In my view, Redwood's analysis is correct. He convincingly shows that, as a narrative, the film simply does not hold together. Here, I wish to focus not on this narrative breakdown, however, but on the dream/reality issue pointed out by all the writers cited earlier. If the film in its entirety is taken to be a dream, it is obvious that this will seriously undermine the narrative interpretation that I have developed in this chapter. More exactly, if the dream is understood as beginning already in what Redwood (2010, 250; Appendix F) identifies as Scene 6 – where Alexander discovers the small model of the family home – then the claim that Alexander is increasingly able to perceive the herding calls while fully awake becomes untenable. This is because, according to the assumption, everything that happens after Scene 6 only occurs because someone (presumably Alexander) is dreaming it. Peter Green argues that this is actually the most plausible way to resolve the alleged dream/reality ambiguity in the film:

> The supposition that this whole central episode is but a dream is supported by a number of circumstances: by the many references to sleep; by the irrational, dreamlike actions that occur; and, more conclusively, by Tarkovsky's use of a differentiating colour code. The entire central nocturnal section of the film, from the time Alexander goes out into the garden to seek Little Man and finds Maria and the model house, to the time he wakes on the couch in the morning, is cast in the form of a dream and is photographed in darkly lit sequences virtually devoid of colour. The everyday waking reality of the beginning and end is painted in the pale, natural colours of a northern summer, framing the interior world of the dream.
>
> (Green 1987, 118)[18]

The problem with Green's argument is not that this "whole central episode" cannot plausibly be understood as a dream. Such an interpretation might be entirely apt, and Green certainly provides some reasons in its favor. The problem, rather, is that Green presents his reading as the only viable one, thereby ruling out the possibility that certain parts of the film's "nocturnal section" can also be understood as taking place while Alexander is fully awake. What Green misses, or chooses to ignore, is that reasons could be given for this interpretation, too. To take just one example, despite the changing color code, several of the scenes occurring within the "central episode" do not exhibit a typically dream-like logic. On the contrary, they depict extended conversations that people

136 *The Voice of Truth*

would normally engage in when fully awake and that must be considered distinctly atypical of most dreams. Moreover, these scenes contrast sharply with what are clearly represented as more or less delirious dream-visions, such as Alexander's walk through the deserted park or the shot of Marta chasing roosters down a long corridor. Even more problematic is that some of these dream-visions are shot in black and white while others are shot in color, which means that Green's appeal to the color code as a conclusive means of differentiating between dream and reality does not hold up. If the color code is made the principal criterion for distinguishing between dream and reality, the dream sequences in color (even if "darkly lit") could just as well be understood as belonging to the latter, since they are equally close in their color scheme to the beginning and the end of the film as they are to the black-and-white sequences that more unambiguously denote dreams or visions.

The point here is that there are no decisive reasons that can be invoked to finally settle the dream/reality ambiguity at the heart of *The Sacrifice*; the film is obviously designed so that it can be construed in both ways (the double injury on Alexander's leg is one example among several of how this ambiguity is achieved). As Tarkovsky himself acknowledged in an oft-quoted paragraph, the impossibility of determining what is actually going on in the film offers the viewer considerable latitude to interpret it in accordance with his or her own religious and metaphysical inclinations:

> I naturally have my own views on the film but I think that the person who sees it will be able to interpret the events it portrays and make up his own mind both about the various threads that run through it, and about its contradictions. . . . It may be that some religious people will see in [Alexander's] actions following the prayer God's answer to the question put by man: "What must be done to avert nuclear disaster?" – namely, turn to God. It may be that some who have a heightened sense of the supernatural will see the meeting with the witch Maria as the central scene which explains all that happens subsequently. There will doubtless be others for whom all the events of the film are merely the fruits of a sick imagination – since no nuclear war is actually happening.
>
> (Tarkovsky 1986, 224)

The interpretive diversity encouraged by *The Sacrifice*'s ambiguous and labyrinthine narrative constitution has important consequences for the approach developed in this chapter. It implies that my narrative interpretation does not have to rest on the claim that in the final analysis Green's understanding of the film is incorrect; it is enough to show that the alternative is viable. So, let me develop this alternative in some more detail. I will focus here on the section that begins with Otto telling Alexander that he must go and spend the night with Maria and ends with the sequence

The Voice of Truth   137

that most writers identify as definitely ending the dream, namely where Alexander wakes up on his couch and exclaims the word "Mama." This section can be understood as consisting of two consecutive parts that contrast radically with each other in terms of how well they accord with the logic of dreams as typically experienced and recounted in everyday life (and also, I believe, in how well they accord with the way dreams are often rendered in film). The first, and longest, part encompasses three successive scenes: Alexander and Otto's tête-à-tête in Alexander's studio, Alexander's bike ride to Maria's home and the encounter between Alexander and Maria. A distinctive feature of this first part consists of the lengthy verbal exchanges between Alexander and Otto and between Alexander and Maria. The comprehensive and detailed character of these exchanges is distinctly unlike the way verbal exchanges, to the extent that they exist at all, are typically represented in dreams. In other words, there is a level of continuity in the dialogue that corresponds to how we would converse with each other in a fully awake state. This continuity is also reflected on a broader level in the way the three scenes are woven into an extended unified sequence, again exhibiting a level of coherence that is seldom found in dreams. In sharp contrast to this, the second part of the section consists, as described earlier, of several brief segments, each of which conveys a distinctly dream-like atmosphere: a view of the debris-littered street (now crowded with people); Alexander and Maria (dressed in Adelaide's clothes and with Adelaide's coiffure) resting under a tree; a close-up of the Virgin Mary and the infant Christ in Leonardo's *Adoration*; and the shot of the naked Marta chasing roosters. The contrast to the preceding three scenes becomes still more pronounced with the sound of Alexander's desperate groaning and the presence of Adelaide's comforting voice on the soundtrack, as she tells Alexander that "everything will be fine." At the same time, Adelaide herself appears in the last segment as the camera tracks right from the corridor with the naked Marta to the studio where Alexander wakes up, her movements thus signaling the transition between dream and reality.

Between the two parts of this section we can identify another transitory sequence that does not so much mark a distinction between dream and reality as display the decisive moment when the spiritual emptiness and confusion of everyday existence turns into an encounter with the true miracle of life: the transformative power of love. I am referring to the shot where Alexander and Maria are seen levitating over Maria's bed. As in *Solaris* and *Mirror*, levitation is here closely connected with deeply felt love, but it can also be interpreted as an allegory for the cataclysmic forces unleashed when we unconditionally devote ourselves to another person, forces that in an instant can change our lives and uproot our taken-for-granted everyday existence. Thus understood, the sequence should not necessarily be viewed as the point where Alexander falls asleep. Instead, and in order to make sense of the fact that Alexander is subsequently

138 *The Voice of Truth*

seen waking up on the couch in his studio, we can postulate that there is actually an unaccounted-for gap in time at this point in the narrative. It is not inconceivable that, after sleeping with Maria, Alexander returns home on his bike, climbs up the ladder and falls asleep on the sofa.[19]

The previously mentioned considerations could be developed into a broader discussion that would take the whole film into account, and further reasons could be given in support of an approach that views some of the film's central scenes as taking place while the characters are fully awake. But it lies in the nature of things that a completely convincing and consistently coherent account of this film can hardly be achieved. In Nariman Skakov's words, "the 'real' linear succession of events becomes impossible to reinstate" (Skakov 2012, 205). However, this is equally true with respect to the alternative "it-was-all-a-dream" version. Both perspectives are destined to contain lacunae and inconsistencies; neither of them will achieve optimal coherence. Thomas Redwood is surely right when he states that "no single *fabula* . . . will find absolute validation in the film's narrative material" (Redwood 2010, 235; emphasis in original). Similarly, Astrid Söderbergh Widding writes that *The Sacrifice* "is constructed as 'neither-nor': it opens for at least two possible interpretations, and at the same time seems to exclude both as the complete explanation" (Söderbergh Widding 2006, 164). But it is precisely the fact that neither alternative can claim more validity than the other that makes it possible to argue that each of them constitutes a legitimate way to construe the film. The central ambiguity and the "chaotic" narrative composition cannot be finally resolved. However, in the light of this insight, tolerable but incomplete accounts can be given on which more specific interpretations of the film can be built.

I therefore must conclude this chapter with the admission that, with the herding calls in focus, I have developed a narrative interpretation of *The Sacrifice* that relies on a perspectivation of the film's dream/reality ambiguity that can never be made fully consistent. But again, given that this perspective is as good as any other, and on the assumption that a hermeneutic enterprise like the one carried out here may afford new insights into the film and ways of experiencing it, the narrative interpretation presented may claim some plausibility.

Notes

1. Throughout *Sculpting in Time*, when Tarkovsky speaks about the filmmaker, the artist, or more generally about spiritual self-realization, he consistently uses masculine pronouns like "he," "his" and "him." It is obvious that he views such occupations and aims as primarily a male concern (cf. Brezna 2006, 107–116). To what extent this view is also reflected in the way the translated version of *Sculpting in Time* uses expressions like "man" and "modern man" can be discussed.
2. A much-debated question in the literature concerns the extent to which the film should be understood as representing Alexander's (or someone else's) dream. I return to this question in the last section of this chapter.

The Voice of Truth 139

3. In the Swedish encyclopedia *Nationalencyklopedin*, the verb "kula" is defined as "locka på kor med sjungande röst" ("call cows with a singing voice"). See "kulning," *NE*. URL: www.ne.se/uppslagsverk/encyklopedi/lång/kulning (accessed 2019-04-12).

4. Björn Hellström and Nicolas Rémy write that *kulning*, as a song technique, "originates from the valleys in the middle of Sweden" and that it "was developed by local women calling their cattle." They continue: "The very high and intensive voice is strongly connected to the reverberating time that exists in the valleys, and the technique doesn't work in the steppe or in the desert. The physical place – the valleys with their intrinsic acoustics – is a prerequisite for the music. This mediaeval song technique was developed in symbiosis with the context of place and from the beginning 'kulning' only had a functional purpose, but over the generations the women developed this song technique and today the musical expression is in focus rather than the function" (Hellström and Rémy 1999, 23).

5. I will use the word "herdswoman" throughout this chapter, since the word "shepherd" (which is the word usually used in the literature on *The Sacrifice*) specifically refers to people who herd sheep.

6. Roberto Calabretto reports a memory of Eduard Artemiev in which the composer recollects Tarkovsky as having said the following about Bach's music: "I know nothing higher than his music. . . . His music gives an immediate impulse to your soul and you feel it" ["Non conosco niente di piú alto della sua musica. . . . La sua musica dà un impluso immediate alla tua anima e tu lo senti"]. Continuing, Calabretto says that with these and other statements by Tarkovsky, "not only is Bach's music constituted as an expression of perfection and universality, but also comes to be held up as a metaphor for the divine order" ["non solo, Bach si configura come espressione della perfezione e dell'universalità, ma viene anche additato come metafora dell'ordine divino"] (Calabretto 2010b, 7; my translation).

7. For a penetrating discussion of Leonardo's painting and its importance for the film's narrative and thematic development, see Skakov (2012, 195–199). See also Lövgren (2010, 10–12, 14–21).

8. The expression "Little Man" occurs, as far as I can tell, only once in the film, namely during the hysterical breakdown of Alexander's wife Adelaide after the outbreak of nuclear war has been announced on the TV. Apart from this occasion, the boy is consistently called "gossen" by the characters, a word that most readily translates as "the boy" in English.

9. As Nariman Skakov (2012, 201) points out, "Hamlet's '[w]ords, words, words' is one of the most famous references to the word as a profane and disingenuous means of communication."

10. Another possibility would be to say that they function as diegetic music and that Alexander's inattentiveness is simply due to the fact that he is so used to them. But this assumption becomes less plausible when we consider Alexander and Otto's reaction of bewilderment upon hearing the calls later in the film.

11. The scene, like the black-and-white dream sequence later in the film (see later in this chapter), was shot at Tunnelgatan in central Stockholm (cf. Lövgren 2010, 10).

12. Maya Turovskaya advances a similar view when she writes that Otto is "a character from the 'boundary' world," further noting that his "'foreignness' is expressed in a tiny detail of his clothing: he is wearing black sandals and shining-white socks which make a striking intrusion on the grey-green harmony of everything else in the frame" (Turovskaya 1989, 143). In the same vein, Magnus Bergh, in a published conversation with Birgit Munkhammar,

140 *The Voice of Truth*

describes Otto as an "occult figure that, at least when appearing in the evening or at night, is visible only to Alexander" ["en ockult figur, som åtminstone i sitt uppdykande under kvällen eller natten bara är synlig för Alexander"]. (Bergh and Munkhammar 1986, 197; my translation).

13. The second act of sacrifice is the burning down of the family house at the end of the film. Johnson and Petrie are very critical in their assessment of the two sacrificial acts, writing that "an unexplained double sacrifice is created when Alexander *both* sleeps with the witch as encouraged by . . . the postman Otto, *and* burns down his house and becomes mute, thus fulfilling his vow to God. This results in a frustrating absence of thematic and philosophical coherence that ultimately damages the film" (Johnson and Petrie 1994, 172). As John A. Riley notes, Johnson and Petrie's critique rests on the observation that the script of *The Sacrifice* "is an amalgamation of two scripts," incorporating "elements of an earlier script called *The Witch* that told the story of a man cured of illness through sexual congress with a magical woman." Riley, however, thinks that Johnson and Petrie's critique constitutes a too literal reading of the film: "Johnson and Petrie attempt to impose a single, straight line onto Tarkovsky's narrative, against his forking conception of time. In fact, the merging of the two scripts means that the entire film is structured along the lines of a double exposure" (Riley 2012, 12–13).

14. Bird (2008, 219) proposes a reading of the herding call's symbolic function that is very similar to Shpinitskaya's, stating that "Maria's mysteriousness can be attributed in part to her musical motif, the Swedish folk singing that appears in the grove and in Alexander's dreams" (Bird 2008, 219–220). In contrast, Green settles for a more tentative approach, writing that the herdswoman's voice "is a cry of warning or exhortation, perhaps the voice of God or the silent call of Little Man, so faint and fleeting, however, that one can never be entirely sure it is any more than a shepherd calling to his [*sic*] flock in the night" (Green 1993, 129).

15. This scene refers back to the very beginning of the film where Alexander had told his son the story of a young monk, Ioann Kolov, who, at the request of his master, climbed a mountain to water a dead tree. Kolov did this every morning for three years before the miracle finally happened and the tree blossomed.

16. For a similar conclusion, see Robinson (2006, 522–523).

17. There has also been some discussion of who is actually doing the dreaming in the film. Peter Green, for example, considers the possibility that the dream could be ascribed to Alexander's son (see Green 1987, 118; see also Redwood 2010, 235).

18. Skakov advances what appears to be a similar view when he writes: "The temporal point when Alexander encounters the miniature replica of the house is extremely important, since from this point on the distinction between reality and illusion is blurred. It may even be suggested that this is the moment at which the protagonist starts to dream" (Skakov 2012, 203; see also Turovskaya 1989, 145; Lövgren 2010, 15). At the same time, Skakov is careful not to push this suggestion too far, emphasizing that "the principal question of whether the nuclear war and subsequent visit to the 'witch' took place or not cannot be resolved in definite terms" (Skakov 2012, 204).

19. Bhaskar Sarkar views the sequence differently, reaching the conclusion that Alexander's visit to Maria "may have been part of a dream" (Sarkar 2008, 254).

7 Music, Meaning and Troubled Utopias in Tarkovsky's Cinema

In a famous radio speech from 2004, Ingmar Bergman invited the audience to reflect on what he regarded as the two most fundamental questions about music: where does music come from, and why is it that human beings, but not other living creatures, produce it? These are indeed very basic questions – even though the first might appear somewhat nebulous, and the assumption behind the second can be questioned – and the response was immediate and overwhelming. Well over a hundred emails and letters were sent to the Swedish Radio, and to Bergman personally, from listeners all around Sweden. This led to a follow-up production – "Letters to Bergman" – in which some of the correspondents were asked to record and send in their answers, which were then broadcast. In the original talk, Bergman's own tentative answer was that music is a gift that we humans have received in order to imagine worlds outside the one we live in.[1] In Bergman's musical universe, the most precious gift of all was the body of works given to us by classical composers like Mozart, Beethoven and Schubert. But towering above them all was German master of counterpoint Johann Sebastian Bach. For Bergman, Bach's music remains unsurpassed in its existential authenticity and its capacity to provide relief from the spiritual desolation afflicting many people in the modern age:

> As far as religion is concerned, we live in a time of reconsideration. Bach speaks directly to the religious feelings missing today in many people; he gives us the profound consolidation and quiet that previous generations gained through ritual. Bach supplies a lucid reflection of otherworldliness, a sense of eternity that no church can offer today.
>
> (quoted in Luko 2015, 66)

As several writers have pointed out, Bergman's veneration for classical music, and Bach's music in particular, is reflected in many of his films.[2] In her 2011 essay "An Unrequited Love of Music," Charlotte Renaud provides a complete list of musical quotations from Bergman's cinematic

142   *Music, Meaning and Troubled Utopias*

oeuvre. According to Renaud, Bergman used music from the classical musical canon in no less than 27 of his films, of which 14 feature music by Bach.[3] This sheer number of musical quotations reveals Bergman's responsiveness to and affection for classical music, a deep and near-religious respect for the art form that he talked about on a number of occasions, for example when he claimed that he loved music "too much to use it as a subordinate factor" in film (Bergman quoted in Luko 2015, 67).

Tarkovsky, too, was a lover of classical music, and judging from several of the quotations in the previous chapters, it seems safe to say that his reverence for Bach was every bit as strong as that of Bergman. Perhaps unlike Bergman, however, Tarkovsky imagined an ideal form of cinema where the proper use of sound would make music superfluous. As Tarkovsky saw it, the problematic status of music in cinema had to do with the close relationship between the two art forms:

> It may be that in order to make the cinematic image sound authentically, in its full diapason, music has to be abandoned. For strictly speaking the world as transformed by cinema and the world as transformed by music are parallel, and conflict with each other. Properly organised in a film, the resonant world is musical in its essence – and that is the true music of cinema.
>
> (Tarkovsky 1986, 159)

In a sense, then, cinema – or the true form of cinema – already is music.[4] In such a "musically organized" cinema, music becomes a redundant phenomenon; in a cinematic world that is already musical "in its essence," there is no need for music, classical or otherwise. Nevertheless, Tarkovsky readily admitted that music "has always had a rightful place in my films" and that it "has been important and precious" (Tarkovsky 1986, 159). Like Robert Bresson, Tarkovsky was highly "sensitive to music's unique power to transform the formal and thematic moments in a film" (Gariff 2012, 5), believing that the best way to incorporate music into film was to use it as a refrain so that it could open up "the possibility of a *new*, transfigured impression of the same material," the implications of which idea I will explore later in this chapter. With specific regard to electronic music, Tarkovsky considered it to have "enormously rich possibilities for cinema"; provided it was "purged of its 'chemical origins'," it had an extraordinary capacity to "accurately produce precise states of mind, the sounds of a person's interior world" (Tarkovsky 1986, 162). And this, of course, is how it is used, at least partly, in *Mirror*. However, while electronic music can easily be combined with other sounds in a film, the use of instrumental classical music will always "involve some measure of compromise," partly because of its status as an autonomous art form but also, and relatedly, because of its character as pre-existing "illustrative" music (Tarkovsky 1986, 162–163). Despite this element of compromise,

Music, Meaning and Troubled Utopias   143

Tarkovsky evidently believed that classical music was of great importance to his cinema, given the fact that he used it in all of his last five films.

In light of Tarkovsky's somewhat ambivalent approach to the question of music's status in cinema, how should we understand the presence of music in his films? What role does music play in them? How is it involved in the construction of meaning? How should we assess its relation to the complex and occasionally indeterminate nature of the films' fictional realities? And how does music participate in the construction of the ethical, existential and philosophical themes running through the films? In this last chapter, I try to answer these questions by summarizing, discussing and further developing the conclusions and insights reached in the previous chapters. The next section focuses on music's diegetic status in Tarkovsky's cinema, an issue that to a greater or lesser extent has been taken up in all the chapters (with the exception of the one on *Stalker*). Picking up the thread from Chapter 2, where I examined possible ways of understanding the diegetic status of the Bach chorale prelude in *Solaris*, I discuss the concepts of interpretive multiplicity and hermeneutic pliability in relation to the other films, and ask to what extent these concepts are relevant for assessing the music's diegetic status in these films. The following section then concentrates on questions of music and representation. I begin by surveying what I consider to be the main representational functions of classical, electronic and traditional music, after which I turn my attention to the different types of musical dichotomies and syntheses that can be found throughout Tarkovsky's cinema. The final section opens up a broader discussion of how the music in Tarkovsky's films relates to his philosophical views on art, his decidedly autonomist conception of Western art music and, most importantly, what can be described as a troubled utopianism that to a greater or lesser extent is present in all his last five films. This is a utopianism that combines an unremitting pursuit of spiritual integrity and perfection with more or less subtly expressed misgivings as to whether this goal can ever be attained.

Music, Interpretation and the Tarkovskian Diegesis

Tarkovsky's brief discussion of music in *Sculpting in Time* does not raise the question of music's relation to the diegesis in his films. The closest we come to a consideration of this kind is his remark (which I quoted in Chapter 3) on music's role and significance in *Mirror*. Tarkovsky claims that in the film "music is often introduced as part of the material of life, of the author's spiritual experience, and thus as a vital element in the world of the film's lyrical hero" (Tarkovsky 1986, 158). It is not immediately clear which kind of music Tarkovsky is talking about here. Is he referring to the classical music in the film or to Artemiev's electronic score, or perhaps to both? Whatever the answer, to the extent that this quote can be said to have any bearing on the question of music's diegetic status in

144 *Music, Meaning and Troubled Utopias*

the film, it can be interpreted as suggesting at least two alternatives. If the music is understood as forming part of the author's (that is, Tarkovsky's) spiritual experience, and hence should be regarded as an expression of this experience, the implication seems to be that it constitutes a form of extra- or nondiegetic music. In other words, rather than belonging to the film's diegetic universe, it constitutes "a direct reflection of authorial stance or personality" (Levinson 2004, 510). On the other hand, if the music is conceived of as a "vital element in the world of the film's lyrical hero," it more readily translates as some kind of diegetic music. With his use of the adverb "thus," Tarkovsky in fact seems to conflate the two possibilities by unhelpfully stating a causal or inferential connection between them. But from the fact that the music is part of the author Tarkovsky's spiritual experience, it does not follow that it must also be an element in the world of the film's "lyrical hero" (that is, Alexei).

However, instead of reproaching Tarkovsky for his lack of clarity and analytical stringency, we should perhaps take the absence of considerations about music's diegetic status as an indication that such considerations are, at best, of marginal relevance for understanding the role and significance of music in his films. Maybe it does not matter much whether Purcell's music in *Mirror* or the Russian folk song in *Nostalghia* are categorized as diegetic, metadiegetic or nondiegetic, or some variant of these. An orthodox disciple of Tarkovsky would probably claim that it is more important to experience and develop a sensitivity for the music's emotional impact insofar as it forms part of the aesthetic totality of each film. And even if we wish to maintain that giving an adequate account of the music's representational and "symbolic" significance is a viable undertaking, this could very well be realized without recourse to questions about its diegetic status. One could even argue that an approach that is excessively framed in terms of music's diegetic status is detrimental to a proper understanding of Tarkovsky's cinema, since it risks excluding other ways of experiencing and comprehending his films (and music's role in them) that do not rely on such considerations.

I certainly do not wish to rule out the possibility and potential relevance of analyses that approach music's place in Tarkovsky's cinema without giving any special attention to its diegetic status. Nevertheless, such considerations seem to me to be central, or at the very least constitute a relevant and rewarding framework, in assessing and understanding music's role and significance in Tarkovsky's films. With the exception of my analysis of *Stalker*, which proceeded by and large without recourse to claims about the music's diegetic status, all the preceding chapters have to varying degrees relied on such claims, and in some of my readings the music's diegetic status and its representational meaning have been inextricably entangled (perhaps most so in my account of the herding calls in *The Sacrifice*). But the critical "usefulness" of discussions about music's diegetic status is only one of the things that make such discussions interesting and

Music, Meaning and Troubled Utopias   145

worthwhile. There is also the intriguing question of the hermeneutic pliability of music in Tarkovsky's cinema, its potential diegetic multifariousness. The scope of this multifariousness is directly related to the more or less porous and uncertain nature of the diegetic realities in the different films, that is, how these realities are constituted and how much latitude the spectator-critic has in defining and redefining them (and, as a consequence, the diegetic status of the music). In this section, I will return to the discussion from Chapter 2 and consider the extent to which music in Tarkovsky's cinema can be said to be hermeneutically pliable with regard to its diegetic status. What are the possibilities and limitations of such pliability? As we shall see, the answer to this question will vary depending on which film we are discussing, and not all the films may afford the same degree of pliability that we detected in *Solaris*. But the answer will also depend on the critical relevance and plausibility of the interpretive approaches, of which claims about the music's diegetic status form an integral part. Before venturing into a discussion of these questions, however, I need to expand a bit upon the conception of diegesis that I have been assuming throughout this book (briefly described in Chapter 1) and how this relates to the specific nature of the Tarkovskian diegesis.

Mainstream and Tarkovskian Diegeses

The distinction between diegetic and nondiegetic music, though not universally accepted, is central to much film music analysis. Regarding the concept of diegesis itself, the film-musicological discussion (paralleling the discussion in other scholarly fields) has revolved around both the definition and the history of the concept.[5] As stated in Chapter 1, the definition I have been assuming throughout this book is best captured by Claudia Gorbman's description of diegesis as "the *narratively implied spatiotemporal world of the actions and characters*" (Gorbman 1987, 21; emphasis in original). In this definition, derived from French philosopher and film theorist Étienne Souriau,[6] the diegesis of a film should be distinguished not only from the film's narration, but also from its narrative. The diegesis is the story world represented by the film's discourse; it is the fictional reality within which the narrative takes place. Thus, it can be equated neither with the narration nor with the narrative itself (cf. Heldt 2013, 50; especially footnote 30; see also Rosar 2009, 110). Even though this understanding of diegesis is not without its problems (see, for example, Bunia 2010), it has become the standard definition within film and film music scholarship. As David Bordwell stated over three decades ago, the term diegesis "has come to be the accepted term for the fictional world of the story" (Bordwell 1985, 16).

However, the diegesis thus understood is not an objectively existing thing. The fictional worlds of films differ from our actual world in that they rely for their existence on the cognitive and imaginative activity of

146 *Music, Meaning and Troubled Utopias*

the perceiver.[7] As Guido Heldt writes: "That the diegesis . . . is constructed by the viewer, that it only takes place in her or his mind, is a basic fact of narrative fiction" (Heldt 2013, 51). Heldt proceeds to demonstrate that this constructivist notion is advocated by prominent film scholars such as David Bordwell, Edward Branigan and Christian Metz. More specifically, Heldt, adhering to a Bordwellian perspective, describes the diegesis as a mental construct accomplished by the spectator "on the basis of three sources of knowledge": the cues that the film itself provides; the spectator's knowledge of narration in general and filmic narration in particular; and the accumulated experience and knowledge of how our actual world works (Heldt 2013, 51). I believe this to be a basically correct analysis of diegesis construction, a process that is sometimes denoted by the term *diegetization*.[8] It should be noted, however, that the construction of a diegesis, even if subjective in the sense that it must be regarded as a mental operation going on in the spectator's mind, is neither an ad hoc nor a radically "creational" procedure. As Heldt remarks, "while the construction of the diegesis is subjective, it is not arbitrary, but guided by the organization of the film text," which means that "most films cue us to construct diegeses that are more or less coherent most of the time" (Heldt 2013, 52, 54). Especially in classical narrative cinema, the constitution of a film's diegesis is not something the spectator can freely decide upon, but is rather something determined by the information provided by the film's representation in conjunction with the conventions of storytelling and the assumption that filmic fictional worlds should behave more or less in accordance with the perceived make-up of our actual world. It might thus be more accurate to speak of reconstruction rather than construction, and although it seems clearly inaccurate to posit an objectively existing diegesis in the strong realist sense of the word – that is, assuming a realist ontology according to which fictional worlds predate and exist independently of our mental operations – a film's diegesis is often objective in the sense that it can be intersubjectively shared and discussed. That the diegesis is a mental construct does not imply that the spectator has complete freedom to create it according to his or her own imagination. In classical narrative cinema, at least, the spectator is typically cued to (re)construct a very specific diegesis for a film, one that is shared with and can be communicated to other viewers.[9] In other words, in mainstream cinema there is most often an intersubjective consensus as to what constitutes the diegesis of a particular film. This seems to be much less true, however, for art cinema in general and Tarkovsky's cinema in particular.

Even though Bordwell's seminal article on art cinema[10] has been much criticized, including by Bordwell himself (see Bordwell 2007, 158–169), it is striking how Tarkovsky's films display many of the traits enumerated by Bordwell in his analysis of art cinema as a distinct mode of film practice. Whether intentionally or not, Tarkovsky's cinema "defines itself

Music, Meaning and Troubled Utopias   147

explicitly against the classical narrative mode, and especially against the cause-effect linkage of events"; it is "realistic" in the sense that it aspires to show us "real problems (contemporary 'alienation', 'lack of communication', etc.)"; it is clearly concerned with "the art film's thematic of *la condition humaine*," in that it "attempts to pronounce judgements on 'modern life' as a whole"; it is full of characters that "tell one another stories: autobiographical events (especially from childhood), fantasies, and dreams"; each film, at least to some extent, "offers itself as a chapter in an *oeuvre*," for example by containing "references to previous films by the director"; several of the films favor an "arbitrary ending"; and so on (Bordwell 2007, 152–156). To this can be added the "familiar 'illusion-reality' dichotomy of the art cinema" (Bordwell 2007, 154), which in Tarkovsky's case has the consequence that the impression of a coherent fictional world – a "stable quasi-space," to use Heldt's expression (Heldt 2013, 57) – is often undermined in favor of an ambiguous, multilayered or even incoherent diegetic reality. (As the quote from Bordwell implies, this is of course not exclusive to Tarkovsky's films.) In *Solaris*, as we saw in Chapter 2, the impossibility of determining the precise nature of the narrative world results from a subjunctive narrative that seems to afford two mutually exclusive interpretations of the film: (1) an "external" interpretation according to which Kelvin actually travels to the space station, where he increasingly is affected by the mysterious powers of the planet Solaris; and (2) an "internal" interpretation whereby everything that happens from the moment we see Kelvin traveling into space can plausibly be viewed as "materializations of mental or subconscious states" (Green 1993, 74). In *The Sacrifice*, similarly, the long central section of the film can be understood as *either* representing happenings that actually took place during the night *or* as depicting a course of events unfolding only in Alexander's or someone else's dream. Again, the nature of the narrative world will be different depending on which perspective one is entertaining. As for *Mirror*, the diegetic reality can perhaps best be described as disjointed. While many writers, including Tarkovsky himself, equate the film's diegesis with the dreams and fantasies of the absent narrator (even though the issue is rarely stated in terms of diegesis), most of them also note that several scenes cannot be accounted for within this approach. In a sense, the film seems to turn the conventions of classical narrative cinema on its head. Whereas in narrative cinema metadiegetic sequences and internal focalizations (that is, focalizations through characters' subjective points of view) are typically "embedded in a framework of objective narration" (Bordwell and Thompson 2010, 95), in *Mirror* such "objective" scenes (e.g. Ignat's meeting with the mysterious woman) constitute an exception that seems to break the narrative coherence of a fundamentally focalized narration. Although the diegesis of *Mirror* can accordingly be described as disjointed rather than ambiguous, there are nevertheless a number of sequences that are open to different diegetic

148 *Music, Meaning and Troubled Utopias*

construals. The documentary sequences in particular can be interpreted either as belonging to the film's primary diegesis (that is, as issuing from the interior perspective of the film's narrator) or, alternatively, as the agonizing reflections of a filmind or an extradiegetic implied filmmaker. One of these sequences, the crossing of Lake Sivash, can even be conceived of as a metadiegetic vision of one of the characters appearing in the film, namely the orphaned boy Asafiev.

Compared to *Solaris*, *Mirror* and *The Sacrifice*, the films *Stalker* and *Nostalghia* may display somewhat more stable diegetic worlds. In *Nostalghia*, the distinction between Andrei's waking states and his dreams or reveries may be reasonably clear, since during most of the film the two dimensions are kept fairly distinct. Yet the film is so intensely preoccupied with Andrei's interior life that the boundary between outer and inner reality seems constantly to be breaking down. Thus, even though on a manifest level there is an external diegetic reality in which Andrei moves around (the wintery Tuscan landscape), the appearance of this external reality is so saturated by Andrei's woeful state of mind that we increasingly begin to question its "realness." Still, *Nostalghia* does not exhibit the same degree of ambiguity between external and internal reality as *Solaris* and *The Sacrifice*. Nor does it display the kind of disjointed diegesis that I argued characterizes *Mirror*. Something similar is true of *Stalker*, where the Zone can be understood as a genuinely alien and mysterious space where the laws of our natural world do not apply. Alternatively, its miraculous powers can be understood simply as an invention of the Stalker's imagination. Furthermore, a multiplicity of interpretations could be, and have been, given as to what the Zone represents or symbolizes (cf. Žižek 1999, 227). However, what basically constitutes the diegesis of *Stalker* may not be open to interpretation to the same extent as in several of the other films. For example, in contrast to *Solaris* and *The Sacrifice*, no one has suggested that the three men's journey into the Zone might be something that actually did not take place, but should rather be understood as a reverie, vision or dream on the part of the Stalker. Regardless of how we conceive of the Zone in terms of its otherness and its symbolic or representational meaning, it seems that we are bound to admit that it exists as an external diegetic reality in the film. In this respect, *Stalker* may be a less complex film than the others discussed in this book.

To varying degrees, then, the diegeses of Tarkovsky's last five films display a level of indeterminacy that invites spectatorial diegetic constructions of a more radical kind than is possible in classical narrative cinema. Put differently, the spectator's construction of the diegesis in Tarkovsky's cinema is more akin to a genuine interpretive act than the spectatorial reconstruction of the diegesis in mainstream cinema, which to a much larger extent is dictated by conventionalized narrative cuing as well as conventions of genre and storytelling. It follows from this that the "narratively implied" element of Gorbman's definition, though certainly not

Music, Meaning and Troubled Utopias   149

expendable, is of comparatively less importance for an account of dieg-esis construction in Tarkovsky's cinema. But more importantly, this mal-leable nature of the Tarkovskian diegesis is an important prerequisite, if not a necessary condition, for the hermeneutic pliability of music's diegetic status in Tarkovsky's films. More specifically, we can say that a particular construal of the music's diegetic status in a film is justified to the extent that it can convincingly be integrated into an interpretation of the film that in turn is congruent with a plausible construal of the film's diegesis. Hermeneutic pliability occurs in situations where two or more construals of the music's diegetic status can be thus justified. But what, more exactly, are the possibilities and limits of such hermeneu-tic pliability in Tarkovsky's films? What interpretive constructions of the music's diegetic status are credible, and what concepts can plausibly by applied? And are there cases where an allegedly plausible understand-ing of music's diegetic status may nevertheless be critically irrelevant or uninteresting? I now turn to a discussion of these questions.

Diegetic Status and Multiple Interpretability: The Possibilities and Limits of Hermeneutic Pliability

In the preceding chapters, I have employed a plurality of concepts in describing the diegetic status of music in the films. The concepts applied have crucially been what can be called cine-ontologically plausible; that is, the diegetic status they ascribe to the music can be given a reasonable justification within the films considered as larger symbolic, phenomeno-logical and aesthetic totalities comprising both diegetic and nondiegetic levels (cf. Yacavone 2012). Also, and even more importantly, the concepts have in each instance been chosen because of their critical effectiveness, which is to say for their utility in advancing the interpretation I have wished to develop. The phenomenon of hermeneutic pliability was of course most explicitly examined in the chapter on *Solaris*, but also to some extent in my analysis of *Nostalghia*, where I tried to show that Ver-di's *Requiem* could be construed both as a metadiegetic reverie issuing from Andrei's subjective point of view and as a bemoaning by the film-ind (Frampton 2006) of the fates of Andrei and Domenico. But to what extent is this kind of hermeneutic pliability an option in the other films?

The analysis of the Bach chorale prelude in Chapter 2 showed that the music's diegetic status may change in relation to the interpretive perspective or context in which it is embedded. However, it also showed that specifications of music's diegetic status can play a significant role in the development of pertinent critical interpretations of Tarkovsky's films. In themselves, however, construals of the diegetic status of a particular instance of music might seem to be of marginal relevance for gaining a deeper understanding of Tarkovsky's films. If we wish to go beyond a purely taxonomic approach, such construals must have critical import;

150 *Music, Meaning and Troubled Utopias*

they must further new perspectives on, new understandings of and new ways of experiencing the films. Beyond the admittedly rather loose criterion of cine-ontological plausibility mentioned previously, an acceptable concept application on the critic's part must therefore fulfill the following three requirements: (1) it must be compatible with basic "describable features" (Margolis 1992, 48) of the given film in question; (2) it must be diegetically plausible, which is to say that it must convincingly position the music in relation to a diegesis, the construction of which is itself plausible; and (3) it must have critical relevance as well as critical force; that is, it must be an integral part of an interpretation or interpretive perspective that engages with existing and relevant interpretive canons while at the same time contributing to a new and apposite way of understanding and experiencing the film.[11] I believe that the concepts I have employed in my analyses of the various films – diegetic, nondiegetic, metadiegetic, implied filmmaker, focalization, filmind, transcendental diegetic music, etc. – have in each instance satisfied these criteria. In the chapters on *Mirror, Stalker* and *The Sacrifice*, I did not, however, consider alternative accounts of music's diegetic status. (Indeed, in *Stalker*, as I noted earlier, I proceeded almost entirely without recourse to such accounts.) To what extent are such alternative accounts possible? In order to keep my discussion within manageable limits I will focus on two musical "refrains" (to use Tarkovsky's term) that I believe could have been given alternative readings to the ones I pursued: Purcell's *The Indian Queen* in *Mirror* and the herding calls in *The Sacrifice*. However, I will also consider what I believe to be some very clear cases of implausible concept application with regard to the two cases, thus outlining the limits of hermeneutic pliability.

In my analysis of *Mirror*, I argued that Purcell's music, and the classical music more generally, can be understood as focalizing the interiority of the film's main character. Accordingly, this was not a focalization of the music itself; rather, the music intimated an interior state of mind, and hence it was the phenomenological quality, the "feel," of that state of mind that, via the music, was being focalized. Alexei is the "focalizing subject" (Buhler 2018, 189), experiencing a specific state of mind that is precisely captured by the emotional quality of the music, and so the music becomes integral to the very existence of that state of mind *as experienced* by Alexei. This way of placing the music within the phenomenological lifeworld of Alexei appeared to me both diegetically plausible and critically productive. But might there be other ways of positioning the music that are equally plausible and productive? I think there are. Toward the end of Chapter 3, I suggested that a credible way to make sense of the music accompanying the sequence of documentary footage that begins with the crossing of Lake Sivash is as a representation of the incomprehensibility of human destruction, articulated from the more abstract vantage point of the film itself. In a similar vein, we can reinterpret Purcell's music as issuing, not from Alexei's subjective point of view, but from the perspective of a thinking filmind. This would significantly change our conception and experience of Purcell's music and, as a consequence, the scenes in which it occurs. Instead of inserting ourselves into the young Alexei's point of view, we will now identify with the position of the empathizing filmind, experiencing the music more as a nondiegetic representation of Alexei's feelings than a musicalized outpouring of those feelings.[12] The situation here thus corresponds to the "double interpretation" of Verdi's music in *Nostalghia*. Moreover, in a further correspondence with *Nostalghia*, I think that the invocation of a filmind works better with regard to Purcell's music (and probably some of the other classical music in the film) than it does with regard to the electronic music that appears in the film's dream sequences. In those sequences, the music is so inextricably tied to the absent narrator's (that is, Alexei's) interior perspective that positing a thinking and experiencing filmind seems largely redundant.[13] In addition to tying Purcell's music to a filmind, however, there is yet another possible way to conceive of its source. This would definitively remove the music from the diegesis by understanding it as a reflection on or an assessment of the scene (and the film more broadly) by Tarkovsky himself. This would more radically relocate the music from an intra-diegetic position to the extra-fictional plane of the actual or implied filmmaker. Tarkovsky's somewhat abstruse statement about music's role and significance in *Mirror* might make this a plausible option, in that the music can now be understood as a direct communication of "the author's spiritual experience" (Tarkovsky 1986, 158) and, accordingly, as an expression of "the artist's *personal vision*" (Bordwell 2007, 154; emphasis in original).

Construing Purcell's music as an expression of a filmind or an implied filmmaker seems diegetically plausible, and there is, at least prima facie, no reason to doubt that either of these construals could be part of a productive and more fully developed reading of the film and its music. The conclusion we should not draw from this, however, is that any account of the music's diegetic status can in principle be made to work. Multiple interpretability is not the same thing as unlimited interpretive freedom. To demonstrate this, I will give two examples of what I regard as implausible concept application. The first should be obvious, and concerns the possibility of construing Purcell's music as diegetic music proper, that is, as music that has an objective existence in the film's represented reality and can be intersubjectively accessed by different characters. (One of the most unambiguous instances of what I here call diegetic music proper can be found in Francis Ford Coppola's *Apocalypse Now* (1979), in the scene where Lieutenant Kilgore attempts to demoralize the enemy soldiers by ordering that Wagner's *Ride of the Valkyries* should blare from the attacking helicopters' loudspeakers.) Any attempt to interpret Purcell's music in this way would fall on its own implausibility, and even if it could

152 *Music, Meaning and Troubled Utopias*

be so understood, it is hard indeed to see what critical relevance such an account would have. If anything, it would turn the music into a kind of ironic, even ridiculing, commentary on the young Alexei's feelings that would give the scene a strangely self-conscious and melodramatic quality completely at odds with the emotional tone of the film. The second example, though perhaps not as obvious, also constitutes an instance of what I would regard as implausible concept application. We could entertain the idea that Purcell's music is positioned in relation to the diegesis of *Mirror* in much the same way as I claimed the herding calls could be positioned in relation to the characters' empirical reality in *The Sacrifice*. In other words, we could claim that the music from *The Indian Queen* can be identified as transcendental diegetic music, and that we thus can view it as being part of an expanded diegesis while at the same time transcending the empirical reality of the film's characters. This, however, is not a reasonable suggestion, for transcendental diegetic music, as I have defined it, is music that, while not tied to a specific sound source like diegetic music proper, nevertheless has an objective presence within the diegesis of a film. Transcendental diegetic music denotes an objective spiritual presence in the diegetic reality and as such does not bear any special connection to a character within the film's diegesis. But this is decidedly not true of Purcell's music, which, even if we choose to understand it as an expression of a filmind or an implied filmmaker, is clearly *about* Alexei's interiority.[14]

The plausibility of conceptualizing the herding calls in *The Sacrifice* as transcendental diegetic music rested to a not insignificant degree on how this conception facilitated the wider interpretation developed in Chapter 6. Could the diegetic status of the herding calls be given an alternative reading? One way to do so would be to make sense of them from an entirely different interpretive framework; for example, by viewing the film as being about the ongoing psychic breakdown of the main character. In this reading, everything in the film would be about Alexander's interiority, and to the extent that it could be fleshed out convincingly we would understand the herding calls as a kind of metadiegetic or focalized music, not as transcendental diegetic music. An option that is perhaps closer at hand would yield the same result: if we accept Peter Green's claim (Green 1987, 118) that everything that takes place during the night should be understood as Alexander's dream, it makes sense to regard the herding calls as part of that dream, that is, as some kind of metadiegetic or internally focalized music (the final scene would probably constitute an exception here). Alternatively, one might proceed from a "mixed account," according to which the herding calls are sometimes metadiegetic (for example, in the visionary dream sequences) and sometimes plainly diegetic (for example, when Alexander and Otto hear them in Alexander's studio, during Alexander's bike ride to Maria and in the film's concluding scene), and from this one might seek to build

Music, Meaning and Troubled Utopias 153

a coherent and convincing interpretation of the film.[15] What does not, however, seems to be a plausible alternative is construing the herding calls as nondiegetic music in the more traditional sense. The herdswoman's voice seems too close to the diegetic world of the film, if not always to the empirical reality of the characters, for this to be a viable option. Also, it is not clear what the critical relevance of such a construal would be, that is, how understanding it as a nondiegetic sonic phenomenon could form part of a convincing interpretive examination of the film.

In conclusion, then, the notion of music's hermeneutic pliability in Tarkovsky's cinema is premised both on the indeterminate nature and resulting malleability of the diegeses in his films and on the possibility of shaping a diversity of interpretive accounts of these films. But the malleability of the Tarkovskian diegesis is not limitless, and some films seem to afford less leeway in this regard than others. Similarly, even if several plausible interpretive accounts are available, they are not inexhaustible. Conditioned on these premises, the diegetic status of music in Tarkovsky's cinema is both hermeneutically pliable and subject to limitations.

Representation, Dichotomies and Syntheses

Questions regarding diegetic status are but one of the issues pertinent to the role and significance of music in Tarkovsky's cinema. In the chapter on *Stalker*, as I noted earlier, such questions did not in fact play a central role in the interpretive argument. At the same time, both the sonic figure and the electronically manipulated main theme in *Stalker* were, perhaps more so than the music in the other films, ascribed an explicit symbolic function. Overall, however, the hermeneutic approach of this study has led me to claims about what music signifies and represents (or, more exactly, what it can conceivably be taken as signifying and representing) in all five films under scrutiny. This section summarizes and expands on the previous chapters' results regarding the representational meaning of music in Tarkovsky's films. It then proceeds to a more extensive discussion of two central aspects of Tarkovsky's handling of music in his films from *Solaris* onward, aspects that to varying degrees have been noticed in all the chapters: the presence of musical dichotomies and musical syntheses.

Classical Music

In his last five films, Tarkovsky uses three kinds of music: Western classical music, electronic music and "traditional music" from different parts of the world (Spain, Italy, Russia, Sweden, Japan, etc.).[16] While classical music is used in all these films, electronic music and electronically manipulated acoustic sounds appear in *Solaris*, *Mirror* and *Stalker*, and traditional music in *Mirror*, *Nostalghia* and *The Sacrifice*.

154   *Music, Meaning and Troubled Utopias*

One salient feature in Tarkovsky's handling of classical music from *Solaris* onward (with the exception of *Stalker*) is how he uses it to establish a musical frame by inserting it at the very beginning and end of his films, a practice that is most consistently applied in *The Sacrifice* and that has since been employed in films by other directors influenced by Tarkovsky, two recent examples being Lars von Trier's use of Handel's "Lascia ch'io pianga" and the prelude to Wagner's *Tristan und Isolde* in *Antichrist* (2009) and *Melancholia* (2011) respectively. This practice has led some writers to argue that classical music in Tarkovsky's cinema functions above all as a way of underlining the films' status as serious art (see Johnson and Petrie 1994, 57, 250; Mroz 2013, 124). In other words, the primary role of classical music, together with references to other art forms such as painting and poetry, is to differentiate "the text . . . in question from the texts produced by Hollywood" (Neale 2002, 104). While this may be one of the ways classical music functions in Tarkovsky's films, I do not think it is the most interesting. Much more significant is the role played by classical music in providing atmosphere and emotional depth to scenes and images. On a more general level, Tarkovsky's "use of classical music heightens affective responses, albeit not necessarily or only to characters and narrative situations, but to the cinematic process of imagining" (Mroz 2013, 123). Equally important, however, are the ways in which this music can be seen as establishing patterns of representation, symbolism and meaning within and across Tarkovsky's films, and how paying close attention to such patterns can contribute to a deepened understanding of the films. This, of course, has been one of the main concerns of the present book. Collecting the various observations and considerations about classical music in the previous chapters, I will here summarize what I consider to be the most significant representational functions of such music in Tarkovsky's cinema.

Discussions of Tarkovsky's use of Johann Sebastian Bach's music has surfaced regularly throughout this book, most explicitly, of course, in the chapters on *Solaris*, *Mirror* and *The Sacrifice*, since these are the films where it appears.[17] What is most striking about Tarkovsky's cinematic appropriation of Bach is the way the music comes to be associated with an ideal of unconditional spiritual integrity. For Tarkovsky, this is music that "expresses a vision of the truth" (Tarkovsky 1986, 154). Incorporating this Bachian vision into his films, Tarkovsky clearly means for it to have an extra-fictional significance, in the sense that it is directly addressed to the spectator. In a passage discussing Bergman's use of the Sarabande from the Fifth Cello Suite in *Cries and Whispers* (1972), Bach's music is described as providing the spectator with "the possibility of filling the spiritual emptiness [of a scene] and feeling the breath of an ideal" (Tarkovsky quoted in Bird 2008, 151). And even though in Bergman's film – depicting the profound rivalry between two sisters visiting their third sister at her deathbed – this ideal "is patently a chimera," the vision

Music, Meaning and Troubled Utopias   155

expressed by Bach's music is nevertheless "what the human spirit seeks, what it yearns for"; it is what "gives the *audience* the possibility of catharsis, of spiritual cleansing and liberation" (Tarkovsky 1986, 192; emphasis added). These last words apply, I believe, to all instances of Bach's music in Tarkovsky's films, even if this audience-addressed cathartic function is perhaps most clearly at work at the end of *The Sacrifice* where the unambiguously nondiegetic aria "Erbarme dich" from the *St. Matthew Passion* floods the soundtrack.

But as should have become clear from the previous chapters, this is not the only way Bach's music can be understood as functioning in Tarkovsky's films. Apart from addressing the audience, it can also be understood as playing a decisively narrative role, in that it is clearly concerned with the interior worlds of the films' characters, revealing the emotional constitution and "feel" of their visions, dreams and fantasies. This seems especially true in *Solaris* and *Mirror*, where Bach's music becomes closely linked to the characters' pursuit of emotional authenticity and existential belonging. In these films, as we have seen, it takes on the role of an interior truthfulness, an unassailable spiritual sincerity, toward which the characters continuously strive. Thus understood, Kelvin's longing for Earth in *Solaris* and the dying Alexei's vision of himself as a small child at the end of *Mirror* – accompanied by the chorale prelude "Ich ruf zu dir, Herr Jesu Christ" and the opening chorus of the *St. John Passion* respectively – express the same need to access and hold on to a "true affirmation of self" (Tarkovsky 1986, 38). This function of signifying interior truthfulness is not, however, exclusively tied to Bach's music. More generally, this is also the role played by Pergolesi's and Purcell's music in *Mirror* and, to some extent, Verdi's *Requiem* in *Nostalghia*. In all these cases, the music might be understood as standing for a deeply felt need to live in a way that, for lack of a better expression, one might call existentially authentic. This musically articulated search for inner truth and spiritual liberation is thus shared by audiences and characters alike.

As the quote about Bergman's *Cries and Whispers* demonstrates, Tarkovsky was well aware that he was not the first director within European art cinema to incorporate Bach's music into film. As pointed out in Chapter 2, already in *Through a Glass Darkly* (1961) Bergman had employed Bach's music in a manner not dissimilar to how Tarkovsky would employ it over ten years later in *Solaris*. And the same year, Pier Paolo Pasolini had made extensive use of the *St. Matthew Passion* in *Accattone* (1961). In fact, by the time of *Solaris*, cinematic appropriations of Bach's music (and classical music more generally) had become something of an art cinema convention. For some people, like Ennio Morricone, it had even deteriorated into a trite cliché. Thus, in an interview in 1979 Morricone peevishly proclaimed: "Mah! Dopo *Accattone*, purtroppo, tutti si son messi a usare Bach nei film; e quindi l'uso di Bach é venuto degenerando" (quoted in Calabretto 2010b, 7).[18]

156   *Music, Meaning and Troubled Utopias*

Tarkovsky nevertheless maintained that the spiritual purity of Bach's music was unsullied by this widespread cinematic annexation, and that he consequently had no qualms about using it in his films. But Bach's music (and Baroque music more generally) aside, there is another aspect to classical music in Tarkovsky's films, one that is most clearly expressed in *Stalker*. As we saw in Chapter 4, classical music – what can be called Post-Baroque music, the *Marseillaise* and music by Beethoven, Wagner and Ravel – occurs throughout that film at dramatically and structurally important points. On each of these occasions, the music is coupled with the sound of running trains, inextricably linking the two types of sound and creating what I have called a sonic figure. Largely due to this coupling, classical music can here be understood as connoting the grand projects of modern Western civilization, crystallized most clearly in the Enlightenment ideals expressed by the *Marseillaise* in the film's post-credit scene and by Beethoven's "Ode to Joy" in the concluding scene. Furthermore, as was also pointed out in Chapter 4, a similarly irrefutable belief in the absolute necessity of a historically continuous socialist project was a central pillar of the Marxist and ultimately Hegelian-derived state policy of Soviet Russia. Thus understood, classical music stands in stark contrast to the electronic music in the film, especially what is sometimes called the "Stalker theme." The deeply meditative quality of *this* music is intimately connected with the peaceful and mysterious Zone, and its spiritual sincerity testifies to the hollowness and futility of the ideas and values connoted by classical music. The emotional incompatibility between this theme and the recurring sonic compound of classical music and running trains thus turns the latter into a sonic signifier for all that is wrong with modern society.

A similar sense of "false consciousness" attaches to Beethoven's Ninth Symphony as it appears in *Nostalghia*, especially the mutilated rendering of it that underscores Domenico's senseless self-immolation at the Campidoglio in Rome. As in *Stalker*, the "Ode to Joy" is here merged with an emblematic signifier of a society that is materialistic and technologically advanced but, in Tarkovsky's view, spiritually impoverished. This time, however, it is not a train but a tape recorder, a child of the technological inventions that for Walter Benjamin signaled the arrival of "The Age of Mechanical Reproduction" and the withering away of that mysterious quality that had previously imbued the work of art with its distinctive "aura" (Benjamin 2008) – a development that Tarkovsky clearly did not approve of: paradoxically enough, since, as Fredric Jameson (1992, 100) has pointed out, his whole artistic project was premised on "the highest technology of the photographic apparatus itself."[19] In any case, *Nostalghia* may in fact go a step further in its deconstruction of Beethoven's music, for the breakdown of technology represented by the malfunctioning tape recorder is also a breakdown of this musically paradigmatic expression of a united humanity, which is here literally taken to pieces and held up as a giant chimera (cf. Quandt 2008, 279).

Music, Meaning and Troubled Utopias   157

At the same time symbolically multilayered and ideologically charged, classical music can be seen to work in two radically different directions in Tarkovsky's films from *Solaris* onwards: on the one hand, it underscores a recurring theme of human and existential alienation under the repressive forces of social, scientific and technological objectivity (as in *Stalker* and to some extent in *Nostalghia*); on the other hand, it holds out a promise of redemption, spiritual transcendence and absolute inner truth (as in *Solaris*, *Mirror* and *The Sacrifice*). Given Tarkovsky's skeptical stance toward what he saw as the deplorable and destructive developments in the post-Enlightenment world, it is not surprising that he uses what I have called Post-Baroque music to characterize and criticize those developments. There is thus a deep musical dichotomy in Tarkovsky's cinema between the true music of the Baroque era and the "false consciousness" signaled by the music of Post-Baroque composers like Beethoven, Wagner and Ravel (the exception here being Verdi's *Requiem* in *Nostalghia*). As we shall see later in this chapter, this dichotomy *within* the broad genre of classical music has consequences for our understanding of the more overarching musical dichotomies in *Solaris*, *Mirror* and *Stalker*, namely those between classical and electronic music.

Electronic Music

In a striking correspondence to how the music of Bach, Pergolesi, Purcell and Verdi form a comprehensive and coherent pattern of representation across Tarkovsky's oeuvre, there is a remarkable consistency in how he makes use of electronic music in his films from the 1970s. Nevertheless, there are also subtle differences in the three films with regard to the ethical and existential implications of electronic music as well as its musical and aesthetic qualities. Working in close collaboration with composer Eduard Artemiev, Tarkovsky incorporated electronic music and electronically amplified sound in all three of his films from the 1970s. When he left the Soviet Union in 1979 to work in the West, however, his cooperation with Artemiev also came to an end, which is probably one of the main reasons why electronic music is not used in *Nostalghia* and *The Sacrifice*. Since the main focus of the present book is music in Tarkovsky's cinema, the discussion that follows will not be concerned with the more straightforward cases of electronically manipulated diegetic sounds (e.g. the electronic amplification of Writer's footsteps as he walks through the "Meat grinder" in *Stalker*). Of course, the distinction between music and amplified sound is often difficult to pin down in Tarkovsky's films, and in some cases may even be impossible to maintain, but this does not mean that there are no clear cases of electronic *music* in these films. This raises the further issue, however, of what should be counted as *electronic* music in Tarkovsky's cinema. Many of the instances that are labeled electronic in the scholarly literature are in fact amalgams of electronic and acoustic

158 *Music, Meaning and Troubled Utopias*

sounds and instruments. As I pointed out in Chapter 1, given this situation I will define electronic music broadly as including all instances of music that have been electronically processed *and* that were originally composed by Artemiev for the film in question. The second qualification rules out the Bach chorale in *Solaris*, which, despite being increasingly infused with electronic reverberations, should not primarily be regarded as electronic music. With these caveats in place, we can summarize the findings from Chapters 2, 3 and 4 as regards the representational function of electronic music.

Toward the end of the fifth chapter of *Sculpting in Time*, Tarkovsky devotes a few paragraphs to considering the use of electronic music in film, concluding that such music has "enormously rich possibilities for cinema" (Tarkovsky 1986, 162). Discussing *Mirror* in particular, he described his motivation for using electronic music thus:

> We wanted the sound to be close to that of an earthly echo, filled with poetic suggestion – to rustling, to sighing. The notes had to convey the fact that reality is conditional, and at the same time accurately reproduce precise states of mind, the sounds of a person's interior world.
>
> (Tarkovsky 1986, 162)

The idea that electronic music is eminently well suited to capture "the sounds of a person's interior world" is a notion I examined in connection with my application of the concept of focalization to the dream sequences in *Mirror*, and I also expanded this idea to cover classical music in my metadiegetic reading of the Bach chorale prelude in *Solaris*. According to Tarkovsky, however, there is a fundamental difference between how the two kinds of music can be adapted to film. Unlike "instrumental music" (i.e. classical music), the use of which "will always involve some measure of compromise," electronic music has an extraordinary "capacity for being absorbed into sound. It can be hidden behind other noises and remain indistinct; like the voice of nature, of vague intimations." As was noted earlier, however, in order to perform this role it "must be purged of its 'chemical' origins," for "the moment we hear what it is, and realise that it's being constructed, electronic music dies" (Tarkovsky 1986, 162–163).

To say that electronic music is always "hidden behind other noises" in Tarkovsky's films, that it always remains "indistinct," however, is to stretch the truth. A variety of examples from *Solaris*, *Mirror* and *Stalker* could be given that would quickly disprove such a claim. But what is much stranger is that Tarkovsky has next to nothing to say about what is clearly a central representational function of electronic music in his films, namely the way in which this music is consistently associated with a sense of alterity and otherness: with the unfamiliar, ominous and incomprehensible. As we have seen, this connection is most clearly established

Music, Meaning and Troubled Utopias   159

in *Solaris* and *Stalker*, where electronic music is one of the central means employed in constituting the specific ambience and atmosphere of the enigmatic planet Solaris and the mysterious Zone respectively. Especially in *Solaris*, Tarkovsky and Artemiev emulate what Jeremy Barham has described as "the continuing historically disinterested development of a restrictive principle of signification that welds Ligeti-like atonality and tone-clusters . . . to the unknown, the threatening, the monstrous, and the evil" (Barham 2009, 263). Rebecca Leydon, in her excellent analysis of the score to *Forbidden Planet* (1956), explicitly ties this principle to the use of electronic music in film, writing that "like dodecaphony, electronic timbres emerged as a monolithic class of sound objects anchored to images of the aberrant," an audiovisual trope that can be traced at least as far back as Bernard Herrmann's score for the 1951 film *The Day the Earth Stood Still* (Leydon 2004, 64). While the "principle of signification" that Barham points to is also at work in *Mirror*, most obviously in the scene where Ignat inexplicably encounters a mysterious dark-haired woman and her maid, it is much less clearly adhered to in the film's dream sequences and in the hybrid electro-acoustic music accompanying the documentary footage. In *Stalker*, the principle seems to have been abandoned altogether in favor of a more lyrical and tonally grounded electronic manipulation of Eastern and Western instruments with an upper part (the flute) exhibiting a melodic curvature reminiscent of medieval plainsong (see Chapter 4). One result of this is that the alternative reality of the Zone appears rather less threatening than the impenetrable and fluctuating nature of the constantly thundering and reverberating planet in *Solaris*.

In any case, if electronic music is more or less explicitly linked with the alien planet and the desolated space station in *Solaris*, and with the Zone and the magical powers of the Stalker's crippled daughter in *Stalker*, it is no less an articulation of an ungraspable and incomprehensible reality in *Mirror*. As I argued in Chapter 3, the sense of alterity established by the electronic manipulation of voices, sounds and orchestral textures in this film arises in connection with what at first sight might seem to be completely unrelated scenes and representations: dream-memories of early childhood, the inexplicable appearance of mysterious characters and newsreel sequences depicting agitated mobs, exploding bombs and the tribulations of war. But, as I also argued, the multiple occurrences of electronic music in *Mirror* are actually linked, in that they all can be understood as sonic representations of experiences that in various ways lie beyond the reach of human understanding and comprehension, thus establishing what might be called a "theme of incomprehensibility" recurring throughout the film. It should now be apparent that this theme of incomprehensibility, as established by electronic music, is actually a recurring trope in Tarkovsky's cinema of the 1970s. And this is what justifies the claim that the central representational function of electronic

160　*Music, Meaning and Troubled Utopias*

music in Tarkovsky's films is that it signifies – or, more precisely, articulates – a radical otherness beyond the grasp of human comprehension. As we shall see in the following, though, this does not mean that electronic music should necessarily be *valorized* in the same way in *Solaris, Mirror* and *Stalker.* Before proceeding to discuss this issue, however, I need to briefly consider the third type of music that Tarkovsky incorporates into his films, what I have labeled "traditional music."

Traditional Music

In a somewhat simplified fashion, I will use the term "traditional music" here to denote all music in Tarkovsky's films from *Solaris* to *The Sacrifice* that is neither "classical" nor "electronic" (see also endnote 16). Thus understood, the category includes the Spanish flamenco music in *Mirror,* the Russian folk song and Chinese music in *Nostalghia* and the Swedish herding calls and Japanese flute music in *The Sacrifice.* In contrast to what has been said about classical and electronic music, the various occurrences of traditional music in Tarkovsky's films do not seem to share any common representational function. Rather, the representational meaning or significance of each of these occurrences seems to be somewhat *sui generis.* Moreover, while a variety of statements about classical and electronic music can be found in *Sculpting in Time* and in various interviews, Tarkovsky did not have much to say about the role of traditional music in his films. Thus, with regard to this third category, trying to pinpoint an overall pattern of signification across the different films would appear to be a fruitless enterprise. Instead, for each instance we should ask what, if anything, could be a sensible account of its representational function and/or meaning.

The reason for appropriating the Russian folk song *Oi Vi Kumusciki* in *Nostalghia* seems fairly obvious. Whatever else the film can be said to be about, on a manifest level it is a depiction of an exiled Russian intellectual who suffers from severe homesickness for his native country and his family. In this context, it is natural to interpret *Oi Vi Kumusciki* as a musical representation of the main character's compulsive occupation with his idealized homeland, whether we understand the music to be a nondiegetic representation of his nostalgic longing or as focalized through his tormented mind.[20] Variants of this interpretation are possible. But it seems to me that however we choose to flesh out the details of our account, our understanding of the music's representational function must be framed in terms of its relation to the (no doubt multilayered) condition of nostalgia. Similarly, if we disregard the complexity of determining its diegetic status, the Japanese shakuhachi music in *The Sacrifice* is fairly clear as regards its representational meaning. Throughout history, the shakuhachi has been associated with practices and rituals of Zen Buddhism; in *The Sacrifice*, it is closely linked with the character Alexander

Music, Meaning and Troubled Utopias   161

and is consistently heard in connection with shots where Alexander is seen turning his home stereo on and off. It also relates directly to Alexander's "obsession" (as his step-daughter puts it toward the end of the film) with Japan: the planting of the Japanese tree, his kimono with a yin and yang motif, etc. It is therefore reasonable to suggest that the music forms part of Alexander's personal philosophy, representing his belief in the importance of attaining inner peace (while, perhaps ironically, also underlining the extent to which he suffers from a lack of spiritual equilibrium). It is certainly no coincidence that Alexander selects this music as the accompaniment to his "major" sacrificial act at the end of the film; the spiritual purity and integrity of the music reflect the spiritual cleansing symbolized by the fire that consumes the house. In contrast, the herding calls can, as I argued in Chapter 6, be conceived of as articulations of a spiritual truth of a more objective order, one that has an absolute validity beyond any personal convictions that might be associated with the film's characters. In other words, their representational significance consists in their denoting a spiritual presence within the diegesis that transcends the empirical reality of the characters. Finally, the flamenco music accompanying the documentary footage from the Spanish Civil War in *Mirror* distinguishes itself from all the previously mentioned examples of traditional music, partly because it occurs only once in the film and partly because it is not mixed with other kinds of music. Two typically Tarkovskian hallmarks are thus absent here: the musical refrain element and the merging of different musical realities. This affects what we can say about the representational meaning of this musical sequence, which seems to be a musical dramatization of the images serving to intensify and emotionally ground the viewer's awareness of this particular Spanish national trauma, when thousands of children were separated from their parents and sent into exile.

Musical Dichotomies and Syntheses

The presence of musical dichotomies in Tarkovsky's films was shown in the chapters on *Solaris*, *Mirror* and *Stalker*. In discussing these dichotomies, I was above all interested in how the *relations* set up between different kinds of music could be understood as participating in the establishment of central thematic binary oppositions in the films. In fact, one should distinguish between musical dichotomies and musically established dichotomies. Whereas a musically *established* dichotomy should be understood as synonymous with a thematic binary opposition, a *musical* dichotomy functions as a central ingredient in the constitution of such oppositions. Again, whereas the identification of a musically established dichotomy is a matter of interpreting a film at the level of its thematic, ideological and philosophical content, a musical dichotomy is identified by pointing to clearly discernible and contrasting *musical* characteristics in two types

162 *Music, Meaning and Troubled Utopias*

of music. In what follows, I will discuss what I see as the central musical dichotomy in *Solaris, Mirror* and *Stalker*, namely that between classical and electronic music. Even though in all three films the dichotomy fundamentally underscores a distinction between the known and the unknown, between the familiar and the unfamiliar, the specific configuration of the dichotomy in each case implies a different treatment of the distinction, and this affects our assessment of the resulting thematic opposition, or so I will argue. In addition to the presence of musical dichotomies and musically established thematic binaries, Tarkovsky's films are also characterized by a striving toward musical integration, and in *Nostalghia* and *The Sacrifice*, musical and musically established dichotomies seem to have been replaced altogether by what might properly be called musical syntheses. I will therefore conclude this section by briefly considering the different kinds of musical overlaps and syntheses that can be found throughout Tarkovsky's last five films.

As the previous chapters have shown, several types of musical dichotomies can be discerned in Tarkovsky's cinema. *Stalker*, for example, exhibited an explicit dichotomy between Eastern and Western music. Another kind of dichotomy, discussed earlier, appears if we move beyond any specific film and view Tarkovsky's cinema in its entirety. This dichotomy, which marks a distinction within the category of classical music itself, is perhaps most clearly apparent in the way the extended passages of Baroque music, and Bach's music in particular, are distinguished from the fragmentized and deformed occurrences of the "Post-Baroque" music of Beethoven, Wagner and Ravel. However, the central musical dichotomy in Tarkovsky's cinema is unquestionably that between classical and electronic music.[21] It plays a central role in all three of his films from the 1970s and should partly be seen as a result of his close collaboration with Artemiev. Qua *musical* dichotomy, it is most clearly pronounced in *Solaris* and *Mirror*. In a manner similar to the divide between Morricone's "abstract" music and the recurring snippets from Mozart's *Requiem* in Pasolini's *Teorema* (1968), in both *Solaris* and *Mirror* the basically atonal make-up of the electronic music clearly distinguishes it from the unambiguously tonal constitution of the Baroque music of Bach, Pergolesi and Purcell. While in one respect this division between the two kinds of music is more consistently maintained in *Solaris* than in *Mirror*, where several instances of electronic music are not so much atonal as tonally ambiguous, in another respect it is not. Whereas in *Mirror* the two musical "realms" for the most part are kept distinctly apart, in the sense that classical and electronic music are (with one exception) never fused, in *Solaris* they become increasingly interwoven as the film proceeds. *Stalker* is more similar to *Mirror* in this regard, and in fact goes a step further in separating the realm of electronic music from that of classical music. In this film, while *La Marseillaise* and the music of Beethoven, Ravel and Wagner are all combined with the sound of running trains, at no point do they

Music, Meaning and Troubled Utopias   163

overlap with the electronically elaborated "Stalker theme." At the same time, the electronic music in *Stalker* also continues the "tonalization" of electronic music that at times appeared in *Mirror*. In *Stalker*, most occurrences of electronic music are unambiguously tonal. It is thus possible to trace a gradual change across the three films with regard to both the internal constitution of the electronic music and how it is combined (or not combined) with classical music: while the electronic music becomes increasingly tonal in character, it also becomes more clearly separated from its classical counterparts. Intriguingly, these changes seem simultaneously to sharpen and relax the dichotomous relation between the two kinds of music. So how do these changes between and across the three films affect our understanding of the thematic oppositions that these musical dichotomies underpin?

Since I believe that *Solaris* and *Stalker* are the two films that stand furthest apart from each other here, I will try to answer this question by making a comparison between these two films. The presence of a musical dichotomy may at first sight appear more clearly pronounced in *Solaris* than in *Stalker*. There are several reasons for this. Firstly, in comparison with *Stalker*, *Solaris* exhibits a much more radical distinction with regard to the tonal organization of the two musical realms it contains, even if the electronic music is rendered basically tonal when adapted to and merged with Bach's music at the end of the film (see Barham 2009, 267). Secondly, while electronic and classical music occur at very different moments in *Stalker*, in *Solaris* the two types of music often appear in close connection, which makes the perceptible contrast very obvious. Thirdly, while in *Solaris* electronic and classical music are explicitly associated with the planets Solaris and Earth respectively, this is not the case in *Stalker*, where especially the classical music lacks a clear signifying function in this sense. Despite this, I would argue that the musical dichotomy is actually stronger in *Stalker* than in *Solaris*. In *Solaris*, the blurring of the two contrasting musical realms serves to mitigate the dichotomy in a way that does not occur in *Stalker*. That the musical dichotomy in *Solaris* is embedded within a process of gradual musical integration also raises at least the possibility of a reconciliation between the thematic oppositions that the dichotomy underpins. In contrast, the musical dichotomy in *Stalker* is much less obvious and may in fact require an elaborate interpretive argument like the one presented in Chapter 4 to become apparent. Once acknowledged, however, it seems uncompromisingly present, and it is very hard to see how the lyrical music of the Zone could be reconciled with the decidedly non-lyrical character of the sonic figure.

Solaris and *Stalker* differ not only with respect to the extent to which the musical dichotomy is kept intact but also in terms of how this dichotomy participates in the construction of meaning in the two films. More specifically, beyond the obvious fact that in *Solaris* the dichotomy signals a division between Earth and Space, there is a subtle dislocation

164 *Music, Meaning and Troubled Utopias*

in how the two poles are evaluatively assessed that changes the representational import of the dichotomy. In both films, beyond distinguishing the known from the unknown, the musical dichotomy establishes a representational pattern by which a true and authentic subjectivity is distinguished from the alienating forces that threaten to destroy it. But this is somewhat differently achieved in the two films, and neither classical nor electronic music is consistently aligned with either side of the dichotomy. In *Solaris*, the austerity of the space station to which Kelvin travels is contrasted with the lush natural surroundings and strong personal ties associated with his family home back on Earth. Within this Earth-Space dichotomy, the continuous reappearance of Bach's music constitutes a leitmotif representing the quintessential human values of love, intimacy and subjective truth, while the drone-like electronic buzzing and rumbling that surrounds and permeates the space station not only underscores the austerity of the place and the threatening radical otherness of the planet Solaris but also emphasizes the ultimate futility and illusory promises associated with scientific knowledge and man's continuous exploration of the universe. Endless technical progress and what Tarkovsky regarded as a misguided and depersonalizing form of human knowledge are the ideological traps that are investigated and exhibited in *Solaris*. In contrast to the severity of the electronic sounds and music, we have the poignancy, the firmly grounded F-minor tonality and the slowly unfolding melodies of the Bach chorale prelude, the latter signifying what is truly human in the film's tormented hero. In *Stalker*, the musical dichotomy serves the same function as in *Solaris*, but now the roles of the classical and electronic music are reversed. As in *Solaris*, classical music occurs regularly throughout the film. As I have repeatedly argued, however, here it is best conceived of as representing the destructive forces of modernity and, in this role, as standing in stark contrast to the peaceful and contemplative electronic music in the film. With reference to its ideological and ethical implications, the dichotomy has thus been turned on its head: if in *Solaris* electronic music represents spiritual alienation, and classical music the idea or experience of an authentic subjectivity, the case in *Stalker* is the opposite. Beyond its close connection to the incomprehensible Solaris and the mysterious Zone, electronic music is thus to an important extent coded, positively or negatively, by the relation in which it stands to a more ideologically charged classical music. In this context, *Mirror* takes a somewhat intermediate position; even if the dichotomy between classical and electronic music can be understood as one of the means by which the film separates a recognizable emotional life-world from the more incomprehensible dimensions of human experience, the electronic music is not explicitly associated with an allegorically replete entity like Solaris and the Zone, and in consequence takes on the appearance of an ethically and ideologically more neutral phenomenon than in the other two films.

Music, Meaning and Troubled Utopias 165

From the perspective adopted in this study, the presence of musical and musically established dichotomies can be understood as one of the distinguishing features of Tarkovsky's cinema in the 1970s. At the same time, the contrast between classical and electronic music was softened in *Solaris* by an antipodal process of musical integration. The practice of merging or "marrying" different kinds of music is in fact a distinctive characteristic of Tarkovsky's way of working with music in his films, one that is not limited to the handling (and possible reconciliation) of specific musical dichotomies. The sonic figure in *Stalker* constitutes a very special instance in this regard, since the arguably nondiegetic classical music is here conflated with what reasonably can be understood as the diegetic sound of trains. Moreover, in Chapter 4, I interpreted this particular amalgamation of music and sound as a sonic *symbol* that functioned as a constituent element in the construction of a more overarching musical and thematic dichotomy in the film. And while the brief combination of the Bach recitative and electronically processed tone clusters in *Mirror* is a clear example of musical merging, it constitutes an exception in a film that otherwise prefers to keep the two types of music strictly separate.

It is in *Nostalghia* and *The Sacrifice*, Tarkovsky's last two films, that the practice of musical merging becomes the predominant way of linking different kinds of music together. Consequently, it is in relation to these two films that we can justifiably speak in terms of musical syntheses. This change in focus from musical dichotomies to musical syntheses suggests that Tarkovsky, even more than before, is concerned with exploring the possibilities of spiritual and existential reconciliation. In a clear illustration of Tarkovsky's ideas about the transfigurative power of the musical refrain (Tarkovsky 1986, 158), the combining of Verdi's *Requiem* and the Russian folk song at the beginning of *Nostalghia* – a film that otherwise "progresses through sets of binary opposites" (Rivi 2007, 79) – is echoed at the film's end. As I pointed out in Chapter 5, in the final two scenes Verdi's *Requiem* and *Oi Vi Kumusciki* are heard in close succession, which is to say that the two kinds of music are not in fact layered upon each other here. Yet, the strong musical synthesis established in the opening scene suggests that a similar synthesis is at work at the end of the film. Indeed, if anything the synthesizing effect is even stronger here, as the "double strategy" of letting the Russian folk song reign supreme in the final scene while still creating the impression that a musical amalgamation is in play is combined with a geographical and at the same time existential synthesis when the Russian dacha appears inside the roofless Italian gothic church. In this way, the sound and image tracks jointly suggest at least a possibility of reconciliation, of overcoming the seemingly unbridgeable rift between the protagonist's incurable longing for his homeland and his current condition of exile.

In *The Sacrifice*, mergings of different musical materials appear at two points in the film. The most explicit one is the combination of the

166 *Music, Meaning and Troubled Utopias*

Swedish herding calls and the Japanese shakuhachi music, which is heard during Alexander's delirious dream-visions after he has slept with Maria. One could view the musical synthesis articulated here as a reconciliation, or attempted reconciliation, between East and West, an interpretation that would place it alongside the "Stalker theme" in *Stalker*, which was constructed from a combination of Eastern and Western instruments and musical resources (i.e. a Westernized medieval-sounding melody and an Eastern-sounding accompaniment). In Chapter 6, I opted for an alternative reading, interpreting the "polyphonic sound space" (Shpinitskaya 2014) emerging from the blending of Swedish and Japanese music as an affirmation of Alexander's newly acquired ability to link his empirical self (the Japanese music) with a higher spiritual reality (represented by the herding calls). The second musical synthesis that can be identified is rather more subtle. It occurs in the film's final scene, where the herding calls briefly overlap with the aria "Erbarme dich" from Bach's *St. Matthew Passion. The Sacrifice* thus once again exploits the approach taken in *Solaris* and *Nostalghia* of juxtaposing different musical universes at the very end of a film. In the interpretation of the film given in Chapter 6, this overlap between traditional and classical music was described as further reinforcing the presence of an absolute spiritual truth, in that the mysterious herding calls here align with the one composer whose "relationship with God is absolutely outside of civilization" (Ishimov and Shejko 2006, 141). This idea of a transcendental spiritual realm, a spiritual mode of existence that is unsullied by the contingencies of history and civilization, is central to Tarkovsky's cinema. But it is an idea, the realization of which is repeatedly questioned, leading to what I will call a troubled utopianism. As I shall argue in the concluding section of this chapter, music plays an essential role in the construction of this troubled Tarkovskian utopianism.

Rapprochement, Transcendence and Doubt: Music and Tarkovsky's Troubled Utopias

In Chapter 4, I argued that *Stalker* can be viewed as articulating a strong utopian propensity, and I traced this propensity in the film by focusing on the recurring cinematic recontextualization of the sonic figure, a recontextualization that culminates in the final scene's transcendental implications. Michael Griffin and Dara Waldron, despite asserting that "there is nothing to suggest an expression of Utopia in *Stalker*," find a *utopian impulse* at work in the film, which they describe as "an impulse to achieve a fullness of being" (Griffin and Waldron 2007, 268). This understanding of the utopian impulse dovetails with that of Petteri Pietikäinen, who describes "utopianism or the utopian impulse" as "the desire for a different kind of modernity" (Pietikäinen 2007, 2), one in which people "identify with their so-called Authentic Self" (Pietikäinen 2007, 6). In

Music, Meaning and Troubled Utopias   167

Pietikäinen's view, this is a kind of *psychological* utopianism, in that its ultimate goal is an "ideal state of consciousness" and, on a broader level, a society where everyone has realized their true human potential. Utopianism so understood is a kind of "social dreaming" (Sargent 1994, 3), but one primarily directed at the fulfillment of the individual's inherent mental or spiritual potentialities, from which the ideal human society is imagined to emerge.

In this last section, I will suggest that a utopian impulse toward "a fullness of being" or an "ideal state of consciousness" runs through Tarkovsky's last five films as an important theme, and that music plays a central role in how it is articulated. Since I believe that this utopian impulse is most explicitly expressed at the end of each film, my discussion will focus on the final scenes of *Solaris*, *Mirror*, *Stalker*, *Nostalghia* and *The Sacrifice*. These scenes can be described as utopian in character insofar as they suggest the possibility of a mode of existence that can never be completely realized in human life, one characterized by absolute spiritual integrity, a unification of the self and a final resolution of conflicting inner forces. Put differently, each of Tarkovsky's last five films stages a kind of aesthetic and spiritual epiphany at its end, signaling the attainment of a mental end state, a spiritual Foreverland or no-place, in which the existential and psychical conflicts that have beset the characters throughout the film have been finally overcome.[22] Music, and more specifically classical music, is essential to the cinematic construction of this impulse toward spiritual transcendence and reconciliation. However, to speak of a utopian *impulse* is of necessity to speak of a *striving* toward an ideal condition, or, in the words of Ruth Levitas, it is "the expression of the desire for a better way of living" (Levitas 2010, 217; see also Levitas 1990, 151). In Tarkovsky's films, this striving is often problematized, thwarted even, by an opposing pull toward uncertainty and ambiguity. In *Solaris*, *Mirror* and *Nostalghia*, such ambiguities are at play even in the films' endings, while *Stalker* and *The Sacrifice* may be more unambiguously utopian in their attempt to affirm that a transfiguration into a more enlightened and authentic form of existence has actually taken place (but see later in this section). In what follows, I will return once more to Tarkovsky's views on art and music, and show that in themselves these views make a strong argument for ascribing a utopian function to (classical) music in his films. I then conclude this chapter with a consideration of how several of Tarkovsky's films, while clearly exhibiting a strong utopian impulse toward spiritual reconciliation and a "fullness of being" in their final scenes, nevertheless seem to end in uncertainty and ambivalence as to whether the sought-for ideal condition is ever attainable. In this way, Tarkovsky's films to varying degrees exhibit what I have called a "troubled utopianism."

As we saw in Chapter 2 and again in Chapter 4, Tarkovsky's conception of art can be described as idealist in character, or even as a kind of Romanticism. The idealist bent of his aesthetic outlook becomes apparent

168   *Music, Meaning and Troubled Utopias*

already from the fact that the second chapter of *Sculpting in Time* is titled "Art – a yearning for the ideal," a title that also discloses the utopian element in his aesthetics. The presence of such a utopian element is further evidenced by the many claims about the nature and function of art that are scattered throughout the book, claims that are repeatedly stated in a teleological and quasi-religious vocabulary of transcendence and timeless human values. Thus, for Tarkovsky, art is a "detector of the absolute"; it is "an instrument for knowing [the world] in the course of man's journey towards . . . 'absolute truth'"; the artistic image sustains "an awareness of the infinite" and is linked with "that absolute truth that is hidden from us in our positivistic, pragmatic activities" (Tarkovsky 1986, 37). Again, we are drawn to art in order to satisfy "a timeless and insatiable longing for the spiritual, for the ideal"; and "the idea of infinity," even though it cannot be expressed in words, "can be apprehended through art" (Tarkovsky 1986, 38–39). Art is of central importance to human life in that its ultimate aim is "to prepare a person for death, to plough and harrow his soul, rendering it capable of turning to good" (Tarkovsky 1986, 43). And so on. Given such statements it is not surprising that Tarkovsky finally claims that "art could almost be said to be religious in that it is inspired by a commitment to a higher goal" (Tarkovsky 1986, 168). This alignment of art with religion, both of which are assessed in terms of a perpetual striving toward an as yet unrealized state of being, is perhaps the clearest expression of utopian thinking one could wish for.

Tarkovsky's conception of music is likewise colored by an air of utopianism. First of all, music (or more specifically Western classical music), qua one of the art forms, participates in art's "yearning for the ideal," and Tarkovsky's idolization of Bach is of course the most explicit example of this view. Secondly, however, on a more specific level Tarkovsky can be seen as an ardent supporter of art music's autonomous status. Again, this belief is most clearly expressed in relation to Bach's music, which means "nothing at all beyond what [it means in itself]," and this, Tarkovsky believes, is the measure of its autonomy (Tarkovsky 1986, 113). This view is echoed by the Stalker, who, when preaching to Professor and Writer about "the unselfishness of art," illustrates his point with the case of music, saying that "less than anything else, it is connected to reality." As Caryl Flinn, among many others, has pointed out, "the idealized conception of music that considers it an autonomous art form enjoys a long, intricate history" (Flinn 1992, 7). What is interesting in Flinn's discussion of musical autonomy, however, is the strong connection she finds between the belief in music's autonomy and the presence of utopian thinking. As an autonomous and non-representational art form that simultaneously speaks to our feelings and affords "a fullness of experience," music "extends an impression of perfection and integrity in an otherwise imperfect, unintegrated world" (Flinn 1992, 9). For Flinn, this creed of perfection and integrity constitutes what she labels the utopian function of music (and

Music, Meaning and Troubled Utopias   169

film music in particular),[23] and this is a function that is particularly relevant for assessing Tarkovsky's use of classical music in his films.

Solaris is arguably the film in which musical and thematic syntheses are most explicitly employed to achieve a state of spiritual reconciliation at the end. In the film's final scene, Kelvin's apparent return to his family home on Earth is accompanied by the electronically saturated Bach chorale prelude. As Jeremy Barham (2009, 267) has shown, in this scene Artemiev's technological score is adapted to the tonal world of the chorale, in that it is incorporated as an added melodic layer that conforms to the harmonic progressions of the piece. This strongly suggests that the alien nature of Solaris has been successfully harmonized with the authentic interiority represented by the chorale prelude. In the psychoanalytical framework presented in Chapter 2, this can be understood as a rapprochement between the conscious and unconscious dimensions of Kelvin's psyche, as a final resolution of inner conflicts that at the same time is the achievement of spiritual wholeness and lasting inner peace: in other words, the achievement of a more enlightened, more profound, more authentic way of being. This achievement is further underscored by the climactic and almost celestial character of the music in this scene, as the chorale is embellished and "enhanced" by Artemiev's "vibraphone-like countermelody" as well as "additional vocal, string, and bell-like textures" (Barham 2009, 266). But the sense of genuine spiritual rapprochement and authenticity thus attained is eventually put in doubt. It is not only that the simulacrous nature of Kelvin's treasured family home becomes apparent as the ascending camera reveals it to be a tiny island on Solaris's vast oceanic surface. What is really disturbing is how this insight is underscored, at the very last moment of the film, by the return of the atonal and sinister electronic soundscape that had constantly radiated from the enigmatic planet during Kelvin's stay at the space station. The suggested fulfillment of the protagonist's utopian strivings is thus shrouded in doubt and uncertainty.

Mirror displays a corresponding troubled utopianism. In the film's final scene, the utopian function of "autonomous" music is in full force as the opening choir of the *St. John Passion* deluges the soundtrack, infusing the images with a sense of closure and finality. Understood as a vision flowing from the dying narrator's consciousness, the scene takes on an atmosphere of fulfillment born of a combination of resignation and reconciliation, the simultaneous presence of the young and the old mother signaling a rapprochement between past and present, mother and son, and even between the unconscious realm of the ethereal dream-visions and the conscious realm of waking reality. What throughout the film has been little more than a utopian dream of "a fullness of being" is here, at the very end of the tormented narrator's life, finally granted him. Like Kelvin in *Solaris*, Alexei seems to attain a state of spiritual wholeness, a transformation and consolidation of his decentered interiority into a

170 *Music, Meaning and Troubled Utopias*

unified and coherent self, one that is mirrored in, or even constituted by, the "perfection and integrity" of Bach's "timeless" music. But *Mirror* too ends with a troubling twist, though this time it is not generated by the reinsertion of brooding electronic music. Instead, it is the compact silence on the soundtrack (broken only by a final occurrence of the mysterious piping sound heard repeatedly throughout the film) that renders the ending of the film ambiguous. As the camera tracks into the wood and the image gradually grows darker, the door is reopened to doubt as to whether the "fullness of being" promised by Bach's music is perhaps nothing more than a utopian dream.

While *The Sacrifice* resembles *Mirror* in how it introduces an extended excerpt from one of Bach's Passions at the end of the film, *Nostalghia* emulates the approach used in *Solaris*, namely the bringing together of two different kinds of music. Yet both *The Sacrifice* and *Nostalghia* deviate in subtle ways from their forerunners. With regard to *Nostalghia*, it is of special significance for the present discussion that Verdi's *Requiem* and the Russian folk song are not allowed to overlap at the end of the film. In her analysis of *Nostalghia*, Luisa Rivi describes it as "a unique ideological film about the clash and encounter between Eastern and Western Europe" and "a historical utopia . . . that bespeaks a reconfiguration of a Europe yet to exist" (Rivi 2007, 77–78). The utopian element here consists of the film's attempt to overcome the antithetical poles of the "decadent West" and the "exhausted Communist East" and incorporate them into a "synthesis that preserves both worlds" (Rivi 2007, 83). Rivi argues, however, that the synthesis achieved is "weak" because the film does not combine the two poles into a "higher unity," but rather allows them to "remain and preserve [their] distinctive traits," and from this she concludes that *Nostalghia* expresses a kind of "weak" utopianism (Rivi 2007, 79). She finds this weak utopianism to be most clearly expressed in the ambiguous nature of the film's final scene, where the combination of Russian and Italian landscapes, as much as it may suggest a merging of the two countries, would also seem to preserve them as discernible and separate entities. As with the endings of the other films, I prefer instead to speak of a troubled utopianism; the main reason for this is my belief that the film is not so much a depiction of the relationship between Eastern and Western Europe as a story about an individual experiencing severe existential rootlessness as a result of his exiled condition. The utopianism at the end of the film consists above all in the suggestion that Andrei, who is presumably dying as a result of his heart attack, is finally able to acknowledge and integrate the realities of past and present and thus comes to experience a "new wholeness" (Tarkovsky 1986, 216). By appearing in close succession yet at the same time not merging into a larger musical unity, the *Requiem* and the Russian folk song simultaneously seem to affirm and problematize this utopian striving toward wholeness. The utopianism of the final scene is troubled precisely because the same juxtapositions that

Music, Meaning and Troubled Utopias 171

suggest the protagonist's attainment of a new kind of wholeness can also be understood as signaling the continuous presence of a "division within him that prevents him from living" (Tarkovsky 1986, 216).

It might appear, then, that the two most decidedly utopian films of Tarkovsky, those that unambiguously affirm that a higher and spiritually elevated mode of existence is a real possibility in human life, are *Stalker* and *The Sacrifice*. Building on my reading in Chapter 6, I argued previously that the overlap at the end of *The Sacrifice* between the mysterious herding calls and the aria "Erbarme dich" suggests the presence of an absolute spiritual truth. This spiritual truth is here doubly emphasized in that it simultaneously appears at the diegetic (herding calls) and non-diegetic (Bach) levels of the film. Yet the utopian promise of spiritual transcendence thus articulated by the herdswoman's voice of truth and a music that "exists absolutely outside of civilization" is perhaps mitigated as the camera, slowly panning up the barren tree, is halted in its tracks just before reaching the utopian vastness of the endless sky. And even in *Stalker*, arguably the most utopian of Tarkovsky's films, there is a hint of troubling ambiguity in that the supposedly failed mission into the Zone complicates the "flight into transcendence" signified by the final scene. It seems, then, that the strong utopian function of music, especially classical "autonomous" music, in Tarkovsky's cinema is never allowed to flourish in its full potential; it is always problematized and compromised by the presence of counteracting sonic, visual and stylistic elements. Far from reducing the value of his films, however, this complex cinematic handling of music's utopian potency is one of the things that lifts them above most other films and makes them worth revisiting, not once but again and again. As I noted at the beginning of this chapter, Tarkovsky imagined a cinema without music, and he also worked toward creating such a cinema, especially in his last two films. Still, I hope that the preceding pages have shown how central music is to his films, and how paying close attention to it can enhance our understanding and deepen our experience of Tarkovsky's work.

Notes

1. Ingmar Bergman in *Sommar och Vinter i P1* (2004). URL: https://sverigesradio.se/sida/avsnitt/373942?programid=2071 (accessed 2019-04-12).
2. See, for example, Bird (1996), Broman (2012) and Luko (2015).
3. See Renaud (2011, 21–26). URL: www.ingmarbergman.se/universum/en-obesvarad-kärlek-till-musik (accessed 2019-04-12). The 27 works enumerated by Renaud include Bergman's adaptation of Mozart's *The Magic Flute* (1975) for Swedish Television.
4. Luko points to a similar conviction held by Bergman, who said that he "attempted to make films that were akin to musical compositions" (Luko 2015, 67).
5. For accounts of the concept's historical development, see Taylor (2007), Neumeyer (2009), Heldt (2013) and Penner (2017).

172 *Music, Meaning and Troubled Utopias*

6. See Souriau's (ed.) preface to the anthology *L'Univers filmique* (1953).
7. Kant and other metaphysical idealists would of course claim that the same is true of our actual, phenomenal world.
8. Buckland (2004, 92) points out that "in Bordwell's terminology, diegetization operates on a film's most basic level – referential meaning." As I have written elsewhere, in Bordwell's theory "referential meanings establish a film's *fabula* and *diegesis*; they constitute the narrated story of a film, and they also refer to and identify elements of the fictional world in which that story takes place" (Pontara 2016, 39).
9. This fact, if it is a fact, is what motivates philosopher Berys Gaut's claim that Bordwell fails to show that his theory is constructivist in any genuinely radical sense of the word (see Gaut 2010, 170–174).
10. Titled "The Art Cinema as a Mode of Film Practice," the article was first published in 1979 in the journal *Film Criticism* and has subsequently been reprinted in several anthologies. The following references are to the text as reprinted in Bordwell's 2007 book *Poetics of Cinema*. (The chapter in question also contains an afterword added to the original text.)
11. See also the methodological discussion in Chapter 1.
12. The filmind, though, is a strange creature that, in being "the film itself" (Frampton 2006, 7), also can be understood as constituting the diegesis that it is thinking about and produces. Thus, "nondiegetic music" should perhaps be put in quotation marks here.
13. See Mai (2017) for a systematic application of Frampton's concept to *Mirror*.
14. One might object that in my reading in Chapter 6, the herding calls clearly seemed to have a special connection to Alexander, and this is of course true in the sense that they were assigned a central role in Alexander's spiritual awakening. However, I would still claim that they are not *about* Alexander's tormented interiority; rather, they are the voice of an absolute spiritual truth that he needs to follow in order to escape his existential turmoil. Moreover, the herding calls are also heard and acknowledged by another character in the film, namely Otto (and also by Maria in the film's final scene).
15. As I pointed out in Chapter 6, however, diegetic and metadiegetic accounts of the herding calls have their own problems. So it is unclear to what extent such constructions of the music's diegetic status could be made plausible within a more developed interpretation of the film.
16. I have put the term traditional music within quotation marks here to indicate that it should be used with a certain caution. But even though "folk music" might better describe some of the examples in this category (e.g. the herding calls in *The Sacrifice*), "traditional music" has the advantage of not misrepresenting any of the examples I subsume under the category. In particular, the shakuhachi flute music in *The Sacrifice* is probably better described as traditional than folk music, given the complex history of both the instrument and the social and religious practices associated with it (see Donald P. Berger, "Shakuhachi." In *Grove Music Online*, Japan, § II, 5).
17. If we count Writer's whistling in *Stalker* of the "Erbarme dich" aria from the *St. Matthew Passion*, we can say that Bach's music also appears in that film.
18. "After *Accattone*, unfortunately, everybody has started to use Bach's music in film; as a consequence the use of Bach's music has become degenerated" (my translation).
19. According to Jameson, it is precisely the lack of reflexivity with regard to "this second hidden presence [of technology]" in Tarkovsky's cinema that threatens "to transform Tarkovskian nature-mysticism into the sheerest ideology" (Jameson 1992, 100). Robert Bird objects to this, however, saying that the problem with Jameson's critique is that it fails to acknowledge that

Music, Meaning and Troubled Utopias   173

"Tarkovsky's entire cinematic project was aimed precisely at exploring the cinematic apparatus and investigating its impact upon human experience – as much sensory as intellectual and spiritual" (Bird 2008, 12).

20. In the latter case, we could opt for an up-front metadiegetic account and claim that what is focalized is the music itself. Alternatively, we might, in the manner of the electronic music in the dream sequences in *Mirror*, conceive of the music as constituting the phenomenological quality of a focalized mental state.

21. *Stalker* provides a good example of this centrality, since in this film the contrast between Eastern and Western music can in fact be understood as contained within, and dependent on, the broader dichotomy between electronic and classical music.

22. P. Adams Sitney expresses a similar view when he writes that "all of Tarkovsky's films end with impressive codas; in every instance it is as if the whole film were a prelude to the final epiphany" (Sitney 2014a, 92).

23. In her book, Flinn is particularly concerned with Hollywood film music of the 1930s and 1940s.

Appendix
The Structure of *Mirror*

Mirror is built up of a series of seemingly unrelated scenes and sequences, many of which can be understood as remembrances and dream-memories of the film's protagonist, the 40-year-old Alexei.[1] What distinguishes the grown Alexei, however, is that although he is obviously a central character in the film, he is never visually present in it.[2] Alexei functions rather as the "absent" narrator whose interior ruminations constitute much of what happens in the film. As Andrea Truppin aptly describes it, *Mirror* "is a journey through the psyche in which memory, dream and fantasy are represented with the materiality of conventional reality" (Truppin 1992, 235). As I pointed out in Chapter 3, however, and as will become clear, the film is not entirely consistent in this regard. Even though *Mirror* is at center a film concerned with a tormented and dying man's contemplations of a more or less distant past, there are nonetheless a number of scenes that cannot plausibly be construed as recollections and dream-memories issuing from the grown Alexei's mind.

The film cuts back and forth between three different time periods. What might be called Time Period Three takes place in present-day time; that is, the late 1960s or early 1970s. The scenes depicting this time period are set in the grown Alexei's apartment and are mainly concerned with Alexei's relationships with his aging mother, his son Ignat and his ex-wife Natalya. In contrast, Time Period Two consists of scenes set during World War Two when Alexei is around 12 years old, while Time Period One unfolds before the war in the mid-1930s, when Alexei is around 5 or 6.[3] Inserted into this mosaic structure are extended sequences of documentary footage. In contrast to the disorienting and non-chronological arrangement of the fictional scenes, however, the documentary sequences are ordered chronologically throughout the film, beginning with footage from the mid-1930s and continuing with newsreels from World War Two until the end of the 1960s.[4]

The film begins in present time with a pre-credit sequence, in which a brief shot of Ignat turning on a TV is followed by a three-and-a-half-minute documentary-style episode featuring the attempted cure of a young stutterer by a female doctor. In what appears to be an effective

Appendix 175

treatment, the scene ends with the boy successfully uttering the words "I can speak." After this rather extended scene come the opening credits of the film, accompanied by the D minor chorale prelude "Das alte Jahr vergangen ist" (BWV 614) from Johann Sebastian Bach's *Orgelbüchlein*. The music continues into the opening scene of the film, taking place in Time Period One and showing Alexei's mother Maria sitting on a fence in front of the family's dacha (although we have not yet seen the house). As the camera tracks in on Maria, Bach's music gradually fades out, and shortly thereafter we hear Alexei explaining, in voice-over, that they (the family) were always waiting for father to come home: "If he turned right from the bush towards our house, then it was father. If not, it meant it was not father and that father would never come." A man is indeed approaching the dacha, but it is not the father. Instead, it turns out to be a doctor who has lost his way while walking to the nearby village. After a brief verbal exchange with Maria he leaves again, stopping and turning around twice as a mysterious gust of wind suddenly blows across the field. Maria goes into the house, where the camera focuses on her while Arseny Tarkovsky's poem "First Meetings" is heard on the soundtrack, read in voice-over by the poet himself.

Outside the dacha, a neighboring barn is on fire. Maria walks outdoors, followed by her children, while the camera lingers for a while on the interiors of the now empty house. Eduard Artemiev's electronic score makes its first appearance as a man and a woman are seen standing in front of the burning barn. Initially, the electronic music is almost indistinguishable from the diegetic sound of the burning barn, but as we see the man running toward the barn, the music gradually becomes more foregrounded. When the scene shifts to the film's first dream-memory, the music comes to dominate the soundtrack. We see the 5-year-old Alexei asleep in bed. He wakes up, and shortly thereafter the scene shifts again, turning from color to black and white. While the camera pans slowly to the left we see trees and bushes bending in the wind. This is followed by a new shot (now in black and white) of the little Alexei waking up in bed. The electronic music continues as the dream memory transfigures into a vision of Maria washing her hair in a dark and sparingly furnished room. The next shot shows us the room again, but now without Maria in it. Big lumps of plaster are falling from the ceiling. Maria is then seen in close-up walking slowly through the room. Trickles of water are pouring down on her from above, and we also see water flowing down the walls. As she looks into a mirror, seeing herself as an old woman, the music begins to fade out. The film cuts to present time and Alexei's apartment.

As the camera tracks slowly through the empty apartment, a poster of *Andrei Rublev* is glimpsed on one of the walls. Alexei talks to his mother on the phone and she tells him that her old colleague and friend Liza has died. This brings us to the extended Printing House scene (in black and white and presumably taking place in Time Period One) showing Maria's

176 *Appendix*

distress over a possible type-setting error and her subsequent relief when she realizes that her worries are unfounded. Liza accuses Maria of being selfish and of always trying to draw attention to herself. Upset by the accusation, Maria leaves to take a shower. The Printing House scene is then followed by a brief shot (in color) of a large fire in a field. This coincides with the second occurrence of electronic music: as we watch the fire, a rumbling electronic cluster resounds on the soundtrack.

We return once more to the present time and Alexei's apartment. Alexei remarks that Natalya looks very much like his mother and tells her she should consider remarrying. It then emerges that a group of Spanish emigrants are also in the apartment. Alexei comments that one of the men is "talking about Spain again" and asks Natalya to go and "try to distract him" so that things "will not end up in a scandal." The film's first batch of archival footage is then introduced. Documentary sequences from the Spanish Civil War depict a bullfight and then small children being separated from their parents and sent into exile. This sequence, underscored by flamenco music, leads into another documentary sequence of the 1934 Soviet balloon ascent, here accompanied by the second appearance of classical music, namely the last movement of Giovanni Battista Pergolesi's *Stabat Mater*. The music continues as the scene shifts to a portrayal of the 12-year-old Alexei browsing through a book with reproductions of works by Leonardo da Vinci. Pergolesi's music only comes to a full stop a few seconds into the next scene. This extended scene depicts Ignat's encounter with a mysterious woman who inexplicably appears in the flat, and to whom Ignat reads Pushkin's famous 1836 letter about the historical fate of Russia. At the beginning of the scene, Ignat helps his mother to collect a number of coins she has dropped on the floor. He receives a sudden mild electric shock and tells his perplexed mother that it is as if he has been here before. At this point the electronic music makes its third appearance, and it will underscore most of the ensuing scene, ending first as the mysterious woman disappears and leaving behind only a slowly evaporating heat mark where her cup had been on the table.

Just after the enigmatic disappearance of the woman the phone rings. It is Alexei, who tells Ignat about a red-haired girl he was in love with when he was Ignat's age. The scene then changes to Time Period Two and a shot of the red-haired girl. As we see her in close up, music from Henry Purcell's *The Indian Queen* is heard on the soundtrack. The music stops abruptly as the sound of a gunshot is heard, taking us to a wintery landscape where Alexei and other young boys are training shooting on a firing range. The young orphan Asafiev throws a hand grenade onto the firing range, but it turns out to be a dummy. An extended sequence of newsreel footage follows, showing the crossing of Lake Sivash by the Red Army in 1943. This sequence is accompanied by a combination of electronic music and ongoing drum strokes, which are subsequently replaced

Appendix 177

by another poem by Arseny Tarkovsky, "Life, Life," again recited as a voice-over on the soundtrack. A cut takes us back to Asafiev who is seen walking up a hill with a Bruegelesque landscape in the background. More newsreels then follow. Fireworks in Moscow to celebrate the end of World War Two are followed by a shot of a look-alike of the dead Hitler, which in turn is followed by a shot of an atomic bomb exploding. Electronic music returns to underscore these images, rising in volume as the mushroom cloud of an atomic bomb is shown. The music continues at a more subdued level as the scene takes us back to another shot of Asafiev. But soon the music rises again in volume as Asafiev stretches out his arm to grab a small bird that has landed on his cap. Another round of documentary footage follows, this time of huge mass meetings in connection with the Cultural Revolution in China, followed by a sequence showing the 1969 border dispute between the Soviet Union and China. As with the Lake Sivash sequence, this sequence is also accompanied by a mixture of electronic music and drum strokes. This complex musical fabric continues for a few seconds into the following scene, which takes us back to Time Period Two and Alexei's recollections.

Alexei and his little sister are in the forest near the family dacha. They quarrel about the book with Leonardo reproductions that Alexei has brought with him. Suddenly their father, who is back on leave from the war, calls out to them and the children run to meet him. As we see the father embrace the two children the recitative "Und siehe da, der Vorhang im Tempel zerriß" from Bach's *St. Matthew Passion* is heard. As the scene shifts to a shot of Leonardo's *Portrait of Ginevra de Benci*, the music culminates in a brief outburst of electronic sound that penetrates the final bars of the recitative and drowns out its final chord completely. This is the first and only time in the film where classical and electronic music are combined. The film then takes us back to the present time, where Alexei tries to convince Natalya that Ignat should come and live with him, an idea that Ignat does not seem to agree with. Alexei tells Natalya about a recurring dream he has been having, which is followed by a second dream sequence in black and white mirroring and at the same time extending the first part of the dream-memory at the beginning of the film. Again, the wind is tracking through the trees. The 5-year-old Alexei is outside the dacha, trying to get in. As the camera pans to the left, revealing the house, a brief segment of electronic music is heard on the soundtrack. When the boy speaks the word "Mama!" (an echo of the first dream sequence where he had uttered the word "Papa!"), the music stops.

Back in Time Period Two, we see the adolescent Alexei escorting his mother, who is visiting a well-to-do doctor's wife to try to sell a pair of earrings. Alexei is asked to wait in another room while the two women negotiate the price of the jewelry. Glimpsing a reflection of himself in a mirror, Alexei contemplates his feelings for the red-haired girl, who is shown in

178 *Appendix*

front of a fire in the subsequent shot. This sequence is accompanied by a second playing of Purcell's *Indian Queen*. The doctor's wife invites Maria and Alexei to have a look at her baby. As the camera slowly zooms in on the sleeping boy, electronic music is heard for the last time in the film. Maria feels unwell and leaves the room, followed by the doctor's wife, who a moment later asks Maria to kill a rooster for her. Maria complies and, after killing the rooster, looks straight into the camera with a demonic expression on her face. This leads into a brief black-and-white sequence. A momentary shot of Alexei's father (also looking into the camera, as if returning Maria's gaze) is followed by a spectacular *mise-en-scène* in which Maria is seen levitating over what is presumably the marital bed. Maria tells her husband that it is a pity that she can only see him when she feels unwell. She then says she loves him. The scene is accompanied by the second and final appearance in the film of Bach's "Das alte Jahr vergangen ist." Back in Time Period Two, Maria and Alexei commence their long walk home from the doctor's house. Arseny Tarkovsky's poem "Eurydice" is heard on the soundtrack as mother and son are seen walking along a river.

A final dream sequence takes us back for a third time to the black-and-white shot of trees and bushes moving in the wind. The sequence continues with the 5-year-old Alexei entering the dacha. Reflected in a mirror, he is seen holding a large pitcher filled with milk. A cut to color then shows us Alexei swimming in a small pond, while his mother washes the sheets in the background. This is followed by the film's penultimate scene, which takes place in present-day time. Alexei is lying in bed (we see only his right arm and get a glimpse of his chest) while a doctor and the mysterious woman previously encountered by Ignat discuss his health. (Also present is the woman's maid, who briefly appeared in the earlier scene.) Alexei assures them that nothing is wrong with him and that everything will be fine. He then reaches out for a small bird that has been sitting on his bed and releases it into the air. This leads into the film's final scene, which presents a panorama over a beautiful late-afternoon field. In what appears to be a blurring of different time periods, Alexei's mother, as an old woman, leads the 5-year-old Alexei and his sister over the field, while the young mother, standing in the background, watches them. The scene is accompanied by the opening chorus from Bach's *St. John Passion*. The film ends in silence, however; no music is heard as the camera draws further into the woods and the screen eventually fades to black.

Notes

1. My use of the expression "dream-memory" is meant to convey that, in the words of Alice Gavin, the "actions that take place when the narrator is a young boy are memories assembled from both reality and dream" (Gavin 2007, 3).

Appendix 179

2. In the film's penultimate scene, we catch a glimpse of Alexei's bare chest and right arm, but we never see his face.
3. Tarkovsky himself said that the boy's ages were 6 and 12 (see Gianvito 2006, 44).
4. Robert Bird (2008, 136) notes that "the three periods covered by the documentary footage coincide with the chronological foci of the autobiographical narration: 1935–6, 1943–5 and 1969." See also Martin (2011, 120).

References

Aguiar, Marian (2008) "Making Modernity: Inside the Technological Space of the Railway" *Cultural Critique*, No. 68, 66–85.

Amengual, Barthélemy (1988) "Tarkovski le rebelle: non-comformisme ou restauration?" in Gille Ciment (ed.) *Dossier Positif* (Andrei Tarkovski: 4). Paris: Edition Rivages, 19–33.

Aspesi, Natalia (1983) "The Gentle Emotion That Is a Mortal Illness for Us Russians" (Interview with Andrei Tarkovsky in Cannes 1983), *Nostalghia.com*. URL: http://nostalghia.com/TheTopics/Tarkovsky_Aspesi-1983.html (accessed 2019-02-04).

Barham, Jeremy (2009) "Scoring Incredible Futures: Science-Fiction Screen Music, and 'Postmodernism' as Romantic Epiphany" *The Musical Quarterly*, Vol. 91, No. 3–4, 240–274.

Barham, Jeremy (2014) "Music and the Moving Image" in Stephen Downes (ed.) *Aesthetics of Music: Musicological Perspectives*. New York and London: Routledge, 224–238.

Barthes, Roland (1972) *Mythologies*. London: Cape.

Bassil-Morozow, Helena (2015) "The Poetics of Maternal Loss in Tarkovsky's *the Mirror*" in Agnieszka Piotrowska (ed.) *Embodied Encounters: New Approaches to Psychoanalysis and Cinema*. New York: Routledge, 194–207.

Beaumont, Matthew & Freeman, Michael (eds.) (2007) *The Railway and Modernity: Time, Space, and the Machine Ensemble*. Bern: Peter Lang.

Beer, David (2006) "*Solaris* and the ANS Synthesizer: On the Relations between Tarkovsky, Artemiev and Music Technology" in Gunnlaugur A. Jónsson & Thorkell Ágúst Óttarsson (eds.) *Through the Mirror: Reflections on the Films of Andrei Tarkovsky*. Newcastle: Cambridge Scholar Press, 100–119.

Benjamin, Walter (2008) *The Work of Art in the Age of Mechanical Reproduction* (trans. J.A. Underwood). London: Penguin.

Berger, Donald P. (revised by David W. Hughes) "Schakuhachi" in *Grove Music Online*, Japan, § II, 5. URL: www.oxfordmusiconline.com.ezproxy.ub.gu.se/grovemusic/view/10.1093/gmo/9781561592630.001.0001/omo-9781561592630-e-0000043335 (accessed 2019-04-14).

Bergh, Magnus & Munkhammar, Birgit (1986) "Den sjunde filmen – ett samtal om *Offret*" in Magnus Bergh & Birgit Munkhammar (eds.) *Tarkovskij: Tanken på en hemkomst*. Stockholm: Alfabeta.

Biancorosso, Giorgio (2001) "Beginning Credits and Beyond: Music and the Cinematic Imagination" *Echo*, Vol. 3, No. 1. URL: www.echo.ucla.edu/article-beginning-credits-and-beyond-music-and-the-cinematic-imagination-author/ (accessed 2019-04-15).

References   181

Biancorosso, Giorgio (2009) "The Harpist in the Closet: Film Music as Epistemological Joke" *Music and the Moving Image*, Vol. 2, No. 3, 11–33.

Bird, Michael (1996) "Music as Spiritual Metaphor in the Cinema of Ingmar Bergman" *Kinema: A Journal for Film and Visual Media*. URL: www.kinema.uwaterloo.ca/article.php?id=315&feature

Bird, Robert (2008) *Andrei Tarkovsky: Elements of Cinema*. London: Reaktion.

Bonds, Mark Evan (1997) "Idealism and the Aesthetics of Instrumental Music at the Turn of the Nineteenth Century" *Journal of the American Musicological Society*, Vol. 50, No. 2–3, 387–421.

Bordwell, David (1985) *Narration in the Fiction Film*. Madison: The University of Wisconsin Press.

Bordwell, David (1989) *Making Meaning: Inference and Rhetoric in the Interpretation of Cinema*. Cambridge, MA: Harvard University Press.

Bordwell, David (2007) *Poetics of Cinema*. New York: Routledge.

Bordwell, David & Thompson, Kristin (2010) *Film Art: An Introduction* (9th edition). New York: McGraw-Hill.

Bould, Mark (2014) *Solaris*. London: Palgrave Macmillan.

Boym, Svetlana (2001) *The Future of Nostalgia*. New York: Basic Books.

Brezna, Irena (2006) "An Enemy of Symbolism" in John Gianvito (ed.) *Andrei Tarkovsky: Interviews*. Jackson: University of Mississippi, 104–123.

Broman, Per F. (2012) "Music, Sound, and Silence in the Films of Ingmar Bergman" in James Wierzbicki (ed.) *Music, Sound and Filmmakers: Sonic Style in Cinema*. London: Routledge, 15–31.

Buch, Esteban (2003) *Beethoven's Ninth: A Political History*. Chicago: University of Chicago Press.

Buckland, Warren (2004) *The Cognitive Semiotics of Film*. Cambridge: Cambridge University Press.

Buhler, James (2018) *Theories of the Soundtrack*. New York: Oxford University Press.

Bunia, Remigius (2010) "Diegesis and Representation: Beyond the Fictional World, on the Margins of Story and Narrative" *Poetics Today*, Vol. 31, No. 4, 679–720.

Burns, Christy L. (2011) "Tarkovsky's *Nostalghia*: Refusing Modernity, Re-Envisioning Beauty" *Cinema Journal*, Vol. 50, No. 2, 104–122.

Calabretto, Roberto (ed.) (2010a) *Andrej Tarkovskij e la musica*. Udine: LIM Editrice.

Calabretto, Roberto (2010b) "'La musica cinematografica per me, in ogni caso è una componente naturale del mondo dei suoni' – La musica secondo Andrej Tarkovskij" in Roberto Calabretto (ed.) *Andrej Tarkovskij e la musica*. Udine: LIM Editrice, 3–51.

Carroll, Noël (1999) "Myth and the Logic of Interpretation" in Michael Krausz & Richard Shusterman (eds.) *Interpretation, Relativism and the Metaphysics of Culture: Themes in the Philosophy of Joseph Margolis*. New York: Humanity Books, 40–60.

Casey, Edward (1997) "Joseph Margolis on Interpretation" *Man and World*, Vol. 30, 127–138.

Cecchi, Alessandro (2010) "Diegetic versus Nondiegetic: A Reconsideration of the Conceptual Opposition as a Contribution to the Theory of Audiovision" *Worlds of Audiovision*. URL: http://www-5.unipv.it/wav/pdf/WAV_Cecchi_2010_eng.pdf (accessed 2019-03-07).

Chion, Michel (1994) *Audio-Vision: Sound on Screen* (ed. and trans. Claudia Gorbman). New York: Columbia University Press.

182 References

Chion, Michel (2001) *Kubrick's Cinema Odyssey* (ed. and trans. Claudia Gorbman). London: BFI Publishing.

Cobb, John B. (1962) *Living Options in Protestant Theology: A Survey of Methods*. Philadelphia: Westminster Press.

Çolak, Metin (2013) "The Functions of Sound and Music in Tarkovsky's Films" *Audio Technologies for Music and Media International Conference 2013: Proceedings*, Ankara, Turkey: Bilkent University, 12–19.

Dahlhaus, Carl (1989) *The Idea of Absolute Music* (trans. Roger Lustig). Chicago: University of Chicago Press.

DeNora, Tia (2000) *Music in Everyday Life*. Cambridge: Cambridge University Press.

Dillon, Steven (2006) *The Solaris Effect: Art & Artifice in Contemporary American Film*. Austin: University of Texas Press.

Donnelly, Kevin (2013) "Extending Film Aesthetics: Audio Beyond Visuals" in John Richardson, Claudia Gorbman & Carol Vernallis (eds.) *The Oxford Handbook of New Audiovisual Aesthetics*. New York: Oxford University Press, 357–371.

Dunne, Nathan (ed.) (2008) *Tarkovsky*. London: Black Dog Publishing.

Dyer, Richard (2010) *Nino Rota: Music, Film, and Feeling*. London: Palgrave Macmillan.

Egorova, Tatiana (1997) *Soviet Film Music: An Historical Survey* (trans. Tatiana A. Ganf & Natalia E. Egunova). Amsterdam: Harwood Academic Publishers.

Epelboin, Annie (1986) "Andrei Tarkovsky on *The Sacrifice*" (Epelboin in interview with Tarkovsky in Paris 1986) *Nostalghia.com*. URL: http://nostalghia.com/TheTopics/On_Sacrifice.html (accessed 2018-12-12).

Fairweather, Elisabeth (2012) "Andrey Tarkovsky: The Refrain of the Sonic Fingerprint" in James Wierzbicki (ed.) *Music, Sound and Filmmakers: Sonic Style in Cinema*. London: Routledge, 32–44.

Figes, Orlando (1997) *A People's Tragedy: The Russian Revolution 1891–1924*. London: Pimlico.

Fitzpatrick, Martin (2002) "Indeterminate Ursula and 'Seeing How It Must Have Looked,' or, 'The Damned Lemming,' and Subjunctive Narrative in Pynchon, Faulkner, O'Brien, and Morrison" *Narrative*, Vol. 10, No. 3, 244–261.

Flinn, Caryl (1992) *Strains of Utopia*. Princeton, NJ: Princeton University Press.

Flinn, Caryl (2000) "Strategies of Remembrance: Music and History in the New German Cinema" in James Buhler, Caryl Flinn & David Neumeyer (eds.) *Music and Cinema*. Hanover: Wesleyan University Press, 118–141.

Foster, David (2010) "Where Flowers Bloom But Have No Scent: The Cinematic Space of the Zone in Andrei Tarkovsky's *Stalker*" *Studies in Russian and Soviet Cinema*, Vol. 4, No. 3, 307–320.

Frampton, Daniel (2006) *Filmosophy*. London: Wallflower Press.

Gariff, David (2012) "Moments of Grace: The Films of Robert Bresson" in *Film notes at the National Gallery of Art*. URL: www.nga.gov/content/dam/ngaweb/calendar/film/pdfs/notes/ngafilm-bresson-notes.pdf (accessed 2019-04-15).

Gaut, Berys (2010) *A Philosophy of Cinematic Art*. Cambridge: Cambridge University Press.

Gavin, Alice (2007) "The Word of the Father/the Body of the Mother: Dimensions of Gender in Tarkovsky's *Mirror*" *UCL Opticon, 1826*, No. 2, 1–6.

Gianvito, John (2006) *Andrei Tarkovsky: Interviews*. Jackson: University of Mississippi.

References   183

Golstein, Vladimir (2008) "The Energy of Anxiety" in Nathan Dunne (ed.) *Tarkovsky*. London: Black Dog Publishing, 176–205.

Gorbman, Claudia (1987) *Unheard Melodies: Narrative Film Music*. Bloomington: Indiana University Press.

Green, Peter (1987) "Apocalypse and Sacrifice" *Sight and Sound*, Vol. 56, No. 2, 111–118.

Green, Peter (1993) *Andrei Tarkovsky: The Winding Quest*. London: Macmillan Press.

Griffin, Michael J. & Waldron, Dara (2007) "Across Time and Space: The Utopian Impulses of Andrei Tarkovsky's *Stalker*" in Michael J. Griffin & Tom Moylan (eds.) *Exploring the Utopian Impulse: Essays on Utopian thought and Practice*. Oxford: Peter Lang, 231–246.

Gunnarsson, Gunnar J. (2006) "In Hope and Faith: Religious Motifs in Tarkovsky's *the Sacrifice*" in Gunnlaugur A. Jónsson & Thorkell Ágúst Óttarsson (eds.) *Through the Mirror: Reflections on the Films of Andrei Tarkovsky*. Newcastle: Cambridge Scholar Press, 238–260.

Hara, Kunio (2016) "1 + 1 = 1: Measuring Time's Distance in Toru Takemitsu's *Nostalghia: In Memory of Andrei Tarkovsky*" *Music and the Moving Image*, Vol. 9, No. 3, 3–18.

Heldt, Guido (2013) *Music and Levels of Narration in Film: Steps across the Border*. Bristol: Intellect.

Hellström, Björn & Rémy, Nicolas (1999) *Space, Music, Sound Environment: What Links Exist between Research on the Sound Environment and Music?* (Publication by CRESSON Laboratory). URL: https://aau.archi.fr/laboratoire-aau/publications/ (accessed 2019-05-03).

Holbrook, Morris B. (2004) "Ambi-Diegetic Music in Films as a Product-Design and Placement Strategy: The *Sweet Smell of Success*" *Marketing Theory*, Vol. 4, No. 3, 171–185.

Illg, Jerzy & Leonard Neuger (1985) "I'm Interested in the Problem of Inner Freedom" (interview with Andrei Tarkovsky in Stockholm 1985), *Nostalghia.com*. URL: http://nostalghia.com/TheTopics/interview.html (accessed 2019-04-15).

Ishimov, V. & Shejko, R. (2006) "The Twentieth Century and the Artist" in John Gianvito (ed.) *Andrei Tarkovsky: Interviews*. Jackson: University of Mississippi, 124–154.

James, Nick (2015) "The Tarkovsky Legacy" *Sight and Sound*, Vol. 25, No. 11, 46–52. URL: www.bfi.org.uk/news-opinion/sight-sound-magazine/features/deep-focus/tarkovsky-legacy (accessed 2019-04-08).

Jameson, Fredric (1992) *The Geopolitical Aesthetic*. Bloomington: Indiana University Press.

Jameson, Fredric (2005) *Archaeologies of the Future: The Desire Called Utopia and Other Science Fictions*. London: Verso.

Johnson, Vida T. & Graham Petrie (1994) *The Films of Andrei Tarkovsky: A Visual Fugue*. Bloomington: Indiana University Press.

Jones, Daniel O. (2007) *The Soul That Thinks: Essays on Philosophy, Narrative and Symbol in the Cinema and Thought of Andrei Tarkovsky*. PhD thesis of College of Fine Art, Ohio University (Ohio).

Jónsson, Gunnlaugur A. & Thorkell Ágúst Óttarsson (eds.) (2006) *Through the Mirror: Reflections on the Films of Andrei Tarkovsky*. Newcastle: Cambridge Scholar Press.

Jordan, Miriam & Haladyn, Julian Jason (2010) "Simulation, Simulacra and *Solaris*" *Film-Philosophy*, Vol. 14, No. 1, 253–273.

184 *References*

Kassabian, Anahid (2001) *Hearing Film.* New York: Routledge.

Kassabian, Anahid (2013) "The End of Diegesis as We Know It" in John Richardson, Claudia Gorbman & Carol Vernallis (eds.) *The Oxford Handbook of New Audiovisual Aesthetics.* Oxford: Oxford University Press, 89–106.

Kramer, Lawrence (1990) *Music as Cultural Practice, 1800–1900.* Berkeley: University of California Press.

Krausz, Michael (1999) "Interpretation, Relativism, and Culture: Four Questions for Margolis" in Michael Krausz & Richard Shusterman (eds.) *Interpretation, Relativism and the Metaphysics of Culture: Themes in the Philosophy of Joseph Margolis.* New York: Humanity Books, 105–124.

Le Fanu, Mark (1987) *The Cinema of Andrei Tarkovsky.* London: BFI.

Levinson, Jerrold (1990) *Music, Art, and Metaphysics: Essays in Philosophical Aesthetics.* Ithaca and London: Cornell University Press.

Levinson, Jerrold (1992) "Intention and Interpretation: A Last Look" in Gary Iseminger (ed.) *Intention and Interpretation.* Philadelphia: Temple University Press, 221–256.

Levinson, Jerrold (2004) "Film Music and Narrative Agency" in Leo Braudy & Marshall Cohen (eds.) *Film Theory and Criticism: Introductory Readings* (6th edition). Oxford: Oxford University Press, 482–512.

Levitas, Ruth (1990) *The Concept of Utopia.* Syracuse, NY: Syracuse University Press.

Levitas, Ruth (2010) "*In eine bess're Welt entru ckt*: Reflections on Music and Utopia" *Utopian Studies,* Vol. 21, No. 2, 215–231.

Leydon, Rebecca (2004) "Forbidden Planet: Effects and Effects in the Electro Avant-Garde" in Philip Hayward (ed.) *Off the Planet: Music, Sound and Science Fiction Cinema.* Eastleigh: John Libbey Publishing, 61–76.

Luko, Alexis (2015) *Sonatas, Screams, and Silence: Music and Sound in the Films of Ingmar Bergman.* New York: Routledge.

Lövgren, Håkan (2010) "Förord – Fäder och söner" in Håkan Lövgren (ed.) *Andrej Tarkovskij. Offret.* Umeå: Atrium, 5–23.

Mai, Nadin (2017) "The Filmind in Andrei Tarkovsky's *Mirror.*" URL: https://theartsofslowcinema.com/2017/12/19/the-filmind-in-andrei-tarkovskys-zerkalo/ (accessed 2019-02-04).

Margolis, Joseph (1980) *Art and Philosophy: Conceptual Issues in Aesthetics.* Atlantic Highlands, NJ: Humanities Press.

Margolis, Joseph (1992) "Robust Relativism" in Gary Iseminger (ed.) *Intention and Interpretation.* Philadelphia: Temple University Press, 41–50.

Margolis, Joseph (2009) "Hermeneutics" in Stephen Davies et al. (eds.) *A Companion to Aesthetics.* Oxford: Blackwell Publishing, 324–327.

Martin, Sean (2011) *Andrei Tarkovsky.* Harpenden: Kamera Books.

McClary, Susan (1993) "Narrative Agendas in 'Absolute' Music: Identity and Difference in Brahms's Third Symphony" in Ruth A. Solie (ed.) *Musicology and Difference: Gender and Sexuality in Music Scholarship.* Berkeley and Los Angeles: University of California Press, 326–344.

McSweeney, Terence (2015) *Beyond the Frame: The Films and Film Theory of Andrei Tarkovsky.* Konia: Aporetic Press.

Miall, David S. (2008) "Resisting Interpretation" in Nathan Dunne (ed.) *Tarkovsky.* London: Black Dog Publishing, 320–333.

Mroz, Matilda (2013) *Temporality and Film Analysis.* Edinburgh: Edinburgh University Press.

References   185

Neale, Steve (2002) "Art Cinema as Institution" in Catherine Fowler (ed.) *The European Cinema Reader*. London: Routledge, 103–120.

Neumeyer, David (2009) "Diegetic/Nondiegetic: A Theoretical Model" *Music and the Moving Image*, Vol. 2, No. 1, 26–39.

Neumeyer, David (2015) *Meaning and Interpretation of Music in Cinema*. Bloomington: Indiana University Press.

Noeske, Nina (2008) "Musik und Imagination: J. S. Bach in Tarkovskijs *Solaris*" in Victoria Piel, Knut Holsträter & Oliver Huck (eds.) *Filmmusik: Beiträge zu ihrer Theorie und Vermittlung*. Hildesheim and Zürich: Georg Olms Verlag, 25–42.

Oushakine, Serguei Alex (2007) "'We're Nostalgic But We're Not Crazy': Retrofitting the Past in Russia" *The Russian Review*, Vol. 66, 451–482.

Penner, Nina (2017) "Rethinking the Diegetic/Nondiegetic Distinction in the Film Musical" *Music and the Moving Image*, Vol. 10, No. 3, 3–20.

Pietikäinen, Petteri (2007) *Alchemists of Human Nature*. New York: Routledge.

Pontara, Tobias (2011) "Beethoven Overcome: Romantic and Existentialist Utopia in Andrei Tarkovsky's *Stalker*" *19th-Century Music*, Vol. 34, No. 3, 302–315.

Pontara, Tobias (2014) "Bach at the Space Station: Hermeneutic Pliability and Multiplying Gaps in Andrei Tarkovsky's *Solaris*" *Music, Sound, and the Moving Image*, Vol. 8, No. 1, 1–23.

Pontara, Tobias (2015) "Interpretation, Imputation, Plausibility: Toward a Theoretical Model for Musical Hermeneutics" *International Review for the Aesthetics and Sociology of Music*, Vol. 46, No. 1, 3–41.

Pontara, Tobias (2016) "Interpretation and Underscoring: Modest Constructivism and the Issue of Nondiegetic versus Intra-Diegetic Music in Film" *Music and the Moving Image*, Vol. 9, No. 2, 39–57.

Pontara, Tobias (2019) "The Music of Sacrificial Acts: Displacement, Redemption: Beethoven and Verdi in Andrei Tarkovsky's Nostalghia" in Michael Baumgartner & Ewelina Boczkowska (eds.) *Music, Memory, Nostalghia and Trauma in European Cinema after the Second World War*. New York: Routledge.

Quandt, James (2008) "Tarkovsky and Bresson: Music, Suicide, Apocalypse" in Nathan Dunne (ed.) *Tarkovsky*. London: Black Dog Publishing, 258–281.

Redwood, Thomas (2010) *Andrei Tarkovsky's Poetics of Cinema*. Newcastle: Cambridge Scholars Publishing.

Renaud, Charlotte (2011) "An Unrequited Love of Music." URL: www.ingmarbergman.se/universum/en-obesvarad-kärlek-till-musik (accessed 2019-04-15).

Reyland, Nicholas (2012a) "The Beginnings of a Beautiful Friendship?: Music Narratology and Screen Music Studies" *Music, Sound, and the Moving Image*, Vol. 6, No. 1, 55–71.

Reyland, Nicholas (2012b) *Zbigniew Preisner's Three Colors Trilogy: Blue, White, Red*. Lanham: Scarecrow Press.

Reyland, Nicholas (2013) "Negation and Negotiation: Plotting Narrative through Literature and Music from Modernism to Postmodernism" in Michael L. Klein & Nicholas Reyland (eds.) *Music and Narrative Since 1900*. Bloomington: Indiana University Press, 29–58.

Riley, John A. (2012) "Tarkovsky and Brevity" *Dandelion*, Vol. 3, No. 1, 1–16.

Riley, John A. (2017) "Hauntology, Ruins and the Failure of the Future in Andrei Tarkovsky's *Stalker*" *Journal of Film and Video*, Vol. 69, No. 1, 18–26.

186 References

Rivi, Luisa (2007) *European Cinema after 1989: Cultural Identity and Transnational Production*. New York: Palgrave Macmillan.

Robinson, Jeremy Mark (2006) *The Sacred Cinema of Andrei Tarkovsky*. Maidstone: Crescent Moon, Cop.

Rodman, Ronald (2010) *Tuning In: American Narrative Television Music*. New York: Oxford University Press.

Rosar, William H. (2009) "Film Studies in Musicology: Disciplinarity vs. Interdisciplinarity" *Journal of Film Music*, Vol. 2–4, No. 2, 99–125.

Sargent, Lyman Tower (1994) "The Three Faces of Utopianism Revisited" *Utopian Studies*, Vol. 5, No. 1, 1–37.

Sarkar, Bhaskar (2008) "Threnody for Modernity" in Nathan Dunne (ed.) *Tarkovsky*. London: Black Dog Publishing, 237–259.

Sbravatti, Valerio (2016) "Story Music/Discourse Music: Analyzing the Relationship between Placement and Function of Music in Films" *Music and the Moving Image*, Vol. 9, No. 3, 19–37.

Schmerheim, Philipp (2006) "Film, Not Sliced Up into Pieces, or: How Film Made Me Feel Thinking" *Film-Philosophy*, Vol. 12, No. 2, 109–123.

Shpinitskaya, Julia (2006) "Solaris by A. Tarkovsky: Music-Visual Troping, Paradigmatism, Cognitive Stereoscopy" *TRANS-Revista Transcultural de Música* 10. URL: www.sibetrans.com/trans/a157/solaris-by-atarkovsky-music-visual-troping-paradigmatism-cognitive-stereoscopy (accessed 2019-02-01).

Shpinitskaya, Julia (2014) "Andrei Tarkovsky's Musical Offering: The Law of Quotation" *IASS Publications: Proceedings of the World Congress of the IASS/AIS*. URL: http://iass-ais.org/proceedings2014/view_lesson.php?id=161 (accessed 2019-02-04).

Sitney, P. Adams (2014a) *The Cinema of Poetry*. Oxford: Oxford University Press.

Sitney, P. Adams (2014b) "Andrei Tarkovsky, Russian Experience, and the Poetry of Cinema" *New England Review*, Vol. 34, No. 3–4, 208–241.

Skakov, Nariman (2012) *The Cinema of Tarkovsky: Labyrinths of Space and Time*. London: I.B. Tauris & Co Ltd.

Slevin, Tom (2010) "Existence, Ethics and Death in Andrei Tarkovsky's Cinema: The Cultural Philosophy of *Solaris*" *Journal of World Cinema*, Vol. 8, No. 2, 49–62.

Smith, Jeff (2009) "Bridging the Gap: Reconsidering the Border between Diegetic and Nondiegetic Music" *Music and the Moving Image*, Vol. 2, No. 1, 1–25.

Smith, Stefan (2007) "The Edge of Perception: Sound in Tarkovsky's *Stalker*" *The Soundtrack*, Vol. 1, No. 1, 41–52.

Snead, James (1994/2016) *White Screen/Black Images: Hollywood from the Dark Side*. London and New York: Routledge.

Söderbergh Widding Astrid (1992) *Gränsbilder: Det dolda rummet hos Tarkovskij*. PhD diss.: Stockholm (Department of Film Studies, Stockholm University).

Söderbergh Widding, Astrid (2006) "Deus Absconditus: Between Visible and Invisible in the Films of Tarkovsky" in Gunnlaugur A. Jónsson & Thorkell Ágúst Óttarsson (eds.) *Through the Mirror: Reflections on the Films of Andrei Tarkovsky*. Newcastle: Cambridge Scholar Press, 152–167.

Sontag, Susan (2001) *Against Interpretation and Other Essays*. New York: Picador.

Souriau, Étienne (ed.) (1953) *L'Univers filmique*. Paris: Flammarion.

Stadler, Jane (2018) "Cinesonic Imagination: The Somatic, the Sonorous, and the Synaesthetic" *Cinephile*, Vol. 12, No. 1, 8–15.

Stecker, Robert (1997) *Art Works: Definition, Meaning, Value*. University Park: Pennsylvania State University Press.

References   187

Stilwell, Robynn (2007) "The Fantastical Gap between the Diegetic and Nondiegetic" in Daniel Goldmark, Lawrence Kramer & Richard Leppert (eds.) *Beyond the Soundtrack: Representing Music in Cinema*. Berkeley and Los Angeles: University of California Press, 184–202.

Strugatsky, Arkady & Boris Strugatsky (2000) *Roadside Picnic* (trans. Antonia W. Bouis). London: VGSF.

Sullivan, Daniel (2012) "Tillich and Tarkovsky: An Existential Analysis of *Mirror*" *Journal of Humanistic Psychology*, Vol. 52, No. 4, 451–466.

Sushytska, Julia (2015) "Tarkovsky's *Nostalghia*: A Journey to the Home That Never Was" *The Journal of Aesthetic Education*, Vol. 49, No. 1, 36–43.

Synessios, Natasha (2001) *Mirror*. London: I.B. Tauris.

Tarkovsky, Andrei (1986) *Sculpting in Time: Reflections on The Cinema* (trans. Kitty Hunter Blair). London: Bodley Head.

Tarkovsky, Andrei (1999) *Collected Screenplays* (trans. William Powell & Natasha Synessios). New York: Faber and Faber.

Tarkovsky, Andrei (2012) *Martyrologion: dagböcker 1970–1986*. Umeå: Atrium.

Taylor, Henry M. (2007) "The Success Story of a Misnomer" *Offscreen*, Vol. 11, No. 8–9. URL: https://offscreen.com/view/soundforum_2 (accessed 2019-04-15).

Temperley, David (2006) "Key Structure in 'Das alte Jahr vergangen ist'" *Journal of Music Theory*, Vol. 50, No. 1, 103–110.

Thomson, C. Claire (2007) "It's All about Snow: Limning the Post-Human Body in *Solaris* (Tarkovsky, 1972) and *It's All about Love* (Vinterberg, 2003)" *New Cinemas: Journal of Contemporary Film*, Vol. 5, No. 1, 3–21.

Totaro, Donato (2007) "Into the Zone" *Offscreen*, Vol. 11, No. 8–9. URL: https://offscreen.com/view/soundforum_1 (accessed 2019-04-15).

Truppin, Andrea (1992) "And Then There Was Sound: The Films of Andrei Tarkovsky" in Rick Altman (ed.) *Sound Theory/Sound Practice*. London: Routledge, 235–248.

Tsai, Lin-chin (2018) "Mapping Formosa: Settler Colonial Cartography in Taiwan Cinema in the 1950s" *Concentric: Literary and Cultural Studies*, Vol. 2, No. 44, 19–50.

Turovskaya, Maya (1989) *Tarkovsky: Cinema as Poetry* (trans. Natasha Ward). London: Faber and Faber.

Winters, Ben (2010) "The Non-Diegetic Fallacy: Film, Music, and Narrative Space" *Music & Letters*, Vol. 91, No. 2, 224–243.

Winters, Ben (2012) "Musical Wallpaper?: Towards an Appreciation of Non-Narrating Music in Film" *Music, Sound, and the Moving Image*, Vol. 6, No. 1, 39–54.

Yacavone, Daniel (2008) "Towards a Theory of Film Worlds" *Film-Philosophy*, Vol. 12, No. 2, 83–108.

Yacavone, Daniel (2012) "Spaces, Gaps, and Levels: From the Diegetic to the Aesthetic in Film Theory" *Music, Sound, and the Moving Image*, Vol. 6, No. 1, 21–37.

Žižek, Slavoj (1999) "The Thing from Inner Space on Tarkovsky" *Angelaki: Journal of the Theoretical Humanities*, Vol. 4, No. 3, 221–231.

Žižek, Slavoj (2000) "The Thing from Inner Space" in Renata Salecl (ed.) *Sexuation*. Durham and London: Duke University Press, 216–252.

Index

Note: Page numbers in *italics* indicate a figure or music example on the corresponding page.

absolute music 40
acousmetre 121
affection 4, 23, 48–58, 113, 142
Amadeus 29
ambiguities *see* narrative ambiguities
Amengual, Barthélemy, *Dossier Positif* 93n3
Andrei Rublev (Tarkovsky) 5–6, 119, 175
anempathetic sound 115
ANS/ANS synthesizer – SYNTHI 100 Synthesizer 30, 34–35, 43n12, 44nn17–18, 94–95n20
Antichrist 19n1, 154
Apocalypse Now 151
appearance and disappearance, in *Mirror* 47, 63–66, 176
art: Tarkovsky on 8–9, 142–143, 167–168; *The Sacrifice* 122; *Solaris* 27–28; *Stalker* 90–91, 95n21
art cinema 44n23, 45n27; and Tarkovsky 2–3, 19n1, 26, 146–147, 155
Artemiev, Eduard 5, 139n6, 157, 162; music for *Mirror* 15, 58–59, *61*, 63, 69, 143, 175; music for *Solaris* 14, 30–31, 34–35, 41, 44nn17–19, 158–159, 169; music for *Stalker* 13, 75, 79, 82–84, 86–87, *87*, 94–95n20
art-religion 90
authenticity *see* spiritual authenticity
Autumn Sonata 26
awakening, gradual awakening in *The Sacrifice* 118–119, 122–134

Bach, Johann Sebastian 4, 20–23, 91, 139n6; and the basic musical dichotomy of *Solaris* 41–42; "Das alte Jahr vergangen ist," *Orgelbüchlein*,

in *Mirror* 48–50, 71, 72n5, 175, 178; denigration of 172n18; and electronic sound 44n17, 44n19; and hermeneutic pliability 36–39; "Ich ruf zu dir, Herr Jesu Christ," *Orgelbüchlein*, in *Solaris* 14–16, 18, 19n1, 20–21, 23–24, 27–28, 33, 35–36, 41, 42n2, 47–48, 70, 120, 149, 155, 169; and leitmotif 43n9; metadiegetic 28–35; nondiegetic 24–28; "Nun seid ihr wohl gerochen," *Christmas Oratorio* 56; in *Solaris*, brief overview 23–24; *St. John Passion* 48, 55–58, *57*, 73n12, 73n16, 155, 169, 178; *St. Matthew Passion* 48, 54–56, 111, 122–123, 134, 155, 166, 171, 172n17, 177; and troubled utopias 141–143, 154–158, 162–165, 168–170
Barham, Jeremy 44n19, 110, 159, 169
Barry Lyndon 26
Bassil-Morozow, Helena 73n21
Beer, David 44n17, 45n28
Beethoven 2–4, 15, 17, 19n10, 75–78; Domenico's Beethoven in *Nostalghia* 99–104, 116n6; "Hammerklavier" 43n9; and *La Marseillaise* 93n6, 94n13; and musical dichotomies between East and West 84–87, 94n18; Ninth Symphony 87–92, 93n7; and *Nostalghia* 98, 114–115; "Ode to Joy," Ninth Symphony 2, 15, 17, 75–76, 78–79, 84, 86–87, 89, 94n13, 98, 100, 102–104, 114, 156; and signifiers beyond intelligibility 81, 83; and signifiers of triumph and progress 79–81; and troubled utopias 141, 156–157, 162

Index   189

belonging: and despair 54–55; and loss and longing 48–50; and love and intimacy 50–52; in *Mirror* 47–48; and reconciliation 55–58; and tranquility 52–54

Benjamin, Walter 156

Berezovsky, Maxym 115n2

Bergh, Magnus 139–140n12

Bergman, Ingmar 3–4, 26, 141–142, 171n4; *Cries and Whispers* 26, 154–155; and diegetic performances 43n6; *Through a Glass Darkly* 26, 43n7, 155

Biancorosso, Giorgio 40, 116n7

Bird, Robert 8, 12, 42n3, 93n8, 140n14, 172–173n19

Bondarchuk, Sergei 5, 97

Bonds, Mark Evan 91

Bordwell, David 11, 45n27, 145–147, 172nn8–10

Bould, Mark 12, 23–24

Brahms, Johannes 40

Branigan, Edward 26, 44n16, 71, 146

Bresson, Robert 142

Bruegel the Elder, Pieter 20, 24, 32–33, 67, *67*, 74n26, 177

Buch, Esteban 79, 94n13

Buckland, Warren 172n8

Bultmann, Rudolf 92

Calabretto, Roberto 43n9, 139n6

childhood, in *Mirror* 46–49, 54–56, 59–63

Chion, Michel 121

Chkalov, Valeri 52

Christian existentialism/Christian existentialist hermeneutics 92, 95n21

cinematic narrator 25–26

classical music 48, 153–157; and despair 54–55; and electronic music 5, 16–17, 22–23, 41, 47, 69–70, 87, 142–143, 162–164, 177; and loss and longing 48–50; and love and intimacy 50–52; and reconciliation 55–58; and Tarkovsky 4-5; and tranquility and belonging 52–54; *see also specific composers*

Coppola, Francis Ford 151

Cries and Whispers 26, 154–155

Dahlhaus, Carl 90

da Vinci, Leonardo 4, 52–54, 72n8, 176; *Adoration of the Magi* 122, 132, 137; *Portrait of Ginevra de' Benci* 55, 177

Day the Earth Stood Still, The 159

Demme, Jonathan 26

DeNora, Tia 10, 19n8

despair, in *Mirror* 54–55

Dewey, John 1

diegesis 6–7, 21–22, 28–29, 36–37, 69–72, 119–122; diegetic instantiation 132–134; diegetic status and multiple interpretability 149–153; mainstream 145–149; Tarkovskian 145–149; *see also* diegetic music; diegetization; intra-diegetic music; metadiegetic music; nondiegetic music; transcendental diegetic music

diegetic music 22, 44n24, 100, 144, 151; and *The Sacrifice* 123, 133–134, 139n10; *see also* intra-diegetic music; metadiegetic music; nondiegetic music; transcendental diegetic music

diegetization 146, 172n8

disappearance *see* appearance and disappearance documentary sequences 53, 66–69, 148, 174, 176

Donnelly, Kevin 13, 15

doubt 166–171

dream-memories, in *Mirror* 47, 52, 58–63, 66, 68, 71

dreams 46–47, 70–71, 73n17, 73n19, 73n21; and classical music 49, 52, 55–56; and electronic music 65–66, 68–69; *see also* dream-memories

East and West 83–87, 95n20, 166

Eastwood, Clint 36

Egorova, Tatiana 14–16, 19n11; and *Solaris* 20, 31–32, 43n12, 44n18; and *Stalker* 95n20

electronic music 58–59, 157–160; and classical music 5, 16–17, 22–23, 41, 47, 69–70, 87, 142–143, 162–164, 177; and documentary sequences 66–69; and dream-memories of early childhood 59–63; and inexplicably appearing and disappearing characters 63–66; *see also* Artemiev, Eduard

expressive doubling 88–91

Fairweather, Elisabeth 73n22

fantastical gap 22, 35–41, 44n24, 101

Figes, Orlando 94n14

filmind 74n29, 99, 104–113, 117n19, 148, 150–152, 172n12

190   *Index*

filmind persona 109–112
Fitzpatrick, Martin 38–39
Flinn, Caryl 93n7, 168, 173n23
focalization 34, 51, 71, 147, 150–152, 158–160, 173n20
folk music and song 6, 17–18; and *Nostalghia* 98, 106–107, 113, 116; *Oi Vi Kumusciki* 105, 108–109, 115, 160, 165; and *The Sacrifice* 120, 132, 134, 140n14; and troubled utopias 144, 170, 172n16
Forbidden Planet 159
Foster, David 93n8
Foucault, Michel 19n9
Frampton, Daniel 74n29, 99, 108–109, 117n19, 172n13

gap *see* fantastical gap
Gaut, Berys 172n9
Gavin, Alice 178n1
Genette, Gérard 29, 71
Gianvito, John 9, 27–28, 74n27, 85, 110
González Iñárritu, Alejandro 19n1
Gorbman, Claudia 6, 29, 58–59, 79–80, 145, 148–149
Green, Peter 12, 152; and *Mirror* 73n19; and *The Sacrifice* 128, 135–136, 140n14, 140n17; and *Solaris* 20–21, 29–30, 38; and *Stalker* 82
Griffin, Michael 166
Gunnarsson, Gunnar J. 122–123

Hamlet 124, 139n9
Handel, "Lascia ch'io pianga" 154
Hara, Kunio 116n9
Hegelianism 84, 122, 156
Heldt, Guido 44n16, 71, 146–147
Hellström, Björn and Nicolas Rémy 139n4
herding calls 6, 18; and *The Sacrifice* 119–132, 134–135, 138, 140n14; and troubled utopias 144, 150–153, 160, 166, 171, 172nn14–16
hermeneutic pliability 16, 18, 22, 35–42; limits of 41–42; possibilities and limits 149–153
hermeneutic window 7, 88
Herrmann, Bernard 159
Hoffmann, E. T. A. 90
Hour of the Wolf 26
human experience 17, 164, 173n19; and *Mirror* 47–48, 51, 58–59, 62–66, 69–72

Id-machine 28–35
implied filmmaker 24–28, 39–41, 42n4, 43n11, 148, 150–152
incomprehensibility 17, 48, 69, 71, 73n16; and electronic music 61–63, 66; and *The Sacrifice* 122, 135; and troubled utopias 150, 159, 164
Insider, The 29, 37
instantiation, diegetic 132–134
intelligibility 81–83
interpretation 7–12, 14, 18; multiple interpretability 149–153; and *The Sacrifice* 134–135; and *Solaris* 28–29, 36–37, 39–42; and *Stalker* 75–76; and troubled utopias 144–145, 147–149
intimacy 33–34, 47–48, 50–52
intra-diegetic music 36–39, 101, 151
Ivan's Childhood (Tarkovsky) 5–6

James, Nick 19n1
Jameson, Fredric 156, 172n19
Johnson, Vida T. and Graham Petrie 4, 12, 15, 45n28; and *Mirror* 61; and *Nostalghia* 98, 102, 115n3, 116–117n17; and *The Sacrifice* 134, 140n13; and *Stalker* 75–78, 83–85, 93n3

Kant, Immanuel 30, 172n7
Kierkegaard 132
Kieślowski, Krzysztof, *Three Colors: Red* 94n15
Kramer, Lawrence 7, 88–89
Kubrick, Stanley 26
Kunstreligion 27, 90–91

Lacanian Real 30
Leitch, David 19n1
Levinson, Jerrold 25–26, 28, 42n4, 43n11, 109–111
Leydon, Rebecca 159
liminal, the 133; liminal music 122; the liminal voice of truth 120–122
longing, in *Mirror* 48–50, 96–97, 108–113
loss, in *Mirror* 47–50
love, in *Mirror* 48–52, 131–132
Luko, Alexis 171n4

Mao 68
Margolis, Joseph 10–12, 19n9, 42

Index 191

Marseillaise, La 14; and *Stalker* 84, 87, 89, 92, 93n6, 94n13; and troubled utopias 156, 162
Martin, Sean 9, 35, 38, 94n19, 134
McClary, Susan 40
McSweeney, Terence 3, 46, 134
meaning 143–144, 148, 153–154, 160–161, 163, 172n8
Melancholia 19n1, 154
memories 46, 48–49, 52, 56, 59, 68–69; *see also* dream-memories
metadiegetic music 15; metadiegetic Bach 28–35; metadiegetic reveries 104–112; and *Mirror* 71; and *Nostalghia* 99, 101; and *The Sacrifice* 120–121; and *Solaris* 22, 36–39, 41, 45n26; and troubled utopias 144, 147–150, 152, 158, 172n15, 173n20
Mirror (Tarkovsky) 5–6, 16–17, 19n11, 34, 42, 46–48; classical music in 48–58; and "Das alte Jahr Vergangen ist" in 48–50; documentary sequences in 66–69; dream-memories of early childhood in 59–63; dream sequences in 73n17, 73n19, 173n20; electronic music in 58–69, *61*; and filmind 74n29; images from *50, 60, 64, 67*; and *The Indian Queen* 50–52; inexplicably appearing and disappearing characters in 63–66; mother washing her hair in 73nn21–23; music, diegesis and dimensions of human experience in 69–72; and *Stabat Mater* 52–54; and *St. John Passion* 55–58, *57*, 73n12; and *St. Matthew Passion* 54–55; the structure of 174–178; and troubled utopias 142–144, 147–148, 150–155, 157–165, 167, 169–170
Moritz, Karl Philipp 90
Morricone, Ennio 155, 162
Mozart, Wolfgang Amadeus 4, 29, 141; *Requiem* 56, 162
Mroz, Matilda 12, 46, 53, 72n9
Munkhammar, Birgit 139–140n12
musical dichotomy 18, 57, 71, 153, 157; between East and West 83–87; of *Solaris* 41–42; and syntheses 143, 153, 161–166
musical offering 104
musical synthesis 18, 143; and classical music 153–157; and

electronic music 157–160; and musical dichotomies 161–166; and traditional music 160–161
music as autonomous art form 142, 143, 168, 171
Mystic River 36

Nakata, Hideo 73n23
narrative ambiguities 134–138
Neumeyer, David 37, 42n1
Nietzsche 124
nondiegetic music 6, 13; and *Mirror* 51, 71; nondiegetic Bach 24–28; and *Nostalghia* 100–101, 104; and *The Sacrifice* 120–121, 124–125, 134; and *Solaris* 21–22, 35–39, 41, 42n1, 44nn21–22; and troubled utopias 144–145, 149–155, 160, 165, 172n12
Nostalghia (Tarkovsky) 6, 15–17, 57, 96–98, 119, 122–123, 134; color scheme in 116n12; folk music in 116n10; images from *103, 105, 107*; metadiegetic reveries and the contemplating filmind in 104–112; music and nostalgia in 98–99; resisting the nostalgia of *Nostalghia* 112–115; the triumphant music of failed self-sacrifice in 99–104; and troubled utopias 144, 148–157, 160–162, 165–167, 170
nostalgia 96–97, 103, 106, 108–111; and music in *Nostalghia* 98–99; resisting the nostalgia of *Nostalghia* 112–115

Ovchinnikov, Vyacheslav 5
Oxford English Dictionary 96

Pasolini, Pier Paolo 3–4; *Accattone* 155, 172n18; *Teorema* 162
Pergolesi, Giovanni Batista 47, 70, 155, 157, 162; *Stabat Mater* 48, 52–55, 176
Pietikäinen, Petteri 166–167
Preisner, Zbigniew, *Bolero* 94n15
progress 17, 79–81, 84, 90, 97, 124, 164
Pulcherrima Rosa 86, 94n19
Purcell, Henry 47, 70, 144, 157, 162; *The Indian Queen* 48, 50–52, 54–55, 150–152, 155, 176, 178
Pushkin 47, 64–65, 68–69, 176

192   *Index*

rapprochement 56–57, 114, 166–171
Ravel 92, 156–157, 162; *Bolero* 14,
    84–85, 93n6, 94n16
reconciliation 55–58, 163, 165–167,
    169
Redwood, Thomas 14, 101, 134–135,
    138
Rembrandt, *The Return of the Prodigal
    Son* 44n20
Renaud, Charlotte 141–142
representation 21–22, 143–144, 150–
    151, 153; and classical music 154,
    156; and electronic music 157–159;
    and musical dichotomies and
    syntheses 164, 166; and *The Sacrifice*
    120–121; and *Stalker* 79–80, 87–90;
    and traditional music 160–161
Reyland, Nicholas 26–27, 36–38,
    94n15
Riley, John A. 140n13
Ring, The 73n23
Rivi, Luisa 170
Roadside Picnic 82
Robinson, Jeremy Mark 43n7, 73n12,
    92–93n2
Rodman, Ronald 43n5
Romanticism 4, 17, 167–168; and *The
    Sacrifice* 122; and *Solaris* 27; and
    Stalker 76, 87–88, 90–92, 95n21

Sacrifice, The (Tarkovsky) 2, 6–7, 9,
    18, 23, 118–120; herding calls in
    122–134; herding calls and Maria
    in 130–132; herding calls and Otto
    in 126–128; images from *126, 131,
    133*; the liminal voice of truth in
    120–122; and *Mirror* 47, 53, 68;
    narrative ambiguities in 134–138;
    and *Nostalghia* 111–112; sacrifice
    in 140n13; and troubled utopias
    147–155, 157, 160–162, 165–167,
    170–171, 172n16
sacrificial acts 111–112, 115; *see also*
    self-sacrifice
Saraband 26
Sarkar, Bhaskar 140n19
Schiller 86, 102–103; *An die Freude*
    94n13
Sculpting in Time (Tarkovsky) 4, 9–10,
    18; and *Mirror* 47, 57; and *The
    Sacrifice* 118–119, 124, 134, 138n1;
    and *Solaris* 27; and troubled utopias
    143, 158, 160, 168

self-sacrifice 98–104, 107–108
Shpinitskaya, Julia 132, 140n14
signifiers 87, 90, 156; beyond
    intelligibility 81–83; of triumph and
    progress 79–81
Silence of the Lambs 26
Sitney, P. Adams 12, 73n19, 116n8,
    173n22
Skakov, Nariman 12, 34, 38–39,
    73n21, 74n25, 138, 140n18
Smith, Jeff 44n24, 93n6, 116n7
Solaris (Tarkovsky) 2–3, 5–7, 14, 16,
    18; and Bach, a brief overview
    23–24; basic musical dichotomy
    of 41–42; and classical music 157;
    and electronic music 158–160;
    hermeneutic pliability and
    multiplying gaps in 35–41; images
    from *21, 25, 31*; metadiegetic
    Bach in 28–35; and *Mirror* 46–48,
    50, 55, 57–58, 69–70, 72; music
    and opening credits in 42n2; and
    musical dichotomies and syntheses
    161–166; nondiegetic Bach in
    24–28; and *The Sacrifice* 119–120,
    137; and *Solaris* 20–23; and
    traditional music 160; and troubled
    utopias 143, 145, 147–149, 153–155,
    167–170
Solaris-Thing 30, 34–35
sonic figure 17; and *The Sacrifice* 120;
    and *Stalker* 75, 79–81, 84–85, 88–91,
    93n6; and troubled utopias 153,
    156, 163–166
Sontag, Susan 9
soothing sounds 96, 113
Sosnovsky, Pavel 98, 113–114, 115n2,
    116n4
Souriau, Étienne 145
spiritual authenticity 18, 120, 122,
    126, 129, 169
Stalker (Tarkovsky) 1–2, 5–6, 13–14,
    17, 44n18, 75–76; and classical
    music 156–157; and electronic
    music 158–160; electronic sound
    in 94–95n20; images from *78, 89*;
    and *Mirror* 47, 58, 69, 72; Monkey
    and Beethoven in 76–78, *78*; and
    musical dichotomies between
    East and West 83–87, 173n21; and
    musical dichotomies and syntheses
    161–166; and *Nostalghia* 102, 104;
    and *The Sacrifice* 119–120; signifiers

Index 193

beyond intelligibility in 81–83; signifiers of triumph and progress in 79–81; "Stalker's theme" 87; transcending the Ninth in 87–92; and troubled utopias 143–144, 148, 150, 153–154, 166–168, 171
Stecker, Robert 28–29
Stilwell, Robynn 16, 22, 29, 35, 37, 101
Strick, Philip 74n27
structural trope 88–89
style topic 26–27, 43
subjunctive narration 38
Syberberg, Hans-Jürgen, *Hitler* 93n7
Synessios, Natasha 12, 52, 59, 61

Tarkovsky, Arseny 49, 66–67, 73n17, 175, 177–178
Through a Glass Darkly 26–27, 43n7, 155
Tieck, Ludwig 90
traditional music 4, 6, 143, 153, 160–161, 172n16; *see also* folk music and song
tranquility, in *Mirror* 52–54
transcendence 76, 80, 86, 166–171; transcending the Ninth 87–92; *see also* transcendental diegetic music
transcendental diegetic music 18, 120–122, 125, 133, 150, 152
triumph 79–81; triumphant music of failed self-sacrifice 99–104
Truppin, Andrea 59–60, 76, 93n6, 121–122, 174

truth 118–119; and diegetic instantiation 132–134; the liminal voice of 120–122; listening to the voice of 122–130; and Maria in *The Sacrifice* 130–132; and Otto in *The Sacrifice* 126–128
Turovskaya, Maya 139n12
Tyutchev, Fyodor, *I love your eyes, dear* 77

utopia and utopianism 17–18, 87–92, 96–97, 143; music and Tarkovsky's troubled utopias 166–171; psychological utopianism 167; utopian impulse 17, 166–167

Verdi, Giuseppe 17, 151; *Requiem* 15, 98–99, 104–115, 122–123, 134, 149, 155, 157, 165, 170
von Trier, Lars 19n1, 154

Wackenroder, Wilhelm Heinrich 90
Wagner, Richard 4, 92, 94n18, 156–157, 162; *Meistersinger* 14; *Ride of the Valkyries* 151; *Tannhäuser* 14, 84; *Tristan und Isolde* 108, 154
Waldron, Dara 166
West *see* East and West Winters, Ben 36, 43n11, 101

Yacavone, Daniel 35, 44n22

Žižek, Slavoj 30, 32, 34, 39, 81–82, 94n9

Printed in the United States
by Baker & Taylor Publisher Services